KU-599-193

Sing Me Back Home

CID 103722S SC

BELFAST PUBLIC LIBRARIES

BELFAST PUBLIC LIBRARIES

784. 5200924

HAE

BELFAST PUBLIC LIBRARIES

DATE DUE	DATE DUE	DATE DUE

SING
ME
BACK
HOME

*My Story
by*

Merle Haggard

WITH *PEGGY RUSSELL*

Times
BOOKS

Permission to quote from numerous songs has been granted by their publishers. These acknowledgments appear on p. *286*.

Published by Times Books, a division of
Quadrangle/The New York Times Book Co., Inc.
Three Park Avenue, New York, N.Y. 10016

Published simultaneously in Canada by
Fitzhenry & Whiteside, Ltd., Toronto

Copyright © 1981 by Merle Haggard

All rights reserved. No part of this book may be reproduced in any form or by any electronic or mechanical means, including information storage and retrieval system, without permission in writing from the publisher, except by a reviewer who may quote brief passages in a review.

Library of Congress Cataloging in Publication Data

Haggard, Merle.
  Sing me back home.

  1. Haggard, Merle. 2. Country musicians—
United States—Biography. I. Russell, Peggy J.,
1934– . II. Title.
ML420.H115A3   784.5'2'00924 [B]   81-50082
ISBN 0-8129-0986-0   AACR2

Manufactured in the United States of America

To Mama, who is still trying . . .

Contents

Sing Me Back Home

To the ramblers and the drifters,
  the seekers and the travelers
  and all the wanderers out there
    on the back roads and
      the highways . . .
I hope that in some small way
for even a minute or two
I've been able to
Sing You Back Home
  one more time. . . .

Prologue

AS SOON AS I heard the voices, I knew whose they were. I wasn't sure of anything else at this point, but I knew for certain who those voices belonged to. They were garbled inside my head along with a pounding roar that kept getting louder every time I tried to move.

At first I couldn't tell if the sounds were coming from behind, above, or below me. All I knew for sure was that they seemed to be all around me. That old familiar gut instinct to run like hell was stronger than it had ever been. Unfortunately any move I made hurt so bad that I just sat there, frozen somewhere between where I'd already been and wherever the hell I was going.

Even blinking my eyes was an act too painful to repeat and I wished to God I could at least shake my head to clear away some of the haze, but I didn't dare. Instead, I scooted myself back in the corner and let the morning face me. I sure as hell didn't have the courage or the desire to face it.

When my eyes got used to the lack of light, I looked around. It didn't take long to get the full picture of a nine-by-five-foot room the color of that cold winter fog that rolls in off the 'Frisco Bay. It was empty except for a toilet and a cement slab that looked like a big step. I guessed they called that a bed. Sometime during what must have been the early hours of the morning, some son of a bitch came and took my danged mattress and blanket.

The sockets of my eyeballs hurt so bad that I thought

turning my entire head might be easier. It wasn't. I had the granddaddy of all hangovers and I couldn't understand why—I'd made the stuff myself. Up till then, I had always thought I was pretty good at making beer.

The voices became clearer. I could make out some of the things they were saying. At first I didn't want to listen. Didn't seem quite right. It was like I was intruding on something very personal. As I tried to change my position, my right hand touched something beside me on the cement bed. Slowly I picked it up and one by one the letters became visible. It was the Holy Bible.

Somebody was trying to tell me something.

I managed to move myself toward the edge of the slab and all at once, for some damn reason, I felt I had to check and make sure I was all there. It was like I needed to take inventory. I looked at my hands first, turning them toward me, palms cupped up. All fingers present and accounted for. I didn't want to look at my hands too long for fear I'd get to thinking about all the things I'd touched. I didn't really want to remember the feeling of power a person gets holding the steering wheel of a fast car on a long stretch of desert road. I tried not to think about the cool, smooth feel of a whiskey bottle, or the thrill of a well-tuned Martin guitar. Most of all I was trying to stop before I started thinking about the most torturing thing a caged man can remember—the touching of a woman. I'd already gone too far. It's nearly impossible to look at your hands and not think about a woman. Hell, it's hard when you're in prison to look at *anything* and not think a woman.

Then I happened to notice my bare chest and realized for the first time that I was naked except for some big loose pajama bottoms. I wasn't even wearing any shoes or socks.

Well, hoss, I thought, you're all here, but all where? I knew damn well where. San Quentin-sixth-floor-north-block. Isolation.

Later, I would find out they brought the mattress and

blanket every night at nine-thirty and at five-thirty in the morning some bastard would come and jerk the som'bitch out from under you, leaving your ass on that cold cement slab with nothing but the fear that tomorrow could, and most probably would, be exactly the same.

The voices. There they were again. I decided to listen. Hell, I *had* to listen.

They were talking and laughing about something. Goddamn! How could they laugh? What could they possibly find that was so funny?

"Guess what I got in the goddamned mail," one voice said. A second voice, a little farther away, answered back. "Can't guess, what is it Caryl?"

"I got a life insurance policy," the first voice said, this time laughing louder while the others joined in. The laughter was strange, though. It was the kind that comes from the mouth and not from the insides. I could feel myself starting to shake. I knew exactly who the first voice belonged to. I knew who had the life insurance policy.

There was nothing funny about Caryl Chessman, "red-light bandit," having a life insurance policy. At this point he'd been on Death Row for eleven or twelve years and his case had been appealed over and over. Sometimes he had already been inside the gas chamber, minutes away from death, when he'd get a stay of execution. Now, he was waiting for still another stay.

Chessman was kind of a hero in San Quentin during those days. In the late fifties and until they killed him in 1960, he was the talk of the whole prison. In fact, all of America, even the world, was talking about Chessman and opinion was sharply divided as to his guilt or innocence.

At San Quentin, any fool could have told you what the verdict should have been. We all identified with him. We knew it could have been one of us. Hell, I shuddered, it could have been me. It almost was me.

It was then, on that first day of isolation, in San Quentin, that I began to take stock of where I was and how far I'd come.

Crime was not all it was cracked up to be, I decided. Listening to the voices of those condemned men really shook me up.

Until now, crime had been almost an adventure. Hell, I had actually enjoyed being a criminal, took a certain pride in it. It was exciting and I felt alive. It fascinated me and scared the hell out of me at the same time.

There comes a time, though, when you have to face the truth. There is no way to describe the pain. It has to be experienced, and if you're lucky, like me, you live to try to tell about it. If you're like Chessman, you don't.

I slid down off the bunk and pressed my face against the vent where I thought the voices were coming from.

"Chessman," I almost choked on his name.

"Yeah," the answer came back.

"My name is Haggard and I've just come up from the yard," I said. "I'm doing seven days in isolation for being drunk." I was having difficulty getting the words out and I didn't know what to say next, so I blurted out that everybody down in the yard was pulling for him.

"Thank you," came his answer. "And you be sure and tell the others how much I appreciate their good thoughts."

"Uh . . . how is your appeal going?" I asked, hesitating.

"Very well," came the answer, and he sounded confident and in very good spirits. "I've just talked to my attorney and he isn't worried at all."

I talked to Chessman several times during the next six days, but nothing is clear about what we said. The rest of the time kinda runs together. My routine was broken only by the food and mattress deliveries. I was reading my only possession and constant companion during that seven-day period. Don't let nobody tell you there's just one way to get comfort from the good book. I read it by day and when night came I used it for a pillow.

To say my life flashed before me during that time wouldn't be true. It would be better to say that my death flashed before me. I didn't do a lot of heavy thinking or soul-searching. I found that the only way to keep from going totally mad was to practice *not* thinking at all.

I took time to reflect on the life I'd had on the outside—the wife, who must be having a rough time of it, a little dark-haired baby girl who wouldn't remember her Daddy, and the son I'd never seen. I had a good, hard-working mother, who should have given up on me by now. In the loneliest of times I convinced myself—as I still do from time to time—that nobody cared at all. I should have known better.

I knew my mother hadn't given up on me, nor had my brother, Lowell, or my sister, Lillian, and her husband, Bill. There were others too, people like my Uncle George and Aunt Flora, their kids, Bob and Sylvia, and Sylvia's husband, Lomar Boatman. Also, the people who meant so much to me after the death of my father, my Uncle Escar and his wife, Willie. These were the people who kept me going. The thought of any of them would bring me out of the darkest times, especially when I was in isolation and struggling so hard for some kind of direction.

Sometimes at night I would close my eyes and see the judge who had sentenced me. I could hear him just like he was in my cell. His words were not all that profound, but they had said it all.

"Looks like you've been on a long, hard journey," he said, looking me straight in the eye. "What you need is a little rest." He then went on to tell me what the law had prescribed.

And he was right. I did need rest. I was so danged tired of it all—tired of trying and failing and tired of trying and not failing. I was tired of getting caught and tired of getting away with things, tired of fighting in the barrooms and tired of the battles at home. Most of all I was tired of searching, mostly because I didn't have a clue in hell as to what I was searching for. It damn sure wasn't in San Quentin. There was a big empty gap somewhere inside me that I could never seem to fill, and God knows I'd tried nearly everything.

Those seven days of isolation may have been some of the most important days of my life because for the first time in my twenty-one years, I looked inward.

I talked to the walls, but they just stood there, cold and silent. I talked to myself, and I listened. Sometimes I even answered.

And I believe I finally grew up in those seven terrible days. I knew, and I told myself as honest as I could, that if I didn't make some drastic changes in my life, take some different directions, I would end up where Chessman was—most likely without his recognition.

I didn't make any plans and I didn't even dream. I do remember wishing to God I could talk to Daddy just one more time. I needed his advice, his understanding, and, most of all, his love. He would have made things better. He could do that with just a smile or a wink. My God, why did he have to die just when I needed him most? Didn't he know that a nine-year-old boy needs his Daddy so damned bad?

The man didn't cry then, but the boy did. It was the last time the boy ever cried. When the tears were finally gone, I was filled with an awful pain and an emptiness that comes only from continual crying inside—and it never goes away.

Go ahead, just ask me about hell. I've been there. Only spent seven days—but that was quite enough.

One

Family

First thing I remember knowin'
was a lonesome whistle blowin'
And a youngun's dream of growin' up to ride,
on a freight train leavin' town
not knowin' where I'm bound,
And no one could change my mind,
but Mama tried.

"Mama Tried"   by Merle Haggard

OVER AND OVER I've tried to get Mama to recall that April 6th, 1937, was very unusual. I've tried to jog her memory so she'd recall there were great sounds of trumpets in the land, or twin-fiddles at least—possibly a choir of angels singin' backup—but she says she don't remember none of that stuff. I can't even get her to stretch a point and say that the sun just might have come up an hour early, or even an hour late—anything that would have indicated what a special event it must have been.

Hell, it ain't as though I wanted her to say that a bright star appeared in the west over the little town of Bakersfield and three wise guys came by smokin' Camels. I only wanted her to say that the birth of her youngest child was really a big deal. But Flossie Haggard still sticks to that dull story about how it was just another day when she gave birth to a healthy six-pound boy. She does admit, however, that the weather was unusually nice that day.

When people ask about my family background and Oklahoma heritage, it's hard to describe them without sounding like I'm bragging. I honestly don't realize how much pride I have in them until I get on the subject of the Haggards and the Harps. I will say, though, that I recognize their flaws as well. Usually when one of the Haggards or the Harps was wrong—he was really wrong.

Both the Harps and Haggards were strong of character and true lovers of the land. They had a deep sense of loyalty to each other as well as to their native state. There was a stubborn streak in the Haggards, but a gentleness too. This sometimes caused a lot of confusion. On my mother's side was a strong sense of wrong and right. Some of the Harps also had pretty bad tempers. Putting it mildly, there were often family clashes.

Before moving to California in 1934, my family had lived in Checotah, Oklahoma, a little town just south of Muskogee, where in just about every other house there lived a relative.

My father was a large, gentle man. The thing I remember most about him now was the way he could smile so easy and make everybody feel everything was all right. He was about six foot tall and had extremely big hands.

My mother was a more serious type person, given to worry when there was little to worry about.

On the Harp side of the family we had what some people called the meanest man on our whole family tree. John Harp was ninety-five the day he died and except for my dad—once—nobody had ever gone up against him.

John Harp was a hard-working man. And for him that was

the only way of life. Two days before he died, he kicked the family doctor in a very delicate place simply because he tried to take his pulse. It was understandable though, 'cause John Harp had never had a doctor until that moment. It was simply "that Harp temper" that kicked the good doctor through the screen door. At least that's what everybody said.

If there was a certain streak of meanness in Grandpa, it was more than made up for by his brother, Escar. Uncle Escar was a large man. He and my dad had been friends since they were children in the Oklahoma cotton fields. They were also champion horseshoe pitchers. Nobody could win against the team of Harp and Haggard.

Escar married a woman named Willie, and if there were ever two people who belonged together, it was them. They became very important to me later in my life when so many other things didn't matter. They were just about the last of the clan to move to California.

Daddy and Mama had moved earlier. The fact is they really hadn't planned to move west at all. Unlike most of the Okies, Mama and Daddy were making it on a forty-acre farm they had leased. As they watched carload after carload head west with mattresses tied to the tops and their belongings and kids sticking out the windows of their old cars, they began to think that they were pretty well off.

The farm was producing at an average rate and Daddy had himself a good team of work horses, a wagon, some farm equipment, and a '31 Model-A Ford. My brother, Lowell, was about eleven years old then and my sister, Lillian, must have been about thirteen. It was early in 1934. Things were not in the best of shape.

Besides being a farmer, Daddy was a fisherman and a trapper. Sometimes he'd go on a trapping trip for a couple of weeks and bring back various animals that would give the family a little cash. For us, things were pretty good.

Then came the night of the big storm.

SING ME BACK HOME

It was one of those typical Oklahoma frog-stranglin' rains, along with a lot of thunder and lightning. The rain slapped against the house so hard that they said it sounded like somebody was standing outside and hitting it with something.

"I think somebody's at the door, Jim," my Mother said after one real hard thud. "Ain't nobody out on a night like this," he said. "Besides it's after ten o'clock."

The noise came again and the kids sat up in bed. "It *is* someone at the door, Jim," my mother said again, and by this time my father was on his feet and headed toward the door.

He was surprised to see a colored man he knew from his trapping trips. He knew the man lived quite some distance away. He stepped back when he saw him. Now in that particular area, at that time, a lot of people didn't have anything to do with the colored, but Daddy never judged a person. Daddy considered this particular man a friend and believed him to be an honest, hard-working man. He was soaking wet of course, and he looked like he was scared to death. Daddy asked him in.

"I can't," he answered, "I've come because of my wife. She's awful sick and I'd like to borry your car so I could take her into town to the doctor."

Well, Daddy always had a hard and fast rule about loaning his car—he didn't. Not under any circumstances, not to anybody, and he told the man that.

"But I would take your wife into town if I could," Daddy said. "Only thing is, the car ain't been runnin' right and I don't think it would make it, especially with the roads the way they are now, we ain't got a chance."

The man stood staring at Daddy for a few seconds, and it was obvious he didn't believe him.

"Look, I tell you what," Daddy said then, "I'll just go out to the barn and hitch up the team to the wagon. It'll be slow, but it'll get us there at least."

Suddenly, the man turned and ran back into the storm. Daddy called out after him. He never answered. He guessed the man thought it was an insult—like he didn't want him in his car.

Not knowing what else to do, Daddy stood there for a little while, then finally closed the door and went back to bed.

A few minutes later a bright red glow began to fill the room.

"Oh, no, Flossie," Daddy said, jumping out of the bed, "the barn's afire!"

Even the heavy rain couldn't stop the flames once they were blazing from inside. It could have been lightning, but no one really knew. Mama and Daddy had to watch any dreams they had of staying in Oklahoma go up in smoke.

In the morning it was all gone. The barn, the wagon, the plows, the cows, the horses, and Daddy's prized Model-A Ford. He set out to town on foot to get himself another car. I don't know if he had some money saved, or whether he had to borrow it, but in any case, he came back home with a '26 Chevy and a little homemade trailer bumping along behind. They gave up the lease on the forty acres, loaded what belongings they had in the trailer, and headed west toward California.

Daddy's faith in mankind never wavered. The fact that his barn was burned, probably on purpose, didn't change his belief in his fellow man in the slightest. According to his way of thinking, everything had its purpose. He always tried to understand a man's reason for doing something. He almost never questioned it.

Even though there was great strength in my father, it was often overshadowed by Mama. She really ran the show in our household. Flossie Haggard was, and still is, a very strong, opinionated lady. She always felt that security is only possible when a person settles down in one place, at one job, and "makes somethin' of themselves."

SING ME BACK HOME

In our house Mama and Daddy didn't argue much, but there were always a few arguments. If Daddy didn't want to join in that was all right because Mama could easily carry both sides of an argument, even when they were from the same point of view—hers.

Sometimes I'd be in bed and I knew without looking out from under the covers exactly what the scene looked like. I'd hear Daddy say, "You know I been studyin' . . ." and that was about as far as he usually got. He'd be sitting by the radio with his elbow up on the table and Mama'd walk from one side of the little kitchen area to the other as she once again got on her favorite subject, "settin' her foot down."

"We're not goin' back to Oklahoma," she'd say. "That's where I really set my foot down. We're not goin' to lose all we've worked for—might as well get this travelin' out of your head."

To others she'd say we wouldn't have anything if she hadn't "set her foot down," then she'd repeat this to Daddy. Mostly he didn't say nothin', but sometimes when I'd raise up on my elbows in bed, he'd wink at me, smile a little bit, and turn the radio up a little louder.

Sometimes I'd toss in bed at night and wonder what it was Daddy wanted out of life. I got to thinking that he must have dreams he was letting go by and I knew he had a great love for music, but he didn't seem to work at it much. I thought maybe Mama had something to do with that because she considered some of it rather sinful. Somehow I got the feeling he didn't really approve either, so he just didn't play music in California. But he talked a lot about playing the fiddle back in Oklahoma.

Later, it seemed almost contradictory when it was Mama who most encouraged my music. Even when I was small, she insisted I take violin lessons. I'm sure she believed I could have a career in music long before I ever dreamed about it. The violin didn't hold my interest much, so I told 'em I wanted to play a fiddle 'cause fiddlers have more style. Through it all, Mama never stopped preaching her way of life to anyone who would listen, or to those of us who wouldn't.

We weren't exactly the Waltons, but there were lots of good times. It was basically a good family—church-going and patriotic, nothing to suggest a breeding ground for a young criminal.

It's hard to explain when or where, but somewhere along the way, when I was very young I'm sure, I decided what I *didn't* want to be. I was determined not to spend my life in some set pattern. I didn't like going to church every Sunday morning, then meeting together with the in-laws, cousins, and church folk on Sunday afternoon.

Mama used to say, and I guess she still does, that I was always real good to go to church when I was little. She also says I was never any problem at all until I was about twelve or thirteen. But I remember from the time I was big enough to tie my own shoes, till the time I quit going to church, I fought it every Sunday morning. Mama even said at one time she had dreams of me being a preacher because I used to get out my little apple crate and practice my sermons on anybody who would listen. That must have been real damn cute. Mostly I remember my favorite thing about church was that final Amen.

My career as a preacher was not all that spectacular. Fact was, nobody listened to my sermons but my very first dog, Jack. I was only three years old when I got him, and I remember it just like it was yesterday. Strangely enough, Jack's life ended when I was in San Quentin, probably just about the time the boy in me died. Even today, I can't imagine being without a dog of some kind. That's probably because of Jack, and the day I went with Daddy to get him.

I remember the way Daddy took my hand and led me

around the side of a big house to see some puppies. I even remember the man's name was Harold Granger, and he was talking to Daddy about what fine dogs they were.

"Go ahead, Son," I heard Daddy saying and I looked up at him because I wasn't sure what he meant. "Pick one out," he said, motioning toward the puppies with his head. I couldn't believe he was letting me actually pick out the one I wanted. I had never been able to make such an important decision. It was really a major event. I squatted down and scooped up the one who had already picked me right from the beginning.

"Is that the one you want?" Mr. Granger asked. I could only nod as I held the little animal against my face. I doubt if I have ever felt more important than at that time. Jack was a fox terrier, like the little dogs I have now. He was black with white on his face and weighed about fifteen pounds when he was full grown. He was the toughest little rascal you ever seen and his hobby was killin' big old tomcats. Really. The bigger the cat, the prouder old Jack was of his efforts. He'd bring 'em home like a hunter brings home a deer. It may sound like I'm bragging too much if I tell you that Jack used to ride a tricycle and play hide-and-seek with me, but I have a picture of him on a tricycle. It's here in the book.

No matter where I went, Jack was right at my heels. We would stand by the railroad tracks down at the end of the street and watch the trains and the men who worked on them. One of those men was my father.

I was nine years old and my world couldn't have been better. Sometimes Daddy took me fishing up on the Kern River and sometimes we'd just go for a ride in his car. I always knew he'd come back down the alley by the railroad tracks so he could put two wheels up on the high side next to the track. I thought any minute it would tip over. I would laugh and tell him to go faster, but a lot of the time I would have to catch my breath for fear we'd turn over.

Then, one Wednesday night in '46 everything changed. Something went out of my world that I was never able to replace.

Me and Mama had gone to church on a Wednesday night and I was having more than my usual difficulty sitting still. It seemed like an eternity till that final blessed Amen.

When the Amen came, I was out the door like a shot. Daddy hadn't gone with us that night because he had to work late, something he seldom had to do. There had been a train wreck somewhere up in the Tehachapi Mountains, and he had to go up there with the work crew. I was anxious to get home and hear all the details. As soon as I got in sight of the house I could see his car and I knew he was home. I began to run toward the house.

As I jumped across the railroad tracks, I could feel the gravel through my church shoes and I knew Mama was gonna be mad that I was scuffing them all up, but I kept running.

Before I even got to the yard, I could tell something was wrong. There was no sign of Jack anywhere. I tried to ignore a chill I felt coming up my back. I slowed down to a walk when I got to the front door, and I tried to whistle for Jack but I couldn't get no sound out. I stopped then and looked back to see where Mama was. She was just coming across the railroad tracks. I looked in through the front door from the porch but I couldn't see nothin'. The light was out in the front room and I could see only one little light at the back of the house. It was so quiet. At first I thought nobody was in the front room at all. Then I saw him.

He was sitting in the shadows in the big chair and he had one of his legs propped up on something, another chair, I think. As soon as I walked inside, I could feel a cold fear coming down all around me. The atmosphere of the house was charged with something I'd never felt before. Everything was so still. I was afraid to move. I couldn't speak and the fact that he didn't say anything either scared me to death. I could hear Mama coming in then and when I moved closer to Daddy, I could see tears running down his cheeks.

I'd never seen my daddy cry before. Daddy had always laughed. He loved, and he lived every minute, but dear God, he never cried, at least not when I'd ever seen him. I was scared and I couldn't even ask what was wrong. Nothing could be wrong with him, I kept thinking. I *love* that man, nothing can happen to him. He's not old. He is *not* going to die. God please, don't let nothin' bad be wrong with Daddy.

Mama was beside him then and trying to find out what had happened. I didn't understand what was happening to my world. "Stroke." What was a stroke? I'd heard the word. It was something real bad. I could hear him trying to tell Mama that while he was driving home something had happened.

"Started to turn left," he said, his voice even sounding strange, ". . . and I put my arm out to give my signal . . . it just fell down . . . went dead on me . . ." He told her then that when he tried to raise his left leg to put his foot on the clutch, he couldn't move it either. He had finally managed to get the car home and had crawled into the house.

"I got myself into this chair . . . ," he said, his voice breaking, ". . . and I been waitin' for you and Merle to come home . . ."

We got Daddy to the hospital in Bakersfield that Wednesday night and he stayed until Saturday morning. It all seemed like such a nightmare that I only remember parts of what happened. Most of the time I just shut it out and hoped the awful pain in my head would go away. He was getting better though, and by the end of the week when he came home, I was relieved to see that familiar smile on his face—a little weaker, but there all the same.

It had been decided at the hospital in Bakersfield that Daddy ought to go to the Santa Fe Hospital down in Los Angeles for more tests so they could find out what caused his stroke.

It was on a Saturday morning in June. I remember it was such a pretty day. Me, Mama, Lowell, and Daddy all got into Lowell's '39 Chevy and took off for L.A.

Lowell was driving and Daddy sat up front. Me and Mama were in the back. Daddy said he felt real good and everybody seemed to be in such good spirits. It was almost like we were going on a family picnic or a drive in the country. I had a headache but remember thinking how good it was that I had it, not Daddy. He looked so good and so healthy that morning and I can still see him so clear in my mind. He was wearing a light blue shirt and he kept turning around talking to me and Mama. He had his arm laying on the back of the seat and every now and then he'd reach down and tap my knee with his finger. I'd try to smile at him but my headache kept getting worse.

It was about a four-hour drive to Los Angeles and we were supposed to check him in at one o'clock in the afternoon. We got there early. Mama had brought some baloney and some other food to fix us a lunch. There was a park across the street from the hospital. We went over there to eat and wait for check-in time. As usual, Mama thought of everything. She had brought along a blanket and put it down for us to sit on. I suppose some L.A. city slicker might have seen us in the park and thought we were just another family of red-neck Okies having our baloney and crackers, and in a way we were. One thing for sure, we were a family about to be torn to pieces.

"Why don't you just lay here on the blanket while I take your Daddy around to Admittin'," Mama said. I had to actually look in her direction to make sure she said this. I could not imagine her tolerating such a thing, much less suggesting it. She was a very over-protective mother and the thought of leaving a nine-year-old boy alone in a big and strange city like Los Angeles was just about as foreign to her nature as anything I could imagine. Even though her suggestion had surprised me, what happened next scared me. As I said, Daddy never argued much with Mama, and never once had I ever heard him overrule anything she decided to do.

"No," he said, and there was something in his tone that caused both Mama and Lowell to look at him. Then he repeated it. "No." If I have ever heard anything totally definite in my life, it was that one word.

"Merle's goin' with us," he said. "Get the things in the car. Merle's going with us."

I knew then Daddy knew something we didn't know. Without a word we all gathered up the things and put 'em in the car. Then we drove around to the back of the hospital to the Admitting Room.

What happened in the next few minutes and in the next few days lies still like crumpled paper inside my mind. Mostly it was a time of blank, dark periods with constant pain inside my head. There were bits of conversations and flashes of scenes—some real and some probably imagined. The only thing I'm very sure about is that I tried like hell to block it all out. I could never quite do it.

"It's hospital policy, Mr. Haggard," the nurse said, and Dad had flashed that easy grin at her. "I don't need a wheelchair," he told her, "I can still walk."

Lowell and Mama said he stood up outside the car and was turning to sit down when it happened. They also said the main artery broke and all the blood came to his face turning him completely blue. Then they said he fell back into the wheelchair. I was there, but I don't, even to this day, remember any of that. I stood there and I saw it, but I don't—or I *can't*—remember any of it.

One major brain hemorrhage can easily kill a man. The hospital staff told the family later it took three to kill Daddy. I have to believe he wanted to stay with us pretty bad.

He had his second stroke the next Tuesday, but by that time, Lowell had driven me back to Aunt Flora's house in Lamont.

I remember that the bed at Aunt Flora's was soft and it felt good to lay down. But I was stiff and wide awake as I felt the covers being pulled over me. I tried to think of anything but Daddy, but that was impossible. I tried to think of Jack and the strange way he'd been acting since Daddy'd been sick, but I couldn't even picture him. Later, the old German lady who lived next door to us in Oildale would tell us how she knew something bad had happened because on Tuesday night that little dog had howled all night long.

I don't know how long it took me to fall asleep. I wasn't aware of anything until Wednesday morning about three o'clock.

I could feel somebody's arms around me and I could hear somebody crying. I could hear more than one person crying but I didn't know if I was one of them. Lowell was sitting on the side of the bed with his arms around me and as he rocked me back and forth, he kept saying over and over, "Merle, we ain't got no Daddy . . . Merle, we ain't got no Daddy . . . do you hear me Merle . . . do you understand?"

I heard him, but I didn't understand. I still don't.

Two

Mama Really Tried

Did you ever steal a quarter
*   When you was ten years old?*
*   Ever wear a brogan with a hole in the sole?*
Did you ever ride a freight train
*   while runnin' from the law?*
I've done it all, Lord,
*   Lord, I've done it all.*

"I've Done It All"   by Merle Haggard

"ALL OFF FOR HUGHSON," the red-faced conductor hollered as he walked past us down the aisle of the train.

Mama picked up the satchel and reached for my hand. I pulled back.

"I ain't no baby," I said. But she didn't let on like she heard me. There was nothing more embarrassing for a nine-year-old boy than to have his mother lead him by the hand.

Through the train window I could see Escar and Willie, my great-uncle and -aunt, but I was always allowed to call them by their first names. That made me feel very grown-up and I liked them both a lot. Looking out the window at them standing by the tiny building that served as Hughson's train station, I began to feel almost good. Then I felt guilty about enjoying anything without Daddy. Still, in spite of myself, I couldn't wait to get off the train and be near Escar and Willie. This was my first time to visit them in their home. It was summer, 1946.

Hughson was a little town up near Modesto, and Escar had talked about it a lot. I guess Mama thought it would do me good to go visit them since I thought so much of them. And, I'm sure she was looking for some way to keep her sanity, too, after losing Daddy. As we stepped down off the train, I looked down by the tracks and saw row after row of one room, canvas-covered cabins, all just alike. It was not till years later when I began to write songs that I realized how much that scene impressed me. That's where the first line of "Mama's Hungry Eyes" came from.

It was just a short ways to their house. When we walked through the front door, I saw only one large room, with a stove in the center for cooking and heating. Although I was never aware of being poor when I was little, I did realize that Escar and Willie were poorer than we were. Where did they put all the relatives when they visited, I wondered? Everybody, when they got some time off, went to visit Willie and Escar. They always had room for one more quilt on the floor for sleeping, and one more plate of fried fish and homemade biscuits on the table. I loved Willie's biscuits and fried fish better than anything. More important, I loved the feeling I got at their house. They knew how to make a person feel welcome because they really liked and enjoyed company. The numb feeling I'd had since Daddy's death faded some when I was at their house.

I don't know if I heard them, or whether I just knew, but they discussed the problems of raising a young boy alone. I knew Willie and Escar wanted me to spend as much time as I could with them and Mama knew I needed a firm hand from a man like Escar. It was decided that I would spend some time up there the following summer and I did, in fact, spend some of my tenth, eleventh, twelfth, and thirteenth summers there.

I loved Escar's rules. They weren't like anybody else's. Besides, he let me smoke.

"Church is somethin' you go to if you feel like it," he'd say, as Willie would get dressed on Sunday morning. "Everybody should follow their own conscience about goin' or not goin'. If you do go, do your church there and leave it there—don't bring it home."

The friendship between me and Escar lasted until his death. I treasured him. I loved Willie, but Escar was my mountain after I lost Daddy. He was one of the few people who could talk about Daddy and not make me sad, or even mad because he'd left me. I even loved his "fish stories" and how he knew where there was bass "as long as my arm." Then he'd stretch out that long slender arm and show me.

Away from Hughson and Escar's wisdom, I began to have problems. Mama, of course, had to go to work. She was well-educated, especially for her day, and her job as a bookkeeper for the Quality Meat Company was an especially good job. Left more or less on my own though, I began to get into some trouble. I hated school. Sitting in the back of the room I could think of all the things I'd rather be doing. I'd listen to the trains go by and watch the birds outside. In fact, anything I could do to keep my mind off school, I'd do. I wanted adventure and I didn't think I was gonna find it in the classroom.

That's when Billy Thorpe and I began to talk about making our own adventure. Billy was a boy who lived down the street from me in Oildale, and we spent a lot of time talking about what we'd do and where we'd go when we grew up. Then we decided that we were grown-up. After all, we were ten years old.

"Let's go on a train, Billy," I said one day as we were walking home from school. "You mean, take a trip somewhere?" he asked and I shook my head. "I mean hop a freight and go wherever it takes us."

Billy's eyes widened and at first I thought he was gonna tell me it was a bad idea. Then he thought about it for a few minutes and said, "Let's go."

"We'll come home from school tomorrow," I said, "and put some food in a couple of pillowcases, and we'll go out by the lake and wait for that train that comes by late in the afternoon."

That's just what we did.

With our pillowcases slung over our backs, we hiked out to the lake and waited for the train.

When it arrived on schedule and pulled off for the switch as we knew it would, we made our move.

"I can't get the door open, Billy," I cried. How embarrassing. The big leap on the train and I couldn't even get the door open.

"Let's just get on the next car, Merle," he suggested. I was not pleased with what I saw. As it turned out, there was no other choice, just closed doors and those cement hauling cars. In desperation we climbed on one of them. It was not an ideal place to ride, we discovered. We edged ourselves onto that piece of iron framework that juts out right beside the wheels underneath the angle that forms the boat-shaped railroad car. We tried to get comfortable, all the time scared to death somebody would catch us before the train started rolling.

Finally, after what seemed like ages, we began to move. As the train gathered speed, we clenched our teeth and held on for dear life.

We found ourselves in Fresno about one o'clock in the morning, and we were stumbling around in the train yard when behind us came what sounded like the voice of doom.

"All right, boys," the voice said. "I think you better come with me." Our first encounter with a yard bull, better known as a railroad detective. He herded us to the detention hall while Billy and I tried to figure out how he knew we were runaways. It never once occurred to us that we stuck out like sore thumbs in the rail yard at one in the morning. Runaways never think they look like runaways.

One look at Mama's face and I was sorry. She looked scared. I couldn't figure out why she'd be scared. I knew she'd be mad, but why was she scared?

"We've been worried to death," she said, as she came into the room with the Thorpes. "We thought somebody had kidnapped you. All kinds of things can happen to young boys out these days." I didn't understand what could happen. We held on tight. We took food. We were fine. Why were the Thorpes upset? What was wrong with everybody? We weren't little kids. Hell, I never wanted to worry Mama. I just didn't really think about her feelings. I was looking for adventure.

"What was so *bad* that you felt you had to run away?" she asked then, and I was amazed. "I didn't run away," I said, and I honestly didn't see it as "running away." "Nothin' is *bad*, Mama. Me and Billy just wanted to hop a freight and see what it would be like."

"You've rode a train before, Merle," she snapped, "and besides, you've got a pass that says you can go anywhere on a train free until you're eighteen." I knew that. I knew that as members of Daddy's family, because he'd worked for the Santa Fe railroad, we had a pass, but Mama'd missed the point completely. I had had my first taste of adventure, and now I wanted more.

The summer I was fourteen I got another chance. I'd seen this new guy around Bunkie's drive-in several times and wondered who he was. Bunkie's was the favorite hangout around Oildale in '51. Everybody came there to see what everybody else was doing and we all kinda stood around and watched each other kill time.

Even though the new guy in town didn't have a car, he seemed cool. He was the kinda guy you see in the movies who ends up with the girl whether he tries to or not. He was tall, and carried himself almost like a soldier. I was not surprised when someone said he had lied about his age at fourteen and spent two years in the Marines before they found out. I was very impressed and the fact that he was from Texas made him even larger in my eyes. I knew he was visiting his brother Frank and his sister-in-law Karen, who lived around the corner from us. Bob Teague was everything I wished I was at that point, especially that magic age of *eighteen*. That's why I was totally shocked when he walked over to me one night at Bunkie's and began talking just as though we'd always known each other—and more important—like I was his equal.

"Somebody told me you can sing just like Lefty Frizzell," Bob said after talking a little while. "Is that right?" I was speechless. Although that was a secret wish of mine, I had only heard it out loud once before. I'd been embarrassed and flattered then as I was now. "Not really," I managed to say, and it was about that time that the jukebox blasted out the steel intro to one of Hank Williams' records. "Well, I've been told I sound a little like ol' Hank there," he grinned, "and maybe we ought to team up."

All at once I heard myself telling him how a friend of mine's mother had heard me singing in the car once and told me I sounded just like that guy on the radio. I hoped she meant Lefty since I was singing "I Love You a Thousand Ways."

"Well, looks like you and me got a lot in common," he said. "You play the guitar?"

"A little," I said, "do you?"

"Some," he answered. "Maybe I can teach you a few

more chords if you'd want me to." Did I ever! Just because I was fed up with learning in the classroom was no sign I didn't want to learn everything I could about music, especially the guitar. I'd been real interested in the guitar ever since Lowell had brought home an old Bronson someone left at his service station when he couldn't afford the two dollars for gasoline. Every chance I got, I tried to make friends with that pitiful old instrument with its strings too high off the frets and a neck that didn't quite line up straight.

"Lefty is gonna be out at the Rainbow Gardens in Bakersfield in a couple of weeks," Bob said. "Let's go." I couldn't wait.

On the *big* day of Lefty's show, Bob borrowed his brother's car, I think, and we bought us a case of "Burgie" beer and headed out to the Rainbow Gardens. There was nothing memorable or impressive about the building, but the magic of being there was well worth the trip. We were early, as planned, and while we waited we lay down on a patch of grass outside the club to wait for the show to start. We both fell asleep. The truth is we both passed out drunk.

"Hey, you boys are missing the great Lefty Frizzell." Somebody was shaking me by the shoulder, and sure enough, the show was in full swing. There were about three thousand people already inside the Gardens, a hall only supposed to hold two thousand. We could barely push ourselves inside the door. And we heard only the tail end of the first show. We couldn't see a danged thing through all the crowd. The sound, what little we heard though, was unmistakable. It was the one and only Lefty Frizzell. Nothing, we decided, was going to keep us from seeing the second show.

When intermission came and the crowd thinned out a little we got inside where we knew we would be in a good place when the second show began. I looked across the dance floor and spotted a girl I knew. Her name was Jeanine

Hilton and I had a pretty heavy crush on her, even though I knew it was useless. You have to understand that in the early 1950's, everybody was locked into a category. Everybody had a label. Well, Jeanine was a *nice* girl. She may as well have worn a big old sign hanging around her neck that said "NICE GIRL," and I might as well have had another that said "BAD BOY." Everybody knows that nice girls don't mess with bad boys.

Whether it was the confidence I'd gained by having somebody like Bob Teague as my friend, or whether I was getting bolder, I decided to hell with all the reasons why I shouldn't—I wanted to ask Jeanine to dance. All she can do is say no, I told myself as I walked across the floor.

"Would you like to dance, Jeanine?" I asked and I was already planning my retreat.

"Sure, Merle," she answered and turned toward me. I almost ran. I couldn't believe she'd said yes. Hell, I thought as I put my arms around her, my luck just might be changing. Here I was dancing with Jeanine Hilton, no less, and what was even more amazing, she looked like she was really enjoying my company. Rainbow Gardens took on a "Burgie" haze, and with Hank Williams coming from the jukebox telling me "You Win Again," I just didn't see how I could lose. So what if I couldn't dance worth a shit—who cared?

Just about the time sweet Jeanine leaned her pretty dark head on my shoulder and I had tightened my arms around her, a guy came out on stage and the jukebox shut off right in the middle of pore ol' Hank.

"Ladies and gentlemen," the man announced, "once again, LEFTY FRIZZELL!!!!!!"

Lefty bounced out on the stage and the crowd was so thick again that I could hardly see him. I pushed myself through the crowd trying to get closer. I looked up as someone passed a chair above my head.

"Stand on this so we can see you Lefty," a voice called

out as the chair was handed onto the stage. And that's what he did. He climbed up on the chair and did his entire second show as we stood watching him—me for one—in absolute wonder.

There is really no way I can describe the effect Lefty had on audiences back in those days. He had the soul of Hank Williams, the appeal of Johnny Cash, and the charisma of Elvis Presley. He had it all—brilliance and clarity. He was dressed in white—heroes usually are—and he was truly an inspiration to me that night. I believe the impact he made on country music, and on *me*, at that time was not even measurable.

I can't be sure, but I think I was still holding on to Jeanine's hand, although I was sure tuned in to the man of music standing in a white suit on a chair.

"I'm happy to be back at the Rainbow Gardens," he said at the show's opening, and after what seemed like only *minutes*, although it was more than an hour, he was talking about ending the show. I just couldn't believe the time had gone so fast.

"I'd like to end my show with a new record I've just had released," he said. "This song is for my mom and my dad." Then he sang "The Mom and Dad Waltz," followed by the record's flip side which was to be one of his all-time hits, "Always Late." When he told us that was the first time he'd ever done those songs in public, I felt like I was being included in country music history in some way. It was a feeling I've never forgotten.

The one thing I don't remember, dammit, was what happened to pretty little Jeanine Hilton that night. I just can't imagine forgetting about her under any circumstances. Besides, I think she was the only virgin I ever dated.

Life, I thought, would have been pretty good for me about this time if people had just let me alone. They didn't. Mama thought I ought to be in school. Lillian thought I ought to be in school. Lowell thought I ought to be in school. Last, but certainly not least, the truant officer thought I ought to be in school. It became quite a game to keep ahead of him and I did not always succeed. Even obtaining a fake ID that moved my age up to eighteen didn't keep me totally out of trouble.

I was discovering new things about myself every day and anxious to try everything before it was "all used up." Bob kept teaching me more chords on the guitar, and the better I got the more confident I became. It was that summer that I played to my very first "audience."

After congregating one night at Bunkie's, a bunch of us piled into several cars with a couple of cases of beer, and headed out on the old China Grade Road. We found a bluff overlooking the river and the party began. All the others were at least two to four years older than me.

It turned out to be one of those nights when the music went on forever. I can even remember the guitars we were playing. Bob had a 1940 Epiphone and I had a D-18 Martin. The later it got, the better the pickin' and singin' seemed. It might have been helped by the amount of "Burgie" we drank, but nevertheless it *seemed* like very good music.

When the sun came up I was still singing my ass off. Everytime I'd sing "Always Late," somebody would holler out, "Goddamn! Sing that som'bitch again." And I would.

Imagine anybody giving this up for something as dull as remedial math and European history. Did they think I was crazy?

I made the mistake of mentioning music as a career to Lowell. He set me straight about it.

"People like us, Bud, can't make a livin' in the music business," he said. "You have to have years of formal trainin' to do any good at all. You might as well just get music out of your head. You won't even go to school to get regular learnin' so how in the world do you expect to ever go to college and learn all the music you need to be any kind of a success?"

I didn't. I couldn't. No matter. I wasn't serious about no kind of music career no how.

A trip to Texas. Now that was something I was serious about. When Bob mentioned going to visit his Grandpa Teague who lived in San Antonio, and maybe stopping off in Big Springs where Lefty lived, I was ready. I don't honestly know, but I guess I thought we could just walk up to Lefty's front door and say hello.

Bob had been working some and had a little money. I believe when we got on the bus in Bakersfield we had about a hundred-and-eighty dollars, pretty well off in those days. The bus proved to be too confining however, and there wasn't a hell of a lot to see through the dirty window of a vehicle that stopped at every crossroad. We wanted to move a little faster, so we took to the highway as soon as we got to Barstow.

I loved the freedom of the road. No family telling me to do this or do that. No teachers trying to get me to learn something I didn't want to know. No truant officers grabbing me by the elbow. No authority figure trying to size me up. There are many definitions of the word "freedom" but at that particular time, I thought this was it. As the road stretched out ahead of us and the California sun burned our faces, I double-timed my steps trying to keep pace with Bob's long strides. He looked over at me and grinned.

"We'll get us some boots when we get to Texas," he said, "then you can keep up with me better." God, I thought, real Texas cowboy boots. It was all too good to be true.

It didn't take us long to get a ride, and even though I was a little disappointed at my first glimpse of Texas, I decided that it was the "state of mind" that set Texas apart, and my state of mind was beyond belief.

Mama Really Tried

The man who gave us a ride took us all the way to Amarillo. Since this was my first Texas town, Bob asked if I'd like to hang around for couple of days. I wasn't hard to please, and even the name Amarillo sounded exciting to me.

"Wanna get our boots now?" Bob asked. I sure did.

Getting fitted for a pair of cowboy boots, even secondhand ones, may not seem like such a big deal to some people. But for a fourteen-year-old boy who was almost "on his own" in a big Texas town—let me tell you it was a *big* deal. And to top it all off I got me a secondhand cowboy hat.

I walked out of that store, not a couple of inches taller, but at least a couple of *feet* taller. I felt like all the cowboy heroes I'd ever seen at the Saturday afternoon matinee in Bakersfield. Look out Johnny Mack Brown, Sunset Carson, and The Durango Kid—here comes Merle Haggard!

"How would you like to go in there for awhile?" Bob asked as we walked down the street past a large, kinda run-down building. I looked up and saw THE TEXAS HOTEL on a sign that looked like it might fall down on the sidewalk.

"You mean get a room here?" I asked. Bob laughed, and headed toward the large double front doors. Still trying to get accustomed to my new boots, I almost tripped as I followed him.

Inside the doors, I looked around the lobby and was surprised to discover it was anything but drab. In fact, it was quite colorful. Big heavy drapes covered the windows and everywhere you looked there were big old potted plants, overstuffed chairs, and quite a bunch of very fancy looking ladies.

"Is this . . . ?" I began, and Bob nodded.

How could I tell him I'd never been in a whorehouse before? What if they could tell by looking at me that it was my first time? They were never gonna believe my ID. Do they ask for ID's I wondered. Hell, I couldn't ask. I wished I knew how I was supposed to act so they'd think I did this kind of thing all the time. One glance at Bob made me feel even worse. It was easy to see he'd been in places like this before.

I began to try to put my shirttail in, and in the process jerked a button off. I could feel the tops of my ears starting to burn as I watched it roll across the floor. It stopped next to a silver sandal. The girl wearing the sandal giggled and whispered something to the girl next to her. They both looked at me. I pulled at the sides of my blue jeans, which had been too short even before I got the boots. As I caught a glimpse of myself in a full-length mirror by the stairway, it was enough to make a grown man cry. Only thing was, I wasn't a grown man.

The first conversation that hit me didn't make things any easier. Bob said something to a tall black-haired woman in a reddish-colored dress and she had, in turn, called the girl in the silver sandals over to where they were.

"Hey, I ain't messin' with no kid," she said, her voice high and sharp. "Get him outta here."

I wanted to run, but I didn't want Bob to be ashamed of me, and besides I was curious about these places. Had to be a first time for everything, I told myself, but at the same time I was wondering how I'd ever live down the story that had me "thrown out of a whorehouse."

Then I saw her standing in the back, kinda observing the situation. She was what you would call almost fat—certainly a bit on the hefty side, and she wasn't very young. She had that kind of bright yellow hair, and it was stacked up on top of her head like an ice cream cone. I could feel her watching me before I ever turned in her direction. As soon as I did, she smiled. I tried to smile back and I felt my dry lips crack.

It was then that "yellow-hair" made her move. She looked very impressive as she walked across the floor in my direction. She had on a long, pinkish gown that drug the floor behind her. For a big woman, she moved like she was a little bitty thing. Some may find this hard to believe but the woman had a kind of class about her I've seen very seldom in my life. I began to feel less uncomfortable. If she was going to throw me out, I thought, at least she wouldn't embarrass me by doing it publicly.

She smiled again and I remember thinking that she was really pretty—old and fat—but really pretty. I liked her.

"What's the matter with you girls?" she said then as she approached the ladies who had been talking to Bob. They turned in her direction but nobody said anything back to her.

She walked over and stood beside me, and with her arm around my shoulders, she announced to the others in the lobby, "This here ain't no kid," she said, and her voice was thick with Texas and cultivated caring.

"This here is a young, healthy specimen of a man." She waited for her words to soak in. I was amazed that none of them laughed.

"Just look at him ladies," she continued, squeezing my shoulder, ". . . take a good long look, and remember what I tell you. There may come a time when you'll stand in line just to have this one *smile* at you."

With that speech she took me by the hand and led me up the stairs. Near the top she turned and called back over her shoulder to the others.

"Bygawd, I'll take this one, be glad to."

I wish I could remember her name.

By the next afternoon we were on the road again. This time we were heading for Big Springs, where we would visit old Lefty for awhile. Wouldn't he be surprised?

All the little Texas towns began to look alike to us, and each one had a cafe with a jukebox. We decided to make the trip a little more interesting by making bets who would be singing when we walked through the door.

"I got fifty cents that says the next place we go into will

have Hank Williams comin' from the jukebox," Bob said, as he pointed up ahead to a neon sign flashing out the word EATS.

"And I got fifty cents that says it'll be Lefty," I came back.

From almost a block away we could hear the sound then and we began to laugh. We'd both won.

> ". . . There's a little bit of everything
> in Tex-------aaaaas . . .
> . . . and a whole lot of Texas in me. . . ."

"Aw, come on in there, Billy Byrd . . . ," Bob yelled out as the cry of the steel guitar cut through the warm Texas evening. We both agreed then if we couldn't hear Lefty or Hank, we sure couldn't complain about hearing another favorite, good old Ernest Tubb and his Texas Troubadours. Other times we'd make the same bet and we'd hear Bob Wills.

"Hey, Merle, we just can't lose, can we?" No, we couldn't, not in Texas, where country music was king and everybody we met was a willing subject.

We were a little disappointed however when we got to Big Springs. Nobody seemed to know exactly where Lefty lived and the ones who talked about him at all seemed to think he was out of town, on the road or something. Possibly they wanted to protect him from two road-weary fans who had shown up to bless him with their presence. We found out years later he had never lived there in the first place.

Our main objective had been to go to San Antonio to visit Grandpa Teague anyway, so we headed that way.

We hated to go in on the old man as close to being broke as we were, so we asked around town about a job. We got the promise of one working on a fence line on a local ranch, providing we showed up early the next morning.

We had just enough money to get us a room in a run-down place over a honky-tonk. If you haven't been in Texas in August, then there's no way I can describe how hot it can get in a little bitty room with no cross ventilation.

But we knew we had to get us some sleep if we hoped to get out to our new job the next morning. I put my boots and hat where the light from the window would hit them and I lay there for the longest time just admiring them.

Just about the time I did drift off to sleep I heard one of the awfulest noises ever was, coming from down below. It sounded like a great big truckload of fruit jars being unloaded in the middle of the floor. What it was, of course, was a severe disagreement among the patrons of the establishment downstairs.

I raised up on my elbows, wide-eyed and worried.

"What was *that*?" I asked Bob, half-whispering.

"That was Texas," he whispered back.

Of course we didn't get any sleep because the fight went on and on, followed by another one that did likewise. We missed our starting time on our new job and lost it before we started it.

We decided just to go on out to Grandpa Teague's house broke. He seemed glad to see us anyhow. We spent a few days with the old man and it was there that I first saw television. I didn't think too much of it. I couldn't tell what was going on. Grandpa said it was "rasslin'" but I couldn't tell heads or tails about it. Sure wasn't gonna be no future in that kinda thing, I thought, as I sat there squinting at a bunch of jumbles, rolls, and flickers.

When time came to go, Bob told his Grandpa we were broke. "We don't want no handout, Grandpa," Bob said, "but we would like to have somethin' to munch on if you got anythin' in the house we could take with us."

"How are you travelin'?" the old man asked.

"We aim to go over to the train yard," Bob said.

The old man got up, went over to the table, and took out

some car keys. We went out back to an old garage where he had the prettiest, cleanest old '34 Buick I'd ever seen. Looked like it just come right off the showroom floor. I wondered if he ever drove it at all. Somehow he made us feel very special because he was getting his car out to take us to the train yards. It was obvious he only did it on special occasions.

A little ways up from his house he stopped at a small grocery store. In a few minutes he came back with a bag which he placed on the back floorboard. Then he drove on over to the train yard.

We got out of the car and I saw the old man fumbling in his overall pocket. He pulled out a crumpled old five-dollar bill and handed it to Bob.

"It ain't much," he said, almost apologizing, "but you might need it." Then he reached inside the car for the grocery sack. "There's a half a stick of baloney," he said, "and two loaves of bread."

"Grandpa, about the money," Bob said, holding out the five-dollar bill, but the old man put his hands out refusing it.

"No, no, no," he said. "You might need it. Just consider it my contribution to your trip. . . ."

"Thanks a lot for the baloney," I said then, hardly knowing what else to say.

"You're welcome," he said with a big grin. As we started to walk toward the trains we turned around to wave at him.

"Remember now," he called out to us, "be careful . . . and just eat the shit out of that baloney."

We hopped the freight laughing, and everytime we'd take a bite of baloney we'd laugh harder. That phrase, according to Bob, was not at all in character for the old man, which made it even funnier for us.

Even though we could have ridden the train all the way to Los Angeles, we liked a change of scenery. So, in El Paso we took to the highway. Before long we got a ride.

Just outside of L.A. the guy who had given us a ride picked up a third hitchhiker. Bob made the mistake of showing him the new gun he'd bought in New Mexico, a P-38. We all got into a big discussion about guns.

A short time later we let the hitchhiker out, then got out ourselves.

What we didn't know was that an armed robbery of a liquor store had taken place in the same area. The first person the cops saw turned out to be the hitchhiker who'd been with us. When asked if he'd seen anything suspicious, he told them he'd just been with some guys who had a gun. He also told them we couldn't be too far up the road. Indeed, we were not.

There had to be, I knew, a better way to end a trip. One minute me and Bob were standing by the side of the road trying to hitch a ride and the next thing we knew we were surrounded by police cars with lights flashing. Cops were coming at us from all directions.

"Awright, punks!" one officer yelled as he grabbed my hands and turned me around, "we gotcha now."

I couldn't believe this was happening. Before we could ask a single question they'd searched us, knocked us around, and thrown us in the back seat of a cruiser. The side of my head was stinging where one of the troopers had hit me with something and I felt like I must be in the middle of a danged nightmare.

"What's goin' on?" I asked Bob, but hell, he was as confused as I was. I didn't see how this could be happening to us. On one hand I had a terrible impulse to laugh and ask the gangbuster cops if they always welcomed people to L.A. that way. On the other hand I wanted to cuss and kick the hell out of the one who'd hit me. On both hands though, I had a pair of cuffs.

"What did we *do*, man?" I asked again, this time to nobody in particular.

"Shut up, you goddamned punk!" was the reply. Thanks a lot.

The police wouldn't throw us in jail, I thought, without at least telling us what terrible crime they thought we'd committed. Somebody would talk to us soon. Things like this don't happen. We had to be innocent, whatever the charge was.

From the window of the cruiser me and Bob could see them going through our things. I watched my clothes being dumped by the side of the road. There is something about having somebody sort through your dirty socks and underwear that does not set well at all.

"The gun," Bob whispered then, "ain't gonna be easy to explain." Oh my God—I hadn't even thought about that. I shut my eyes and laid my head back on the seat of the cruiser. I heard one of the officers call out to another one.

"Looks like this clinches it." I didn't have to open my eyes to know he was holding up the P-38. To make matters even worse they found a switchblade as well. None of this made us look very innocent. Lincoln Heights jail was no longer a probability. It was a sure thing.

"Oh, shit!" Bob said then, under his breath. I couldn't imagine what else could be wrong. "Your ID says you're eighteen." I looked at him and shrugged.

"Don't you know what that means, kid?" he asked. I shook my head. "It means you're about to face your first arrest as an adult. They sure as hell ain't gonna believe you're just fourteen, and whatever they think we've done is damned serious."

Well, what would everybody say this time? I guess I shoulda been spending the summer with Willie and Escar. Too late to think of that now.

"What day is this, Bob?" I asked, and he looked at me like I had two heads.

"What kind of a damnfool question is that at a time like *this*?"

"What day is this?" For some reason it was important for me to know.

"It's August 15th."

"Aw dammit," I yelled, "I know it's August 15th and I know it's 1951 too, but I was just wonderin' if it was Monday, Wednesday, or what?"

"How the hell should I know," Bob said. "You're lucky I know the date is August 15th, the day of your first arrest as an adult. You're playin' with the big kids now."

How come I didn't feel lucky?

Three

My Rough and Rowdy Ways

Dear old Daddy, rest his soul,
left my Mom a heavy load,
She tried so very hard to fill his shoes,
Workin' hours without rest,
Wanted me to have the best,
She tried to raise me right
but I refused.

"Mama Tried"   by Merle Haggard

AS I WALKED up the alley in back of the boxcar house, I could see Mama at the kitchen window. She was leaning over the sink with her face close to the glass, squinting her eyes against the early morning sun. As I turned into the yard, her face disappeared from the window.

"Merle," she called out from the back door. I couldn't remember ever hearing her voice sound so relieved—or so happy. It was plain to see that she was very glad I was home. I was really glad to see her. The Lincoln Heights jail had not been the best place I'd ever been and five days had been at least a week too long.

We'd not been offered that one phone call and I doubt we would have used it if we had. It was not something we wanted talked about, our being arrested as robbery suspects, carrying concealed weapons, and so on. Bob had suggested from the beginning we wait it out. He was sure justice would prevail, and it had. When they found the real robbers they released us—on August 20th, an hour before supper.

Of the five dollars Bob's Grandpa had given us, we had sixteen cents left. We flagged down a bakery truck early the next morning and asked him what sixteen cents would buy. He gave us a baker's dozen of doughnuts. I ate all my stomach would hold, and found out right away it was even *more* than it could hold.

We got a ride outside of San Fernando with some guy who played the organ on an early morning radio show in Bakersfield. He dropped us off within walking distance of Oildale. So I was very tired and hungry as I made my way down the alley that morning. My trip to Texas was simply personal history as I stood there looking at Mama holding the screen door open for me.

I waited a few minutes, and although she was never one to show emotion or offer a great deal of affection, I thought she was going to reach out and grab me. Then she noticed that her hands were dripping wet.

"Oh my goodness," she said turning to grab a towel. "My hands are drippin' all over the place. I was washin' out some clothes in the sink when I saw somebody comin'." She stopped then and motioned me on inside the house.

"I bet you're just starved," she said, taking the eggs out of the ice box.

"I sure am," I told her. "I ain't had much decent to eat at all this whole trip." Now was her chance to say "I told you so." I waited, but she let it pass, and went right to work on my breakfast. She only stopped long enough to comment about how tired I looked, and mention at least a couple more times how glad she was that I was home.

In no time at all, she set my meal in front of me. She had fried nearly half a slab of bacon and six eggs, and fixed a side platter of peanut butter and syrup, a treat she knew I loved, and a bunch of fresh sliced tomatoes.

"That'll put the color back in your cheeks," she said, sitting down across the table from me.

"You already eat, Mama?" I asked when I noticed she didn't have a plate in front of her.

"Oh yes," she said. "It's time I left for work already."

I looked at the clock. It was almost eight.

"It's past time, ain't it Mama?" I said. It wasn't like her to be late for anything.

"Oh they won't mind if I'm a little late," she said as she watched me attack my breakfast. "It's not everyday my boy comes home from Texas." I smiled at her. No, it wasn't everyday her boy came home from Texas. That was, indeed, a fact. Her boy saw no need in giving details of the complete trip either.

When she left, she insisted I take it easy, get some rest, and promised me a supper that night to match the breakfast she'd fixed for me that morning.

"Better get you some rest while you can," she said as she was going out the door. "School will be startin' in about two weeks."

That was the only disturbing thing she said the entire time. Only one bad word in the whole conversation. School.

I made the effort though. I decided to give high school a chance. And I went for nine whole days. Hell, I thought, that was enough. High school was no more interesting to me than grade school. I had better things to do.

The truant officer did not share my opinion, nor did my

mother or anybody else in the family. So, it was back to Juvenile Hall. I knew more people there than at the school anyway.

First chance I got I ran away again, stopping only long enough to find Bob Teague before heading north to Modesto.

"I don't think there'll be any problem gettin' a job up there," Bob said, as we stood by the road with our thumbs out again. "We'll work out the season, help get the hay in, then move on."

That was fine with me.

Now "making hay while the sun shines" is an old saying I won't argue with, but making hay by the headlights of a truck until ten or eleven o'clock at night is not my idea of a good time. I mentioned this to Bob and he reminded me that I could be back in the classroom or at Juvenile Hall. Except for a lil' ol' gal named Dolly Ruggs I'd had my eye on back in Juvenile Hall, I never wanted to see that place again. Now I might mention that Dolly's last name wasn't really Ruggs, but considering a story I tell about her later, I think maybe I should protect her identity. Hell, she may be a deacon's wife somewhere today—though I seriously doubt it.

"Hell, this is work," I said to Bob as we put the last of the hay on the truck at the end of the first day.

"It sure is," he agreed. "But listen, we're gettin' paid a dollar and a quarter an hour plus room and board. Not too many places give you food and shelter." We worked from seven in the morning until ten or eleven every night. Mercifully, on Saturday we got off at noon. Still, that gave us fifteen or sixteen hours a day for six days, and another five hours on Saturday.

It was during these hot days in the hayfields that the subject of music came up again. Our boss, Slim Rayford, had asked about Bob's interest in the guitar and the conversation got around to places that had live country music.

"There's a bar out on Crows Landing Road," Slim said, "where they play some pretty good hillbilly music I understand."

"Maybe we'll go out there some Saturday night," Bob said. The following Saturday at noon, we headed in that direction. At a little music store in Riverbank, I found a guitar for five dollars. Me and Bob went together and bought it.

"What's the use of makin' good money," I said to Bob, "if you can't spend it?" Then the three of us, me, Bob, and our brand new guitar, took off for the bar.

The Fun Center, we discovered, as we walked through the door, was completely square. I'm talking about its dimensions, not its atmosphere. It had a twelve-foot ceiling with dirty white walls and a rough cement floor. There was a bad-lookin' old bar with cheap stools that didn't seem to match, the kind where none of the legs are the same length. The only way they sit quite right is when you're too drunk to know the difference.

There musta been about fifteen or twenty drunken old guys and gals in there. I noticed they all looked somewhat alike—hard-looking, tough, and weather-beaten. Hell, they'd probably worked in them damn hayfields all their lives. That'd age anybody. The Fun Center was the kind of place where they didn't give you a glass when you ordered a beer, just slapped the bottle down on the bar. You got the distinct feeling that it would not be in your best interest to ask for a glass either. The bartender was a cross between Charles Bronson and Clint Eastwood.

Over toward the middle of the floor was a microphone that looked like a World War II model and beyond it in a far corner stood an old guitar. It looked like it had been abandoned, rather than left by mistake.

After we'd had a couple of beers, one guy at the bar, without even looking in my direction, asked if I could play that thing hanging on my back. For a minute I'd almost forgotten I had the new guitar with me.

"Well, yeah," I kinda stammered, "a little."

"Well, then how about it?" There was something in his voice that sounded more like a command than a request. I asked the bartender if Bob could play the guitar over in the corner. He said okay.

We walked over to the mike and Bob began tuning up the old guitar.

> *"Al . . . waaay . . . sss . . . late . . .*
> *with your kis . . . ses . . ."*

It was only natural I started off with one of Lefty's songs. Bob followed with one of his favorite Hank Williams' numbers:

> *"Your cheatin' heart . . . will make you weep . . .*
> *You'll cry and cry . . . and try to sleep . . ."*

We couldn't tell at first if we were going over or not. There was no applause, and very little reaction.

We were beginning to get a little nervous after doing about four songs. Then we noticed the bartender heading in our direction.

"Uh," I said out of the side of my mouth to Bob, who was getting ready to do another song. "Here comes trouble I think."

"Hey, would you boys like to play for the rest of the night?" Before we could answer, he said, "All the free beer you can drink, and five dollars if you will."

Hell, I felt like we'd hit the jackpot. We was aimin' to play all night anyway if anybody wanted to hear us. As for the free beer, that meant we wouldn't be using up all the money we'd made working in the hay that week. As Bob started singing "I'll Sign My Heart Away," it occurred to me that we were actually working on our first *paying* gig. Hot damn!

When the place closed around one-thirty in the morning, I noticed three guys who'd been sitting over in the corner heading in our direction. I nudged Bob. He saw them too. You've seen guys like 'em in every Western movie. There was trouble written all over them.

"We liked your songs," one of them said, much to our surprise. "You boys live around here?"

"We're working at Rayford's hay farm out by Modesto," Bob answered.

"Need a ride?" We did.

"Everything's gonna be all right," Bob said as we followed them to the door. Fool-like, I believed it would be.

There was a souped-up '35 Ford sedan outside. Me and Bob got into the back seat and the three of them got in the front. We headed toward Modesto. I looked at the backs of their heads and realized that these guys were really *big* son of a bitches. They were much older, probably in their late twenties. The closer we got to town the better I felt. I would feel a lot better once we were out of the car.

Back in the early 1950's, the big sport was boxing, kinda like football is today. When the conversation in the car turned to boxing, I was hoping these guys only liked to watch, not participate.

"You know who I really like," the guy on the right-hand side of the car said, after we'd discussed people like Jake LaMotta, Sugar Ray Robinson, and Bobo Olsen.

I asked who.

"Tough little lightweight boxer named Jenkins—Lew Jenkins." Well, as it happened, Lew Jenkins was Bob's cousin. I'm sure if he'd stopped to think about it, he would have known the men wouldn't believe him.

"Lew Jenkins is my cousin," Bob said, and you could have heard a pin drop. Conversation stopped.

The silence only lasted a few seconds however, and we could hear the beginning of a snicker coming from the front seat.

"What's that you say, kid?" the driver asked, stretching his neck, trying to see Bob in the rear-view mirror.

"I said Lew Jenkins is my cousin," he repeated. This time he knew it was unlikely they'd believe him, but he couldn't take back what he said. Hell, it was the truth.

It began quietly at first, then it grew louder. The three guys in the front doubled up with laughter. The driver almost lost control of the car.

"You know what," the driver said to them, trying to keep from laughing as he talked. "I once beat the hell out of Lew Jenkins' cousin."

For a minute Bob didn't answer. Then slowly he took a deep breath and said real low, "Well, it wasn't *this* cousin."

Without another word, the guy driving slammed on the brakes, throwing us all toward the front of the car. He came to a dead stop and jumped out. He left the door open on his side and invited Bob outside.

If there was one thing Bob Teague didn't like, it was fighting. He was a big, quiet, soft-hearted kind of guy, basically a gentle person. I've seen him talk his way out of many situations that most people would have turned into a fight. However, when push came to shove, he would, and could, fight as well as any man I've ever seen. He moved almost like a dancer; each step looked like it had been planned. One-two-three-four. He was graceful and cat quick. Hell, you were *down* before you could duck.

All at once I felt Bob take a lunge across me. Before I knew it he was out of the car on my side. He knew if he went out on the driver's side he was a sittin' duck for a sucker punch. Once out on the other side he had gained the upper hand. The other two piled out, one on the same side as Bob and the other with the driver. I was nowhere near the fighter Bob was, but I rolled out too. The only thing I heard Bob say was, "Keep 'em off my back."

Suddenly, I was face to face with the guy who had been sitting in front of me. I threw what I hoped would be a good punch. Somehow it connected and he went sailing back on the pavement. I just stood there amazed at what I'd done.

About this time, I spotted this other guy headed for Bob. He threw a punch and Bob moved just enough for the guy to miss, then took advantage of that few seconds when he was off balance. He came down with a chop on the back of the guy's neck, bringing him down. Just before he hit the ground, Bob brought his foot up and caught him square in the mouth, knocking six teeth out of his head. The third guy dived at Bob, and instead of helping, I just stood there watching. Bob took him out too. Looking down at both of the guys he had put on the ground, I couldn't help but think that it was too bad old Lew Jenkins couldn't see his cousin in action.

Then I noticed the one I'd hit was coming around and all three of them were trying to get up. The one with the missing teeth searched his pockets for his handkerchief so he could stop the bleeding while the two others managed to get to their feet.

I moved closer to Bob, not knowing what in the hell would happen next. All at once Big Dude started laughing, and hell, it couldn't have been easy for him with half of his teeth gone.

Once he got started, he just kept getting louder and louder as he sat there by the side of the road. The others joined in, too.

"You guys are some fighters," Big Dude said then, wiping his mouth with his bloody handkerchief. "You beat us fair and square, whaddya say we all get back in the car and go on into town?"

"Might as well," Bob said. Nobody else said anything as

we all crawled back into the Ford. Once the car was back out on the road, Bob leaned forward and said in that easy-going way he had, "I really *am* Lew Jenkins' cousin." There was no response.

When we got into Modesto, Bob told the driver we'd just get off at the Greyhound bus station. He had bought some more boots that day when we got our guitar, and rather than carry them around, he'd put them in a locker at the bus station.

"We'll just walk on to the farm from here," Bob said. The men wouldn't hear of it.

"Send the kid in for the package," Big Dude said as he pulled up outside the station, "and we'll wait for him. No point in you boys walkin' home. I mean, it's the *least* we can do for you." When I came out of the bus station, there was the goddangest fight going on inside the car. I couldn't tell one person from another—the winners from the losers—if there was either.

Then Bob kicked the door open with both feet, came out of the car, and landed upright on the street. One look at his face and I was horrified. God, I'd never seen anything like it. I never would have known who he was—there was so much blood on him. I could tell he couldn't see where he was going and I reached out and took hold of his arm. The Ford began to burn rubber as the driver took off. Damn. The son of a bitches were gettin' away.

Don't let anyone ever tell you that you can't find a cab and a cop when you need them, because that September night in Modesto, we got both, at *exactly* the right time.

First, the cab came.

"Follow that car," we told the driver. I suppose we tried to sound like Robert Mitchum or somebody, but I suspect it came off more like the Keystone Kops.

About four or five blocks away, the "getaway car" ran a stop sign. Then the red lights began flashing. A patrol car had been waiting for somebody to run the stop street. By the time we pulled up in the cab the cops were rousting the three fighters out of their car.

The law in Modesto seemed to know them and when we pointed our accusing fingers, they were hauled off to jail. At least it was somebody else that time, not *us*.

Bob explained that the men had decided to take him on with a crescent wrench once I went inside the bus station. This had made him mad. Before he had only been fighting because he had to. After he'd been hit in the face, he *wanted* to fight. Even though the blood was gushing everywhere, he nearly beat the hell out of all three of 'em.

On the following Tuesday we went to court. It was a day off from the hayfields at least. Besides we weren't even charged with anything. We only went to tell our sad story, but they claimed we had started the whole thing.

The judge called us up front. He looked us over real good, then he looked at the three men. We were all a mass of bruises—black eyes and bandages.

"How old are you *boys*?" he asked us then. Bob and I exchanged looks. Honesty was, of course, the best policy.

"I'm eighteen," Bob said. There was a low rumble from the three men to our right.

"And *you*, young man?" The judge directed his gaze at me. I gave him what I hoped was my most honest expression.

"I'm fourteen, your Honor."

"Would you speak up a little louder, son," the judge said. "I'd like everybody to hear this."

"I'm fourteen years old," I said. This time there was a loud moan coming from our former good buddies.

"It looks to me," the judge said then, choosing his words very carefully, "like three grown men picked on some boys and found out they just couldn't handle them."

We never saw them again, and I imagine they were as pleased about that as we were.

When the hay was all in the barns, we said goodbye to

Slim, stuffed our money in our pockets, and headed back toward Oildale. For a kid always dying to get away, it seemed like I was always anxious to get back. I honestly don't know whether it was simply the feeling of home, my roots, family, or what, but there was always a clear and simple pull back to Bakersfield—usually followed by a burning need to leave Bakersfield.

My homecoming this time was not as memorable as my return from Texas. Mama mentioned that *word* again and again. She really wanted me to go to school.

It was only a matter of time until I was back at Juvenile Hall. Charged again with truancy. I was beginning to feel like a regular guest there. In fact, I'd been in and out so much I even had my own record collection in the day room. Mama had written my name on some tapes and put them on my country records.

I spent Christmas of '51 in my home away from home. Old Santy never seemed able to find me there, but Mama did. She brought me the first brand new Martin guitar I ever had. It cost sixty-five dollars, and I'll never forget how that mahogany shined.

I really hated to leave it behind, but me and D.D. Warren and Bobby Cox already had plans made to break out.

The Juvenile Hall building was still new then. There was one door without bars. It only had chicken wire that runs through glass—very strong, but still not like bars. We put gum wrappers in our doors where the main bolt went. That kept the latch from going all the way in. The hall lock was easy to crack. We used a playing card.

When we got out in the hall that night, we could see the guard at the desk. The plan was to push a heavy wooden bench through the chicken wire glass. The damned bench musta weighed a hundred and fifty pounds, and we were scared to death they were gonna see us struggling with it before we could get it aimed at the glass.

Once the glass was broken, we did a forward roll the way

we'd learned in tumbling in gym. We hit the floor running.

As we came charging down the hall, the guard hollered, "Hey, where are you boys goin'?"

"We're leavin'," I called out as we hit the cement walk. It was about four hundred yards to the corner of the fence, a chain link deal about twelve foot tall with barbed wire on the top.

We climbed to the top and I turned around long enough to see everybody back at the hall running around asking, "Which way did they go?"

We had to roll off and drop down on the other side. As I waited for my feet to hit the ground at what I figured to be twelve feet, I found myself still falling into space. What we hadn't known was that the exercise yard had been built on a riser. Son of a bitch, I thought, as I kept falling. Where was the bottom?

Because of the riser, it turned out to be about twenty-five feet instead of the expected twelve. Our luck was not all bad, though. The landing place turned out to be a freshly plowed field.

We had made it. We were free—for a time anyway. I'm not sure what finally happened to Bobby and D.D., but I'd built my record up to the point where they were running out of space in my folder.

There'd been talk when I was taken to Juvenile Hall that last time that there was a possibility of sending me to a boy's school somewhere. If no one could handle me, it was probably the only thing left to do, they said.

I doubted that would happen though. What had I done except skip a little school? Maybe a *few* other things, but hell, I wasn't bad like some people were saying. All those threats about turning me over to the California Youth Authority—hell, that was just a lot of talk.

Four

Institutes for
Lower Education

One and only rebel child,
from a family meek and mild,
my Mama seemed to know what
lay in store,
'Spite of all my Sunday learnin'
towards the bad I kept on turnin'
'Til Mama couldn't hold me anymore.

"Mama Tried" by Merle Haggard

RED BRICK. God how I hate red brick buildings. I guess maybe that's one of the reasons I have such a dislike for the big eastern cities. Everywhere I look I see those goddamned red brick buildings.

I'm not too crazy about February either.

It was kinda foggy that day and the clouds were low and depressing. By the time we had got to the big iron gates it had started to drizzle. I knew before I stepped out of the car there would be that California chill that's more noticeable during February. It was no way to begin a new year. It's for sure '52 was gonna be a lot different from '51.

It had happened. The thing they—the people who always predict the worst—had been saying would come to pass. I was sent away. I had finally gotten into the kind of trouble they always said I would. Only thing was, I couldn't figure out exactly what I'd done that had landed me in the custody of the California Youth Authority.

I took my first look at the place that was gonna be my home for the next several months. I was not quite fifteen years old but somebody thought I was a menace to society.

The Fred C. Nelles School for Boys in Whittier was a huge, red brick structure, with a twelve-foot cyclone fence all around it. On top of the fence were nine strands of barbed wire, slanted toward the inside of the compound. On top of that was a large roll of more barbed wire.

School for boys, reformatory, concentration camp, prison, house of correction, rehabilitation center. I hated it on sight and it really scared me. There was a helpless, sickening feeling that had settled in my stomach like a rock, and my throat kept getting tighter until I thought I would actually choke.

My only hope was that there might be somebody there who would understand—somebody who might help me understand. I guess I'd seen too many movies where some kindly soul comes along and rescues the misunderstood boy.

It didn't happen.

"Line up," the angry voice boomed out.

There were about eighteen or twenty of us new boys. We had been issued our uniforms and were standing outside what they called the receiving cottage. At Nelles there were nine cottages, all of them named after Presidents. Later I would be assigned to the Lincoln Cottage.

We were introduced to our supervisor, a Mr. Morris. We soon named him "Prune Face." He was a weight lifter, as was Mrs. Prune Face. They were in their sixties, I guess, but they both looked like they were about a hundred and twenty years old. They had this old leathery-looking skin, dry and parched like they'd spent most of their life out in the hot desert sun.

I hated old Prune Face on sight. He was a sadistic son of a bitch, and I don't think he ever really thought of us as individuals long enough to single out any one boy to dislike more than another. He hated us all equally and was hell-bent on dishing out his own personal kind of punishment. As I look back now, it was the Prune Faces of the world who were the real "criminals," responsible for more boys going wrong than any other one thing.

In all fairness, there was another side of the coin. There were some good people inside those places as well. The one who stands out most in my mind was a black man named Alexander. He was a very large man, about six-foot-four, and had once been a sparring partner for Joe Louis. As big as he was though, he was a very gentle soul, extremely kind when it was possible. You knew right away that he really cared about people and treated us as individuals—as human beings. He let us know though at the beginning that we could not whip or outsmart him. He was always fair and straight with us. He was the one—maybe the only—consolation at Nelles.

There was a third kind of guard—the indifferent ones. To them, prison was just another place of employment. They weren't necessarily cruel, nor did they take much time to try to be understanding.

The Prune Faces were the ones who made the most lasting impressions and left the deepest scars, both physically and mentally.

While we were lined up in front of the receiving cottage,

SING ME BACK HOME

Prune Face began his walk down in front of the new recruits. One by one he looked us over and told us, in no uncertain terms, what was expected of us at Nelles.

By the time he got to me, I was braced for whatever he had to say. I'd wanted reality, but this was too much.

The denim outfit they had issued us hung loose on my shoulders, and I tried to make myself taller as old Prune Face moved in front of me. The outfits didn't have a collar and in the middle of the V-neck there was a little sew-patch, an extra triangle of material stitched down at the points. Prune Face looked me over, then let his eyes rest on the sew-patch in the middle of my chest.

"Do you know what that's for?" he asked. I didn't know whether he wanted any kind of response from me or not. I was afraid to answer.

"I asked you," he said, leaning in closer to my face and raising his voice several tones, "if you know what this is for?" When he asked this time, he folded his fist, took his index finger knuckle, and hit me right on the sew-patch, directly over my breast bone. It really hurt bad. I shook my head and hoped to God Prune Face couldn't see how much he hurt me.

"That patch is there for two reasons," he said, jabbing at me even harder.

"One reason is to teach you to say 'sir' when talking to me." He punched again and again, each time harder than before.

"Another reason it's there," he said, and by now he was accenting each word with a hard punch, "is so I'll know where to hit you to make sure it hurts you the worst."

God, don't let me cry. He wants me to cry, I thought. Please don't let me cry. I clenched my teeth together and stood as straight as I could. I went back to my old method of simply shutting out any pain I couldn't deal with. I became aware only of the sound of his words, not what he was saying. There was something about boot camp, something about being in the receiving cottage twenty-some days, and on and on, with the knuckle drumming on my chest. Both the voice and the pain became distant as I directed my mind toward one solitary goal—getting the hell out of Nelles. Damn if I was gonna spend eighteen months in this insanity.

And I would get out. I would escape those bastards four times, but I would also get caught four times.

By the time I was assigned to Lincoln Cottage, I had already tried to get away two or three times, and as a result, spent most of my time in the disciplinary cottage. Wherever I was, my mind was still set on getting out any way I could.

In the mornings at Nelles they gave us five minutes from the time the lights came on until the supervisor came through for an inspection. No siren, no trumpet, no bells, nothing—just lights on.

Another supervisor was named Troup. He was cut from the same bad cloth as Prune Face—just a different color. He was black. Troup never walked in front when he was making his morning rounds. He always walked behind and it would give you the creeps to hear him coming. He always wore those heavy taps on his boots. You could hear the clamp-clamp-clamp against the hardwood floors. Sometimes the steps would stop right behind us. All we could do was wait. Sometimes he'd make us wait a few seconds, and again maybe five minutes before he'd make his move.

Wham!

His blow was usually strong enough to knock a boy across a couple of beds. Usually the boy wasn't standing straight enough for Troup, or his head moved. Anything could set him off, even the blink of an eye. We never knew when in the hell he was gonna hit us. Sometimes he just stood there for several minutes while we waited for the strike. Sometimes it never came. The effect was almost as bad either way.

Finally my chance for escape came. There were eight of us working in the yard area in the afternoon, and we had planned to make a run for the fence when someone gave the signal. The fence was about fifty or seventy-five yards away and when somebody said, "Hit it," we all ran like hell. They caught us, of course.

We were totally exhausted as they herded us back inside the compound. We had been out on a work detail all day, and because of our escape in the afternoon, we had missed our evening meal. We were tired and hungry and didn't know what to expect in the way of punishment.

I don't know exactly what happened to the others, but there were four of us who were marched into the main yard in front of our old friend, Troup.

The blacktop courtyard was square and surrounded the disciplinary cottage. It was about eight feet long and sixty feet wide.

"So you boys like to run, do you?" Troup asked as he looked us over. "Weee—lll, that's *good*. If you really enjoy runnin', I think you oughta be allowed to have some pleasures here at Nelles . . . so run, goddammit, run!"

We all started to run. At first it didn't seem too bad, but everytime we'd slow down, old Troup would beller out at us and we'd try to pick up speed. I was having an added problem. They had given me size eleven shoes to wear, and I only wore size seven. The only thing holding them on was the strings I had pulled up and wrapped around my legs. Before long, they began to cut into my flesh and my legs got red and raw. When I mentioned this to Troup, he just laughed and asked me if they had hurt while I was running away.

"Keep on runnin', you little bastard," he said. He was laughing as he looked down at the shoes flopping on my feet.

It didn't take long though to get enough. When the strings cut the blood outta my legs, I knew better than to mention it to Troup. It was getting dark and I was weak, tired, and hungry. I honestly didn't think I could run another step. I turned in toward the middle of the courtyard and waited for Troup to come to me.

He walked up and didn't say a word. At least he was standing in front of me, I thought. He's not coming from behind as he usually does. I was unsteady on my feet, but trying to hold my ground. I kept waiting for him to say something but he didn't. I didn't know how much longer I could stand there, eyeball to eyeball.

"I ain't runnin' another fuckin' step," I heard myself saying.

The look on his face was one of total amazement. I could tell he hadn't expected this from a little dude like me, and for a minute, I actually thought he might, at least, respect my courage to stand up to him. Hell, my ability to stand up, *period*, at this point was quite an accomplishment.

I watched as that ol' grin began to spread across his ugly face. I didn't know what in the hell he was gonna do next. I didn't care much either.

"Yeeeaaahhh . . . you willlll . . . ," he said then. The tone of his voice was low, almost soft. "Yeeaaaaah . . . you will!" he repeated, and this time the volume and the tone of his voice had changed completely.

Troup walked over to the wall and picked up a leaf rake. I don't remember how many times he had to hit me before I started running again.

I ran completely into oblivion. Had to run a lot longer than anybody else. I knew some of the boys were watching from the windows of the cottage, but there was nothin' nobody could do. Every time I slowed down I could feel that leaf rake. He didn't aim at any one particular part of my body—just swung it against me again and again. There was no sound except the slap of the rake and the clump of my shoes on the blacktop as I kept running on into the chilly California night.

Just wait till Mama and them get here, I kept thinking. They'll get in touch with somebody who'll do something about this shit. They'll be shocked at the things that go on here. They'll get something done about it. I can take it till they come up here for a visit—then we'll fix Troup and Prune Face and this whole friggin' place.

When Visitors Day finally arrived I didn't waste any time telling my story to Mama, Lillian, and her husband, Bill. One look at Mama's face told me she didn't believe such terrible things. I'd lied to her so much, and there was no way I could support my story. The rake marks had faded and the places around my legs were just caused from bad-fitting shoes. There was no crime in that.

I looked at Bill and I think he believed me. I couldn't tell whether Lillian did or not. She hardly looked at me at all. What was the matter with them?

Looking around though, I could *see* what was the matter with them. Nelles on the surface looked like a nice place, if you were a visitor. The officials who talked to the visitors were polite. It looked like a fine place for a boy who couldn't seem to fit in at the regular schools. Except for the fence and the barbed wire, it could have been any good private school for boys.

What would the visitors do, I wondered, if just once they conducted a tour and let 'em see how they tied the boys to a post and whipped 'em. If they could only see some of the other things that happened to boys in here. Maybe things would change.

I watched the family leave, and with them went the last hope for help. Nobody was gonna get me out. I'd have to do it on my own. And I intended to do just that.

My life at Nelles was not only complicated by the guards but by the other boys as well. I was a country hick in the midst of a bunch of Mexicans, street-wise blacks, and the cool L.A. cats who'd been sent to Nelles for drugs and all kinds of gang activities. I didn't fit into any of the categories, and anytime you were different, that was reason enough to become a target.

Fortunately, there was a big farm boy from Eureka named Pierce who didn't fit in either. We formed our own group of two, but we still had to take a lot of abuse before we earned the respect of the others. About the only way to do this was simply fight as long as you could, take what was given you, and when you couldn't fight anymore, keep your mouth shut about it.

Once after me and Pierce had taken a beating out on the football field, a Mexican named Gilbert decided to give me a few extra kicks with his Bonaroos Brogans. That was a kind of shoe they wore. It was the old farmer brogan, polished up and shined, with the soles doubled and built-up a couple of inches. A kick in the midsection with one of them bastards would set a person back quite a bit. As I lay there bunched up in a ball, I cussed old Gilbert with every thud, swearing to myself I'd even that score someday—one way or another.

Sleep, as it turned out, wasn't even safe at Nelles. One night I'd gone to bed in the disciplinary cottage, and the boy next to me started talking. The cots were real close together and sometimes when you went to bed, depending on who the guards were, you could carry on a conversation with the guy next to you if you talked real low. I'd seen this kid around some. He'd been in the Lincoln Cottage too. He was kinda quiet, almost a loner, but he seemed glad to have somebody to talk to that night. His name was Beck and he was just a little guy. Didn't look to be over eleven or twelve, but I'm sure he was older.

"What do you aim to do when you get outta here?" he asked, half-whispering.

"Put all the distance I can between me and this shittin' place," I answered, and he laughed. It sounded good to hear somebody laugh.

"You got folks?" he asked.

"My daddy's dead," I said. I don't know why I didn't mention the others.

"You like fishin'?" I asked him then, changing the subject. He nodded. "But I ain't never been," he said. "I know I'd like it, if I ever got to go."

"I got an Uncle Escar who lives up close to Modesto," I told him, "and when we get out we'll go up there fishin'." Beck's eyes got real big. You would have thought I told him we'd just been handed a million dollars.

"Do you think he'd take us, your uncle?" he asked. I told him I was sure Escar would be tickled to death to take us both.

"And the fish up there," I added, "why there's bass as long as my arm." I put my index finger at my shoulder and stretched out my arm the way Escar used to do. Beck was impressed.

I went to sleep laying on my stomach with one arm over the side of the bunk and my hand laying on the floor. Next thing I knew somebody's knees hit me in the middle of my back. I moved my hand and could feel something wet and sticky on the floor. As I opened my eyes I could see Beck layin' there in a big puddle of blood. I don't know what it was that gave me that extra strength, pure fear I guess, but I raised up with a twist and threw this big black dude off my back. Turning around I caught a glimpse of his knife. I jerked up my blanket and held it between me and him till the guards got there.

Later I found out there'd been a fight between the blacks and the whites. When they'd put the black in the disciplinary cottage with us, he just continued the fight with whatever white boys he could find.

Beck finally got all right, but sleep, which never was too easy at Nelles, was even harder to come by after that.

I figured the only solution was a successful escape.

It all started out well enough. I planned to wait for the right time and just walk away from a work detail out in the fields. It wasn't much of a problem, and this time I didn't get caught right away.

Once I was several miles away from the place, I couldn't believe how good it felt being free. I had just walked away from it all, away from Prune Face, from Troup and his leaf rake, and from Gilbert's goddamned Bonaroos.

After laying low for several hours, I got out on Highway 10 and headed east toward Indio. In no time at all I saw a car coming. I put out my thumb and he started slowing down. Another few seconds and I would have been on my way. Then I spotted that familiar black and white—the California highway patrol. I couldn't take the chance. The cop would be even with me by the time I could get in the car that was stopping for me. There was nothing I could do but head back into the potato fields.

I hid underneath one of the sheds alongside the field. I buried myself in a bunch of sawdust until nothing was sticking out but my head. I lay there till almost daylight. Then I figured it was safe enough to head back out to the highway. Just about the time I started to crawl out I heard a bunch of people talking. They sounded real mad.

"The cops saw him right about here, I'm sure," one of the men said. "He can't be too far away." I could see the beams from a bunch of flashlights and I thought, good God, there must be fifteen or twenty of 'em.

"Well, by God, if he's around here," another one said, "we'll find his ass—then goddammit, we'll kill the son of a bitch." This could *not* be happening, I thought.

"We've got to turn him over to the law," the first voice said.

"Hell we will," was the answer. "We'll not turn him over to no law. We'll handle the bastard in our own way, here and now."

I was shaking so bad by that time I was sure the whole shed must be rocking like crazy. Don't move, I kept thinking to myself, or you're a goner. My God, why did they want to kill *me*? I'd only escaped from a boys' school. Did they think I was Jack the Ripper?

For what seemed like hours they searched the area. Several times the lights flashed across my mound of sawdust and I held my breath. Finally, they moved on.

God only knows how long I lay there before I got the courage to make a run for the highway again. When I did, the first car to come along was a highway patrol car. I didn't even make no effort to run—hell, I think I was relieved. I walked over to the side of the road where he had pulled over to wait.

"No point in checking me out," I said, as I got into the back seat of the patrol car. "I'm an escapee from Nelles and I'm ready to go back." The officer laid his clipboard down and looked at me.

"Were you around here this morning?" he asked. I told him I was. He began to shake his head.

"You fit the description all right," he said then. "Do you know that you are one lucky boy?"

"Why's that?"

"We had a bad thing happen here a couple of days ago," he said. "There was a young girl raped and killed. Her daddy, brothers, and a bunch of neighbors had 'em up a posse. They were out of their minds with grief and anger. If we hadn't found the kid first, they'da strung him up or beat him to death. You fit the description perfectly. If they'd found you, you never could have convinced them you were the wrong boy. You're *really* lucky."

Sure. How come I felt sick then if I was so goddanged

lucky. I was on my way back to Nelles and to Troup, Prune Face, and Gilbert's Bonaroos.

Although I tried to follow some of their rules and serve out my time I just couldn't. I kept getting out. By the time I had four escapes on my record they decided it might be best for all concerned, them especially, if I was transferred. They used the word "incorrigible." Next stop: Preston School of Industry (PSI), located up near Stockton. It almost sounded academic. In my imagination I could hear the families exchanging bits of news about their scholars.

"*My* son is getting his masters from UCLA," one would say. Another would comment, "*My* son is getting his doctorate from OSU." My Mom would have to say, "*My* son is studying Life Survival Techniques at PSI."

Like Nelles, Preston was also built out of them goddamned red bricks. The buildings looked like something out of a Frankenstein movie and there was a big bell tower right in the middle of the whole deal that looked spooky as hell.

The only major change in me by that time was my ability to hide my feelings. I could be totally scared to death but nobody could tell by looking. I learned early that it's not how brave or how tough you are—but how brave or tough they *think* you are. I'd reached the point where I could convince the ones I needed to convince that there was no use trying to scare me. I had proven I could survive all the shit at Nelles. Hell, I'd got myself promoted to PSI, hadn't I?

PSI was a lot more military than Nelles. We didn't have names for our cottages. We were divided into companies. I was assigned to "N" Company.

It was six months before I escaped from Preston. Don't know why it took me so long. Me and a kid named Rick had been given a job in the dairy just outside the school, and one morning we just decided to throw down our milk buckets and take off.

Instead of running to Stockton though, which would have been the logical choice, we decided to hide out in Ione, a little town right next to the school.

"Everybody gets caught," I told Rick, "running from Ione to Stockton. They'll never suspect we've stayed in Ione. We'll just lay low here for a couple of days, then when their search lets up, we'll make a run for Stockton."

It couldn't hardly fail.

Once in Ione, we began looking for a good place to hide. It was still a couple of hours before daylight, and as we walked along the empty streets we passed by a nice looking car pulled up in the front yard of one of the houses. Even though I was sure there wouldn't be no keys inside, I reached inside to feel anyway.

"Good God, Rick," I said then. "This damn car's got the keys in it." Talk about your good luck. We decided we'd be fools to risk staying in Ione now that we had good transportation that would get us at least a hundred miles away before they would know we were gone.

We eased inside, careful not to close the doors 'til I'd started the engine. I put it in reverse and let out on the clutch. I've never heard such a damned noise in all my life. All at once every light in town flashed on and we could hear doors slamming all around. We knew we'd be surrounded in no time so we made for the first shelter we could find— which was underneath the house where the car belonged.

It seems the natives of Ione were very much aware of the escape attempts made by the boys from PSI. They didn't worry about leaving their cars unlocked though, or even leaving the keys in them. They didn't worry, that is, if they'd done what this guy did. He had his danged car chained to a big old tree. Had a goddanged log chain around the bell-housing of the car and wrapped around his shade tree. That son of a bitch thought some of them old bad boys from Preston might come and try to steal his damned old car. It was getting to where you couldn't count on nobody.

Me and Rick lay there under the house all day while the search went on. We could see patrol cars go up and down the street and hear the helicopters out from town searching the fields.

It was sometime along late in the afternoon when the man who lived in the house came outside again. We could see his feet walking over to the edge of his yard where another set of feet stood.

"Hey, did they ever catch them boys that tried to steal your car?" his neighbor asked.

"Naw," the man answered, "never did. Can't never tell about boys like that. They may be a hundred miles away by now or still hiding in town somewhere."

"Aw, I doubt they'd be dumb enough to still be in town," the neighbor said.

All at once another set of feet came out of the house. These were small and wearing little scuffed-up cowboy boots. We could see only up to his waist where he had a little toy gun strapped on.

"Daddy," Little Feet said. "Daddy, where are the bad boys who tried to take our car?" Big Feet didn't answer. He and his neighbor went ahead talking. They had got off the subject of me and Rick, and we felt relieved about that. Little Feet hadn't forgot us though, and it looked like he wasn't gonna let his daddy forget us either.

"Daddy, where are they?" he asked again, pulling at his dad's pant leg. It didn't take long for Little Feet to get on his nerves.

"I don't have the foggiest idea where they are," he said. "Now run along and play."

"But Daddy," Little Feet whined.

"Go on," he said. "Better get on in the house with your Mama. For all I know them old bad boys are right there under the house and any minute they may just jump out and grab you."

There was nothing we could do but watch as Little Feet

began his slow walk in our direction. Closer and closer the scruffy little boots came. He had his little gun out of the holster and aimed right at the hole in the latticework where we'd crawled in.

Then Little Feet got down on all fours and looked under the house. As soon as his eyes got adjusted to the light he let out a scream. We couldn't do nothin' but stare into the barrel of a dime store pistol. By the time we crawled out with our hands in the air, there were real guns pointed at us.

The authorities came, and as they handcuffed us, Little Feet still stood there with us dead in his sights.

I didn't want to look out the back window of the patrol car as we drove outta town. Hell, I was afraid Little Feet would be standing in the middle of the dusty street with a John Wayne look on his face.

There is just so much humiliation a man can take.

Five

Dolly & the Hobos

People like us
  Never find each other
Love is our greatest loss
Lady I know you're
  Out there somewhere
But our paths may never cross.

"*Our Paths May Never Cross*"

by Merle Haggard

HELLO DOLLY. I don't remember ever being any happier to see anybody than when I saw Dolly that night. Hell, I felt like if anybody deserved somebody like her at that point in my life, it had to be me.

One look and I knew she was just as glad to see me as I was to see her. I didn't have no trouble tellin' what was on her mind either 'cause it was the same thing that was on mine. Still, I had no way of knowing that I was about to take off on one of the wildest, craziest, and most exciting times of my life. Of course with Dolly it had to be something special, because hell, she was sure something special.

SING ME BACK HOME

Dolly introduced me to all the wonders of sex I'd only heard whispered about, or seen in those dirty little comic books. She offered me all the things a lot of us back in the 1950's were too embarrassed to even discuss. And, hot dang, I accepted—asked for seconds, thirds, so on and so off. To her, sex was one big banquet, with me being the guest of honor and her the main course.

In the middle of this story it occurs to me that there are people out there, like somebody's old Aunt Margaret, who'll be too cheap to buy this book. She'll sneak into the bookstore, and while the clerk is busy over in the cookbook section, she'll grab a couple of peeks at the "good stuff," turning right away to this part about Dolly. But she won't get to finish the whole section and she'll just naturally jump to the wrong conclusion. Imagine her running home to call her best friend on the phone.

"Oh Nadine, you just ain't never gonna believe this"— and she's real shocked—"but I just read this book and you oughta hear what that awful, dirty old Merle Haggard says about that sweet, nice lil' Dolly Parton."

And Nadine—well hell, she's just about shocked outta her drawers.

No, to set the record straight and stop the leg pullin', it's not Dolly Parton I'm talking about here. It's Dolly Ruggs, the girl I first met at Juvenile Hall when we were both fourteen. Even then she looked like Anita Ekberg. Now, at sixteen, she looked even better. Her hair was longer and blonder and she was built like that well-known brick house. The fact that I'd spent the past fifteen months locked up seemed to make her even more exciting.

I'd served my time with the California Youth Authority and was back home again. I was making pretty good money on a job Lowell got me at a potato packing shed in Edison, but the hours were long and I hated it. As I got on the bus one night for my long ride back to Oildale I found myself wondering how much longer I could stand it.

"I don't believe it," I heard somebody say just about the time I got settled in my seat. "If it ain't the *baddest* boy in Juvenile Hall."

And there she was.

"What are you doing here, Dolly?" I asked, as I sat down next to her. I was trying not to stare but I couldn't help myself. She was really something.

"I'm workin' at Tiny's Waffle Shop," she answered, making a face.

"Like it?"

"Hell, no."

"I know what you mean," I said. "I'm workin' in a damned potato shed and I'm beginnin' to see 'em in my sleep."

"Well, how'd you like to look at waffles all day long?" she asked, laughing.

"I wouldn't like that either," I said. "Maybe we oughta just take off and leave the potatoes and waffles behind."

We both laughed at such a crazy idea.

Four hours later we were on the Southern Pacific Daylight, a fast north-bound passenger train, headed for Eugene, Oregon.

Why? We'd never been to Eugene, Oregon.

The train ride took about twenty hours and there was nobody on the train but Dolly and me. Oh, there were people riding the same train, in the same compartment even, but we didn't see them. We were so wrapped up in each other that Jesse James coulda robbed the train and we wouldn't have known a thing about it. I'll bet some of the passengers are *still* talking about the terrible behavior of those two wild kids on that train.

Once we got to Eugene we decided we would "settle down" for awhile and set up real housekeeping. For all I know she registered her china pattern down at Woolworth's and subscribed to *Better Homes and Gardens*. We thought we were very domestic. We had pooled our money before leaving Bakersfield and musta had about two hundred dollars. With that we rented us half a duplex and got us some groceries. A couple of days later we both had jobs— me at another packing plant and Dolly at another Tiny's Waffle Shop.

Life together was, for about thirty days, pretty damn good. Almost ideal, you might say. We didn't bullshit each other. There was nothing said about love, marriage, or forever. We just flat out enjoyed each other. There was a real freedom about our relationship that is hard to find at any age and I was convinced that I'd found myself a real treasure.

Then, along came Sherman.

Now Sherman is not the complication you might think he was. He lived on the other side of the duplex from us and he was a real friendly sort. Only thing that bothered me was the fact that I was pretty sure the old boy was a homosexual. First thing I knew me and Dolly were having a few misunderstandings about our next door neighbor.

"He's all right," she'd say when I'd make my snide remarks. "I like him, Merle."

"Sure, you do," I said. "He's just like you are—a *woman*. I bet he wears underwear just like yours."

"He's a nice person," she'd insist, "so just hush up about him."

The fact that she didn't seem to put much stock in my opinion irritated me. I didn't understand how she could be so tolerant of something like that. All I'd had from birds like Sherman was trouble and I guess I wanted Dolly to agree with me that he was a little strange. She wouldn't. She just accepted people for what they were and instead of admiring her for her tolerance, I felt like she was doubting my ability to size up the situation.

One night I got home from work before she did. She had the key and usually got home first, but for some reason she was late. I sat down on the front porch to wait for her.

Before long Sherman poked his head out the door.

"You waitin' on Dolly?" he asked. I told him I was.

"Well, why don't you come in and have a glass of wine while you wait?"

"No thanks, I'll wait for Dolly."

Ain't no way, I told myself, I was gonna go in and have a glass of wine with some middle-aged queer. God, what would the gang at Bunkie's drive-in think if they ever heard I did that?

A few minutes later Sherman was back again.

"I've got some good spaghetti," he said then. "Why don't you just come on in, have a little spaghetti and a glass of wine? Dolly must be workin' late and I'm sure you're hungry."

"No thanks," I mumbled, but he was sure right about one thing. I was starving, and I could smell the spaghetti sauce. It was really getting to me. Next time he came to the door I thought, well hell, why not?

The meal was great. I'd never tasted better spaghetti, and the wine sure wasn't that cheap stuff I'd been used to. Dolly, damn her, was no where in sight. My wine glass kept getting empty and old Sherman kept filling it up.

I must have emptied my fourth or fifth glass when he leaned over to pour another one.

"I don't think so," I said, putting my hand across the top of my glass. I was surprised that I was being quite civil to him. What was worse, I began to think he wasn't such a bad sort after all.

"Might as well have one more," he said then, holding the bottle up against the light. It was almost empty.

"Oh hell, why not?" I moved my hand off my glass.

As he leaned over to pour, he put his head next to my face and before I knew it the goddanged son of a bitch was kissing me.

As unsteady as I was, I managed to get up. Without a word I belted him one and knocked him across the table and into the refrigerator. He was laying there covered with spaghetti, wine, and a little blood when Dolly walked in.

She took one look at Sherman and ran to get a wash cloth. She washed his face and helped him into the bedroom while I just stood there getting madder by the minute. She came back out and started cleaning up the kitchen. I just about ran out the door slamming it behind me. I was waiting for her when she came back over to our side of the duplex.

"What did you expect me to do, Dolly?" I hollered out at her. "That son of a bitch *kissed* me. I mean, he actually put the make on me. He flat out planted a big old smackeroo right here on my cheek." I pointed to the place. She glanced in my direction but didn't say a word.

"I *told* you he was a damned fairy," I said then.

"You didn't have to *hit* him, Merle," she said.

"Well, what did you expect me to do, say, 'No, no, now Sherman, you oughta not do that . . .'?" I was mocking his voice.

"You're making too much out of it," she said.

"You don't *believe* me, do you?" I said then. "You think I hit him just for the damn fun of it."

She didn't answer, just turned and walked into the bedroom. By the time I crawled into bed a little later she was sound asleep. I lay there next to her trying to decide what I wanted to do and where I wanted to go. Why didn't she run to *me* when she came in the door? How come she was so sympathetic to that old queer? I felt hurt, and even though I wouldn't admit it at the time, I was just plain jealous—jealous of old Sherman for gawdssake.

The next day when I came home from the packing shed she was there. She had supper on the stove and was ironing one of my shirts. I walked over to her, dug down in my pocket, took out all the money I had, and laid it on the ironing board. She looked at the money, then at me. I

Dolly & the Hobos

reached over and took a quarter back and put it in my
pocket.

The time for playing house was over. I couldn't say it
hadn't been great but it was time to move on to something
or someplace else. Hell, it wasn't like we didn't have a good
thing going—it lasted well over a month.

I got my things together and started toward the door. I
thought maybe she'd say something to me at least but she
didn't.

"See you sometime down the road," I called over my
shoulder as I went through the door. She didn't say a damn
thing. I walked down to the end of the street where the
main railroad line crossed. Almost on cue, a slow freight
came in sight. I walked out by the side of the tracks where I
grabbed onto a gondola car and watched Eugene fade right
outta my sight. I never did see Dolly Ruggs "sometime
down the road," like I said I would. Still, she was some fine
kind of a woman—too bad about our little misunderstand-
ing.

As the freight picked up speed I scrambled over the top of
the car and settled down inside. Best I could tell we were
headed up into the mountains. Wasn't long till it started to
snow and I climbed up in the corner to see if I could find out
where in the hell I was. As the train slowed down I could
tell we were getting into a little mountain junction. The
sign on the switching station said Crescent Lake. The
weather was getting a little too cold for me and I just had a
light jacket. I figured I'd better try to find me a freight
heading south. I rode on as far as Klamath Falls before I
jumped off and caught another one.

As I bellied myself onto the only open freight car I saw, I
felt like I was getting pretty good at this hobo stuff. I was
boarding one of those cars with no handholds and had
already learned to head in, chest first, pushing my weight
toward my head as I let my feet and legs dangle outside.

SING ME BACK HOME

While I was still struggling to get all the way in, I got a distinct feeling I was being watched.

That son of a bitchin' boxcar was loaded. Musta been at least eight seasoned old hobos in that car. They were lined up around the side of the car and it was too dark in there to see their faces. There was one old man out in the middle on an old crate. I figured he must be their leader. I would have been scared if I hadn't been so tired and hungry because I wasn't sure this bunch of 'bo's would accept me.

"Why ain't you in school, boy?" one of them said from back in the shadows.

"I quit."

"He quit school," another spoke up. "I bet he knows all there is to know, so he jest quit."

"No, I don't," I said. I knew they were making fun of me. "I don't know it all but I'm out here tryin' to learn."

Everybody laughed and a loud splat to my left told me one of 'em was chewing tobacco. The place was damp and chilly and smelled like sweat and stale food.

The old man in the middle kept watching me but he didn't say nothing. I thought he was one of the most impressive people I'd ever seen. He was old, in his seventies at least, and he had the kindest expression I've ever seen on a man's face. He looked like he was smiling all the time. His skin was wrinkled and rough looking, with a stubble of beard covering the lower half. He had a short nose that came down in a little ball making him look a little like a Santy Claus who had fallen on to hard times. He wore bib overalls and an old blue flannel shirt. Over it all he had on an old dirty-looking sweater with one button left. It was fastened in the wrong hole. His hair was long, gray stuff and he had it pulled back and tied with a grass string.

"You goin' to California, kid?" somebody from the back called out. I told the voice I was going home.

"You got a home?" another hollered out. "What's the matter with yore brain. Or doncha' got one?"

I patted my shirt pocket for a cigarette but somewhere along the way I'd lost my Camels. Right away a sack of Bull Durham slid across the floor and stopped a few inches from me. It was from the old man. I pulled out the papers and began to roll my smoke.

As the train began to slow down my stomach was sure my throat was cut. I was starving.

"I'm gonna get out of here and see if I can find somethin' to eat," I said. "There's some refrigerated cars up ahead that look like they might have food on 'em. I aim to get some."

"Don't you break none of them seals, kid," one yelled. "They'll put you in the federal penitentiary for fifty years, you break a seal." Another told me I'd be ruining things for everybody if I did that.

I'm sure if I'd stopped to think, I never would have done it. As it was, my gut simply chewed away any fear I should have had from the hobo's warnings.

Up ahead I could see a car with a beautiful four letter word written on the outside. FOOD. It was like an invitation. Reaching up, I pulled the metal strip down and broke the seal. Hello, federal pen! Swinging the door back, I was faced with case after case of Libby's tomatoes. On top of all these tomatoes was one solitary case of green beans— waiting just for me. I *loved* green beans.

They didn't exactly welcome me back in the boxcar.

"Now, you've done it," one said. "You've ruined it for all of us. You've done what we told you not to, you little punk, and now we oughta whip your ass."

The old hobo who had not said a word in all the time raised his hand. I couldn't even tell what it was he said. Everybody turned to look at him. Nobody even moved.

He reached down in the breast pocket of his overalls, pulled out a rusty old can opener, and tossed it over to me.

"Open up them green beans, son," he said slowly, and I was amazed at the absolute kindness in his voice. Then he kinda smiled and folded his arms across his chest.

SING ME BACK HOME

"Ain't had no green beans in a real long time," he continued, "and I do really love green beans."

For a minute I couldn't open the cans. I could only stare at that old hulk of humanity and wonder why he decided to come to my rescue, especially after I'd broken one of their laws. I wanted to tell him how grateful I was. And I wish I could have talked to him a long time. All I could do though was open the first can of beans and take them to him. He pulled out an old spoon from his pocket and began to eat. Even though he was obviously their leader, their king, actually there was a childlike quality about him. I still remember to this day that old man's face as he held on to that can. Like me, the old man had been hungry and he just *loved* green beans.

I drifted off to sleep late that afternoon surrounded by hobos and a bunch of empty green bean cans. Nothing makes a man sleep as well as a full stomach and the sound of a train rolling you home again.

The silence woke me up. It was pitch black in the boxcar, but looking out the door I could tell we were in a train yard. I was alone. All the hobos had gone.

I got off the train. I didn't know where in the hell I was. I could see a big light. Looked like about a mile away. I started walking toward it. It was early morning, and somewhere I could hear a dog barking. Up ahead I could see what looked like a little town.

When I got to the main street, it was deserted. As I got closer I could see a sign—DUNSMIER GREYHOUND BUS STATION. So that's where I was. Only trouble was, I didn't know where the hell Dunsmier was. I'd never heard of it. Later I found out it was in California. It was a mountain town, a railroad exchange between California and Oregon.

I walked into the bus station, and except for a ticket agent behind a wire cage who looked as though he was asleep, and a man who was asleep on one of those big old

88

wooden benches, it was empty. I sat down and immediately nodded off.

It couldn't be, I thought, jerking my head up real quick. God, I smelled bacon frying. For a second or two, I thought I was home. Turning around I noticed a clock up on the wall and saw that it was almost six o'clock. The bacon smell was coming from a doorway to my right, where a small sign overhead told me it was the diner.

Mama would be cooking breakfast at home about now, I thought, and home sounded real good to me. Mama would be glad to see me. Even when she was mad at me—and this time I knew she'd be mad—she'd still be glad to see me. It wasn't gonna be no picnic facing Lowell. Hell, he'd gone to the mat for me and got me that job at the packing shed and I'd run off—let him down. My reason for leaving wouldn't exactly put me in good standing with the family either. Running off to Oregon with some girl I'd only seen a couple of times before was not the kind of thing you could really explain to your mother.

I got up then and walked toward the smell of bacon. At the counter, this big-assed lady in a green uniform and orange hair turned to greet me.

"Can I hep ye?" she asked, and I saw the name "Helen" stitched over her left pocket.

"Uh, yeah, Helen," I said. "Is there someplace I can have some money wired to me?"

She frowned at first, trying to figure out how I knew her name, then looking down at her uniform she broke into a big smile.

"Sure hon," she answered. "Just ask the ticket agent out there, he's the one who takes care of that. You broke, huh?"

"Well, I got money for coffee." I dug into my pocket and held up my quarter. Her smile got even bigger as she poured my coffee. I lifted the cup to my mouth and jerked it back real quick.

"Ohhh, watch out honey," Helen said reaching across the counter to push my cup back toward the saucer. "That's hot! Don't want to burn that purty lil' ol' mouth, now do we?" I shook my head and laid the quarter down by my coffee.

"Keep your money, sweetheart," she said, moving over to the next customer. "I'm old enough to be your mother and young enough to appreciate your good thoughts. Coffee's on me."

"Could I have some change?" I said, pointing to the quarter.

"Sure can, good-lookin'," she said, reaching into her apron pocket and laying five nickels on the counter.

If I sent home for some money, I thought, I could get me some breakfast and a bus ticket to Bakersfield. Well, what was I waiting for? As I headed for the telephone just outside the coffee shop, I passed an old jukebox.

Dropping in a nickel, I pressed down a button and walked on to the phone. From the other end of the line I heard a voice telling the operator a call from Merle Haggard would be accepted.

Inside the coffee shop, I heard the record hit the turntable. The voice of one of country music's original outlaws began:

> *"Heee . . . eeey good look . . . in'*
> *Whaaaa . . . cha . . . got cook . . . in' . . .*
> *Howsa 'bout cookin' somethin' up with*
> *meeeeeeee!"*

Helen, with the big ass and orange hair, just beamed in the direction of the jukebox, then gave me the okay sign with her thumb and index finger. To the man sitting at the counter, she mentioned something about my good taste in music and women.

". . . I'm free . . . and ready : . .
so weee . . . can go steady . . ."

I turned around and leaned up against the wall. I held the
receiver up to my ear.

"Hello, Mama . . ."

Six

Summer of '53

I was born the runnin' kind—
leavin' always on my mind,
home was never home to me
at anytime.

"Running Kind"   by Merle Haggard

"A GRAY FENDER! Good God Dean, that ruins the look of
your car. A gray fender on a blue car looks like shit."

"Yeah, it does, don't it?" he answered, kinda grinning.

I throwed another empty beer can down and shook my
head again as I looked at the '41 Plymouth coupe settin' at
the curb. It would have been a pretty little car if he hadn't
had to replace one of the fenders with a damned gray one. It
didn't seem to bother Dean none though. That was the kind
of guy he was. He'd been that way ever since I'd known
him—just able to accept things pretty much like they were.
He wasn't a worrier, and even though he loved a good-
lookin' car, he was much more concerned about how fast
the danged thing would run.

I'd known Dean Halloway, or Deanrow as most people

called him, most of my life. The older we got the closer friends we became. He was a tall, thin guy, kinda self-conscious about being skinny, and he had the kind of disposition that made people like him right away.

Having just come home from Oregon with a lot of stories I couldn't exactly share with my family, I was having a great time telling them to Deanrow, Junior Warren, one of my old school buddies, and his girl friend, Pat Ballard. Pat was only about fifteen, I think, but her and Junior were talking seriously about getting married. They were especially interested in my stories about housekeeping with Dolly up in Eugene.

It was the summer of '53. When I'd come back from Oregon, I'd found out the son of a guns over at the potato shed hadn't even held my job for me. There were no really big scenes at home about me just taking off, but things were a little chilly. When I'd run into Dean a week or so later I was glad to get out with a bunch of people for a few laughs. One of our old "beer parties" sounded fine to me, and as the evening wore on, I was beginning to run out of stories.

"All this talk about travelin' makes me wanna go to Arkansas," Deanrow said then as he leaned up against the side of his two-tone Plymouth. "I've got lots of kinfolks there."

I asked Pat and Junior what they thought about a trip, and they thought it was a real good idea.

That's the way we started out. We left late in the evening planning to see as much of the country as we could on our way to Arkansas.

As we passed through the checking station in Arizona, Dean let out a low whistle as he looked at one of the cars pulling out ahead of us.

"Look at that black limo, man," he hollered. "Ain't that Lefty Frizzell and Wayne Rainey?"

"It sure as hell looks like it," I said, leaning forward

trying to get a better look. "Step on it, Deanrow, let's catch 'em. This is a one-in-a-million thing, burn rubber!"

Dean pushed his toe as far as it would go on that little Plymouth, and off we went in a cloud of smoke and cheers for good old Lefty.

We were just outside of Ash Fork, Arizona, when the red flashing lights showed up in our back glass. Caught. And we never even got to see Lefty and Wayne.

"Let's see the registration and the IDs," the officer said as he leaned down by the window of our car. He looked them over. He looked us over, then walked back to his patrol car. He stood there a few minutes talking to the other cop who was on the radio.

"Wonder what they got us for," Junior asked, leaning forward with his head over the back of the front seat.

"I bet my folks called the police," Pat said, and for the first time we realized we might be in serious trouble. We'd crossed the state line with a fifteen-year-old girl and her folks were not gonna be too pleased with the likes of us. We were all older men, sixteen and seventeen.

"Maybe they just thought we looked suspicious," I said, "or they stopped us 'cause this car is so ugly."

"Knock it off about my fender," Dean said. "If you'd stop and think you'd know why we're caught. Hell, I musta' been doin' ninety when he stopped us."

When the cop came back to the car it turned out they did have an APB out on us because of Pat. In addition to that we were speeding, and we did look a little suspicious.

"Awright kids," the cop said, and he was very nice about everything. "We've got another call we have to go to, but we've radioed ahead. The police in Prescott are expecting you."

He warned us about getting any ideas about not turning ourselves in. He pointed out that there were no roads off that route and if we didn't show up in Prescott in about an hour we'd be in big trouble.

"Oh, another thing," he said as he started to walk away. "Better keep that little car under the speed limit or next time you might mess up more than a fender."

"See, I told you the car looked ugly," I said, laughing, as Deanrow pulled back out on the road. He showed me his fist.

The road from Ash Fork to Prescott is Route 89, a stretch of straight road about fifty miles long.

After we'd gone about twenty miles, Dean reached out with his fist and hit the windshield so hard it busted, leaving a big spider-lookin' crack right in his vision.

"What 'n hell's the matter with you?" I asked.

"Well, dammit," he said. "I don't like the idea of just drivin' into town and turning ourselves in."

"Let's not do it then."

"Shit, we ain't got no choice," he hollered. "Look around us. The cops got us. They're in back of us. They're in front of us, and there's that damn desert with tumbleweeds and prairie dogs on both sides. That leaves up and down—what do you suggest?"

"Hit it!" I nodded in the direction of the desert. For a minute Deanrow looked at me like I was nuts. Then he looked toward the desert. Slowly a little bit of grin started across his face. All at once he turned the steering wheel real sharp and started out across the desert.

Everybody was bouncing all over the car and Deanrow never let up on the gas. The brush and tumbleweed flew up against the windshield and we couldn't see a damn thing. Didn't matter; we were getting *away*.

Dean must have drove for twenty-five miles out through that desert as fast as he could—with us yellin' and laughin' all the way. Sometimes Junior and Pat were thrown up so high they hit their heads on the roof of the car. We all scrambled around to find something to hang on to.

By the time we stopped we were all wore out from the ride and the laughin', but we were all patting each other on the back because we had outsmarted the cops.

We stayed out there all that night, the next day and the following night. It was about forty-some hours I think. The first night we drank beer and sung songs. I'd brought along my guitar, and if I ever had a captive audience, this was it. By daylight on our second day, our daring escape was not near as exciting or as smart as we had once believed. We all began to notice how hot the damn sun was and we froze our asses off at night. We were *not* having a good time. By the time we'd killed our last few cans of beer, we'd run out of anything interesting to say. We were tired and sleepy and had started criticizing each other. Pat and Junior were no longer considering the possibility of getting married. They were, in fact, hardly speaking. Pat and I were getting along fine—which may have been part of the problem.

The sun got hotter. Dean sulked more. I was dying from hunger. Ain't my fault we're out here. Nobody was forced to come. What do we do now? Well, we could stay out on the desert and let the sun bleach our bones.

"Hell, let's go back," I said. Nobody wanted to go but nobody had a better idea. We had no choice.

The ride back across the desert was not near as much fun. The bumps were uncomfortable and the tumbleweed coming across the hood of the car was now an aggravation. The laughter had been replaced by cussin' and complainin'.

If we thought the police at Prescott had given up, we were wrong. As we came into sight a cop was standing outside of his car talking to some guy in another car. He had his back to us and we hoped we could make it to a little side road before he saw us.

"Cut into that alley, Dean," I yelled. Just as we cleared

96

the edge of a building, the cop turned. He'd seen us.

"Double back," I called out again to Dean and I felt the back end of the car fishtail as he made a left turn up a small street. One more turn and we'd be headed back west. They'd never expect us to get back on Route 89. We had to do the unexpected.

We'd made it. Straight road ahead. Behind us the city limits of Prescott kept getting smaller. Damn, we'd out-foxed the foxes after all.

"If anybody wants to know what time it is, ask now," Deanrow said as he pulled into a gas station.

"Why's that?" I asked.

"Because, our money, which wasn't much to begin with, is all gone," he said. Money. Hell, it hadn't even crossed my mind.

"We've got to have gas," Dean said, pulling his watch off his arm, "and this is one way to get it." Looking at me he kinda grinned. "I know there are other ways, but this is better." I grinned back. At least he was talking to me now.

Dean got enough money for his watch to get us some gas, hamburgers, and four quarts of beer—although not necessarily in that order.

It was back to Bakersfield. Things were beginning to look familiar. By the time we headed off the ridge route coming into town we were all feeling great again. I reached for my guitar and began to pick out an old Jimmie Rodgers song:

> *"Well, I'm going to California . . .*
> *where they sleep out every night . . ."*

"Aw, sing it Jimmie," Deanrow hollered as he looked through the busted windshield.

> *"All around the water tank . . .*
> *a waitin' for a train . . .*

SING ME BACK HOME

A thousand miles away from home . . .
a sleepin' in the rain . . ."

I glanced in the back seat. Pat and Junior were still sitting in their respective corners. They didn't seem too hostile to each other anymore but they were still aways from being friendly.

"I walked up to the breakman . . .
I give him a line of talk . . .
He said if you got money . . .
I'll see that you don't walk . . ."

Dean joined in and before long Junior and Pat added to the harmony. Down the mountain we came. Hey Bakersfield, we're back!

"Yodel . . . la . . . eee . . . heee . . . ohhh . . .
lad . . . eee . . ."

We sung every Jimmie Rodgers song we could think of as we rolled into town. It was one of those small-town Saturday nights in California during the 1950's which was like no other time before or since.

"Hey, look at the crowd they've got at the Rainbow Gardens," I said, leaning out the window and hitting the side of the car with my hand. "Wanna stop awhile Dean?" He shook his head.

"I think with all we've been through and the trouble we're still in, we'd better go home."

"I want to go home," Pat spoke up from the back.

"I don't," Junior said. "Let me off at the Rainbow Gardens." We let him out and drove on toward Pat's house. We let her out a block from her house and waited while she ran down the street.

"I'd hate to face what she'll have to face when she goes through that door," I said.

"What about you?" Deanrow asked.

"Nothing new for me," I said. "I've heard it all before, two or three times at least."

What I hadn't heard though were charges of "white slavery," which they accused us of when they hauled us all off to Juvenile Hall the next day.

"White slavery," I whispered to Dean. "What in the hell is white slavery?"

"It's taking a girl across the state line for immoral purposes," he answered.

"That's the craziest thing I ever heard."

"Her folks don't think so."

Junior and Deanrow were released right away because they didn't have a record. The girl hadn't been harmed, everybody decided, and with the help of my parole officer, they let me go, too, after awhile. He convinced the authorities that we were just a bunch of crazy kids out having a good time. All considered, it wasn't way up on my list of all-time good times.

Although we had a car for this trip, that wasn't always the case. During that long, hot summer of '53 being without wheels was one of the worst things that could happen to a young man. It could put a damper on everything. We'd never resort to *stealing* though—that was dishonest. We might have been a little wild, but hell, we were as honest as the day was long. We'd borrow a car once in a while but we'd always put it back where we got it. Sometimes we'd even clean it up a little and leave more gas in the tank than when we found it. That's the kind of guys we were—very thoughtful and considerate.

Without a way to travel there wasn't too much to do except maybe walk over to the Kern Theater and watch Ernest Borgnine beat the hell outta Frank Sinatra in *From*

Here to Eternity again. Our interests ran more to the parties out on "beer can hill" and girls. Now you could always have a car without a girl but hell, it was really hard in those days to get a girl without a car.

So, there we were one night, me and Dean, without a car, and we heard about this great party going on up in the mountains. We didn't have no way to go. We walked around town cussin' 'cause we didn't have no way to travel.

"Looky there, Dean," I said, pointing to a big shiny Lincoln parked by the curb. "Ain't that a beauty?"

"It is that," he agreed.

"Well, what do you say?" I asked. "Wanna go to the party in style?"

Dean grinned, and instead of answering, he just opened the door on the driver's side and slid under the wheel.

"The keys are here," he said.

"Well, that means whoever owns it don't mind if we borrow it for a little while," I said, running around to the passenger side. It was on a little grade and we pushed it down aways from the house before starting the motor. Then we drove it away—simple as that.

There was a problem though. The gas gauge was pointing to empty. So was our pockets. We figured though we'd be able to drive it around long enough to find us another vehicle with a little more gas.

Finally, out near the airport, we spotted a 1950 Mercury convertible parked on the street. They were fast machines back then and this one was all fancied up—jet black with lots of chrome and big fuzzy dice hanging from the rearview mirror.

Deanrow pulled up alongside while I checked for keys. The top was down and the upholstery really shined in the streetlight. What a prize! Now, if the son of a bitch just had the keys in it. By gawd, it did! It's kinda funny, looking back, I think we were always more excited by taking the cars than by our reason for needing transportation.

My hand touched the keyring, and I gave a signal to Dean. As I reached for the door handle, I felt something fuzzy. At first I thought it might be a dog and I half expected to feel big teeth closing on my hand. But the fuzzy thing moved, and I knew then I had my hand in the middle of some guy's bearded face. Why in the hell was he sleeping in his car? Did he think somebody was gonna come along and take it? I guess it must have been quite a shock for him to wake up with a hand in his face, but hell, he hadn't done nothin' for my evening either. He leaped about three feet off the seat and screamed loud enough to wake the dead.

Dean had the Lincoln ready to roll and I ran toward him—barely grabbing the door before he peeled rubber for at least a half a block down the street. In the meantime the guy in the convertible got hisself together and took off after us. We had a head start but he had a fast little car and he sure gave us one hell of a race. We kept making right turn after right turn until we were circling a very small area. We knew that any second our big old Lincoln was gonna sputter and die. The needle was way below empty now.

We made one turn the Mercury didn't and almost ran over him at a stop street. We pulled up and stopped as he went by, still thinking he was close on our tail. He never even saw us.

We assume the party went on without us. We never did get there. We managed to get the Lincoln back to its parking space where we dusted off the seats and cleaned the windshield. I told you we were very considerate. All we neglected to do was leave a thank-you note.

All that summer we pulled stunts like that. Sometimes we didn't have any place to go—just wanted to see if we could borrow another car.

It was easy to remember the last car we took that summer. It was a '52 Olds—fast car in those days. We wanted to try it out for speed so we picked a nice summer morning and headed out toward the cotton fields. We picked us out a long stretch of road and Deanrow pushed his foot toward the front. We watched the needle move up to eighty-five, then ninety to ninety-five, and on past a hundred. There was still a lot more power left under that hood and Deanrow was anxious to find out just how much. He was, thank God, an excellent driver. If he hadn't been, I'm sure we would have been killed the first week of that summer. But he was one of the best men behind a wheel I've ever seen. When I got into the music business I remembered his driving talents and hired him as my bus driver. He worked for me several years.

The needle on the Olds was way past one hundred. Up ahead there was a slight curve in the road but I was sure Dean could hold it between the ditches.

Out of nowhere, then, there was a farmer on a damn tractor puttin' right across the road in front of us. He had picked that damned time to cross from one of his cotton patches to the other. Up ahead, coming directly at us from the other side of the two-lane highway, was a '39 Chevy.

That poor soul in the Chevy could see what was going to happen and he hit the ditch on the right side of the road. We took the left lane, barely missing the farmer on the tractor. As I looked out the back glass I saw the other car go into a roll.

"Good God, Dean," I said, "somebody's *hurt* in that other car." I was afraid to say what I really thought.

He lifted his foot off the gas and started to hit the brakes.

"No, you *can't* stop," I yelled. "There's a farmer back there. He'll call for help, but Dean, we can't stop. This is a stolen car."

I'd said it. Stolen car. Not a borrowed car to have a little fun in. We weren't joy-riding, we were auto thieves, pure and simple. Now somebody was hurt, maybe dying— because of us. I began to feel a little sick. I could tell by looking at Dean he didn't feel no better.

Our little game was no longer any fun. We were not just messing with a grand theft auto charge, but could be responsible for somebody's death. Was that manslaughter—murder?

We were lucky. So was the man in the other car. We heard a newscast on the radio later that night that described the accident, even to the unidentified vehicle which caused the whole thing. I never knew the words "there were no injuries" could sound so good.

Our joy-riding summer was over, and best I remember Deanrow got a job out of town someplace. In any case, I still wasn't working and I was drifting more and more into the kind of life that wouldn't do me any good.

A visit from Bob Francis didn't improve my situation any either. I'd met him when I was doing my time in Preston. He'd said he'd come by Bakersfield when he got out, but I'd forgot about it. A lot of guys say that but they hardly ever do.

Bob was a big rough kind of boy, only a little older than me. He was out of a job too, and to tell you the truth, I don't think either of us really wanted one too bad.

What we wanted was something easy—something quick—something wrong. As it turned out, something very wrong.

I'll never stop feeling bad about what I did. There is no way to justify myself. I can't blame it on Bob. It was as much me as him. I knew better. I can't even blame it on whiskey, drugs, or hunger. I was just plain mean. I don't know any other way to say it. Even telling this story is almost a plea for understanding—not for what I did, but so you'll know how much I'd changed from that little boy who wanted to be just like his daddy. He was sure a hell of a long way from it at this stage.

There was a kid who lived not too far from our house in Oildale. He wasn't retarded, but some people said he was slow. He was harmless and certainly not a mean person. The neighborhood kids often made fun of him and hollered out names and unkind things. That included me. We all thought he was just a big dumb kid who wore bib overalls back when they weren't the rage they are today. He mowed lawns all day long with a push mower—very hard and hot work. I don't think he made much money, but what he made he saved. Word was out that he carried it with him. Some said he probably had two or three hundred dollars in his overall bib pocket all the time.

It sounded real easy.

Me and Bob figured the two of us could jump him and take the money with no problem at all. It would be like taking candy from a baby. It didn't work out like that.

What we hadn't counted on was his ability to fight back. We figured that because he had never fought before, he probably couldn't. That was our second mistake. We couldn't believe the strength of that guy. We had to get rough with him. When that didn't get the job done, we got rougher and rougher, until we beat him to a bloody pulp.

We had mistakenly believed a couple of punches would put him out, but he fought us tooth and nail. We finally knocked him unconscious but it took us so damn long to do it. It seemed like once we started we couldn't find a stopping place. We couldn't believe how tough he was. We hurt him bad. Broke his jaw in fact, and he had to go around with his mouth wired up for a long time after that. He finally recovered but I don't think I ever did. It was the sickest and most degrading thing I ever did. I don't even think we got his money after all. I would have remembered the amount if we had. For months, even years after that, I'd shake every time I'd think how close we came to actually killing that pore ol' boy. It could have been the end of the line for all of us.

He was able to identify us to the police and as a result I was sent back to Preston for another thirteen months.

As a second timer at PSI, I wound up being an officer in "A" Company, which is the receiving company. I hadn't been in too long when I looked up at the new crop of lawbreakers one day and who do I see but my old buddy from Nelles. It was my old Mexican, Bonaroos-Brogan, asskickin' friend, Gilbert.

He was assigned to me, proving things do have a way of working themselves out. I don't think he even recognized me. "Evidently you don't remember me," I said. "I'm the old country boy you kicked the shit out of one day on the football field at Nelles."

He didn't say nothin'. I still couldn't tell if he knew me or not, but he knew I had the upper hand regardless of who I was.

"You and I are a long way from being even," I told him then, "but now that you are under my care here at Preston maybe we can fix that." He just stared at me.

"You have a certain amount of time to do here in this company," I went on, trying to sound as official as I could. "And as an officer, I'm going to try very hard not to take advantage of your ass. But I want you to know I'll be watching you real close. You better not miss any steps or get out of line in any way."

He turned around. There was something about his attitude that hit me wrong—or maybe I was looking for an excuse. In any case, I put my boot square in his ass and kicked him past the two guys in front of him. He was really surprised.

As he started to get up he looked to the Mexican leader for support. The Mex turned his back. The same happened with the black who was leader of his group. I'd already told them about my beef with Gilbert and they agreed to let me handle it myself.

When Gilbert realized he was alone, he didn't look quite so confident.

"Well, what are you waitin' for?" I said. "Jump on out here. It's just one to one now—not like it was back at Nelles." I wasn't sure I could come near whipping him but as long as he believed I could I had the edge.

For a long time he stood there looking at me. Finally, without a word he turned around and straightened up in line. I never touched him again but I was just mean enough to make him believe that every day I might.

Later I lay on my bunk and thought about what had happened. The satisfaction felt good for a little while until I began to make comparisons between myself and the people I'd hated so much at Nelles. Here I was using my authority to bring misery down on somebody—just like old Troup and Prune Face. Hell, maybe I was no better than them, or Gilbert. Maybe I was even worse. What I'd done to the kid back in Oildale was worse than what Gilbert and his friends had done to me.

What was happening to me? Was I going to become just like those goddamned people I'd hated so bad? I felt bad. Worse, I felt *guilty*. For the first time in my life I actually felt guilty. I'd made so many excuses before—and sometimes with good reason, but I was in Preston this time because I deserved to be. There would be no escape tries. Hell, I realized that I actually wanted to be there.

Maybe, I thought, as I drifted off to sleep, this is where people like me belong. Maybe I shouldn't be allowed to associate with good people like Escar and Willie . . . and Mama. Poor Mama. What must she think of me now?

I wondered if she cried at night too.

Seven

Listen to the Music

The man that hath no music in himself
Nor is not moved with concord
of sweet sounds,
Is fit for treasons, stratagems and spoils . . .

—William Shakespeare

BY NOW SOME of you may be wondering why I've said so little about my music. The general public probably thinks of me and my music in the same breath. I hope that's the case, because in the past eighteen years, music has been my constant companion.

Like a dear friend, it's puzzled me at times, but never disappointed me. Like a good woman, it's given me comfort and pleasure, and asked only respect and attention in return. Like a religion, it has offered me a reason for being when other things have slipped away. But most of all, it has become an extension of my feelings, allowing me that little piece of immortality everybody dreams about.

I didn't always believe I could make it in music. I think that was partly due to that awful fear of failure that hides inside most of us. When I say I didn't chase after my musical dream—even to the point of denying that I had one—I'm not saying I didn't express myself musically. There was always music in my life, but sometimes I was only a listener. It was not until years later that I realized that even as a listener, I was trying to *learn* all I could.

There was a point when I thought music was just too much fun to be called work. It's funny now, with a certain amount of success, how it can sometimes be too much work to be fun.

Because of the constant warnings that "people like us" could never succeed in the music business, I almost believed it. It was true, I had no formal training, and it was hard to believe I could really make a living doing something that gave me as much pleasure as music. Work, to me, was digging ditches, working in the hay fields, eight hours on a factory line, or picking cotton—not strumming on a guitar and singing some songs.

Traveling around now the way I do, I see thousands of people doing work they hate, simply because they don't believe they could make it doing something they really love. Some of these people are great successes at their jobs, if you measure success by how much money you make or how high up the ladder you climb. Almost to a person they talk about how they're not happy because they'd rather be doing something else. When you ask them why they don't do that, they usually answer by saying, "Oh, I could never do *that*." It all adds up to one thing—the fear of failing.

There was a time when I was afraid to admit how much I wanted the music. But from the first time I picked up a guitar, or maybe even heard one, I wanted to be a good musician, or an excellent guitar player, and have people accept me. It was a long time before I finally admitted to myself that I had a hunger for music that would never be totally satisfied.

I'm sure my dad's love for music influenced me a lot in my early years. He would have been proud to see I've made it my life's work. Even when I started winning awards and getting recognition, someone was always missing. There was always an empty spot where *he* would have been. Nobody can fill that place reserved for my loving father. He would have understood how thankful I am to be a part of this music that I love so much.

It is only now when I look back that I realize how much music has meant to my life. Lillian said Mama was determined long before I was born that music would be part of my birthright. She even named me after some musician friend of the family. My name would have been Merle even if I'd been a girl. I don't know about that story that has me keeping time to the music "under my little covers" long before I could walk, but if that's the way Mama tells it, you can believe that's the way it was.

In the God-only-knows-how-many interviews I've given, there is always that same old question about how I got started.

Well, hell, I'd heard that question so many times. I decided the next time I heard it, I'd just make up a story. I don't know exactly what year, but it's not been too long ago that some lady came on my bus to do an interview. I was tired and not ready for that question again.

"How did you get started in the music business, Mr. Haggard?"

"I was in church with my mama and daddy," I said, keeping what I hoped was a very serious expression on my face. "They got up to sing, and in a few minutes I got up there with 'em." I went on to tell the lady I was only eighteen months old and could hardly make myself understood, but with my da-das and goo-goos, I gave it a good try.

I told her I was a real hit and she scribbled down her notes. "Everybody encouraged me, and told my folks I had natural talent," I went on. "Only thing was, I wasn't singin', I was trying to tell 'em about my terrible diaper rash."

The story actually came out saying I got my start singing in church with my folks when I was only eighteen months old. So, if I get a little upset with interviews, this is one of the reasons. And now, to set the record straight, no, I didn't get started in the business because of a pain in the ass, though I've heard that some people, from time to time, do refer to me that way.

If there was a beginning to my guitar playing, it had to be when I was about ten and Lowell brought an old guitar home.

When I first began to make reasonable sounds on it—ones that wouldn't send the dog under the house—I made a very important discovery. I found out that as soon as I'd pick up the guitar, strum a G or a D, people would stop talking and pay attention to me. What was even more important, my number of friends increased too. For a boy who was shy—and regardless of what some people may think, I was extremely shy—that guitar gave me a new and exciting way of saying something.

By the time I met Bob Teague, I was so hungry to learn more about this marvelous instrument that I felt like he had been sent to me.

There were others in my neighborhood who could play one or two musical instruments. One guy about my age was very good on the guitar and when the gang would get together out on "beer can hill," Delbert Smart was usually in the group. Like me, Delbert had a little problem with the law now and then, and we eventually ended up as neighbors years later—in San Quentin. But, as teenagers in Oildale, we shared love for the guitar. It was from Delbert and Bob Teague that I learned the basic music I live with today. Of course, over the years there have been many others who have been kind enough to share their knowledge with me.

The more I learned about music, the more I wanted to know. Besides the great Jimmie Rodgers, a lot of other artists have had quite an effect on me. I think the first to impress me with his good singing voice was Tommy Duncan, the man who used to sing with The Bob Wills Show.

During the late 1940's and early 1950's in California, especially around Bakersfield, Bob Wills was a national hero. The Okies who had come to California in the 1930's had not found that promised land. Our people were often looked down on by the natives as being dumb and ignorant Okies. We needed a hero, and Bob was certainly that and more. He had come from Oklahoma to California during World War II, and it was like he brought some of home with him. Actually, Bob Wills was more important to some of us than the President, and you know how everybody liked Harry.

One Tuesday every month, there was a live broadcast from the Beardsley Ballroom in Bakersfield. I listened to it every time. Once I even rode my bike out there, propped it up against the side of the building, stood on the seat, and looked through the window. I remember I didn't even want to go in and watch. It was enough just to be in the general vicinity of Bob Wills and his Texas Playboys.

As I listened to the radio at home I knew there was something special, something extra I didn't hear anywhere else. I didn't realize it was that beautiful fiddle of Bob's that was piercing little holes right through my head. I liked all the music and I especially liked Tommy's singing. But when Wills wasn't fiddlin', I knew something was missing. I just didn't know enough about music then to understand exactly what it was.

Bob Wills spent fifty years in the business I've come to love. He laid all the groundwork for country music today. He fought the unions back in the 1930's when country music wasn't accepted at all unless the musician had a lead sheet and could do all the things some union official said a "musician" ought to do. He was really the ramrod, the trail boss in the drive that has taken country music all over the world.

Bob Wills was such a character, and there was so much more to him than his music. And, God knows, there was a lot to his music.

My favorite Bob Wills story—and almost everybody I know has his own favorite—was told to me by Eldon Shamblin, now the oldest living member of the Texas Playboys. Eldon, along with Tiny Moore, still plays music today, and they are both part of my band.

Bob was about thirty-nine, so Eldon said, when he got drunk and joined the Army. I suppose he got overly enthusiastic about "doing his part" after doing more than his part of drinking.

Eldon was already in the service. He was an officer, and when he heard Bob had enlisted he went over to the processing center to find out about his old friend.

As Eldon walked around the corner of a building, who did he meet but this awful-looking person coming down the steps. The old Western Swing King was recovering—and none too well—from a terrible hangover. The clothes he had been issued were too damn big, and there was a bunch of tags hanging all over him. Eldon said he "looked like a man between pukes." Finally Eldon said, "Well, Bob, I don't know what to say to you." Bob just flipped back and said, "Well, Eldon, just don't say a fuckin' thing." And he walked away.

A short time later they said he cussed out some big brass, and they sent him straight to the brig. He never went to boot camp or nothin'—just directly to the stockade. Once there, he got into an argument with some big old sergeant who kept needling him about being a hillbilly singer. Bob told the sergeant he was a soldier, not a singer, and asked to be left alone. Well, the sergeant kept on till he got Bob madder'n hell. They got into a big fight.

In the end Bob was discharged from the service, probably having seen more combat than some of the guys who stayed in for the duration.

I might add that it wasn't just Bob Wills and Tommy Duncan who impressed me. Although I believe they were two of the strongest influences, I was aware of other music during the late 1940's and 1950's. There were so many great songs and singers. Seems like the worst times bring out the best in all kinds of art, music especially. There were the big bands like Tommy Dorsey and Glenn Miller, and the popular singers like Eddie Howard with "I Wonder," Ted Weems whistling all through "Heartaches," and one real smooth crooner by the name of Bing Crosby. What I learned to admire most, even as a child, was talent.

Although I was really influenced by Bob Wills and Jimmie Rodgers, I was also listening to that ol' boy from Alabama who sang as though he knew every teardrop and felt every pain—Hank Williams.

When Lefty Frizzell first came on the radio, everybody talked about him. People usually mispronounced his name, and it came out sounding like it rhymed with drizzle. More and more I found myself trying to sound like him, sometimes without even realizing it. Lefty gave me the courage to dream.

So, when people ask me when I got into music, I honestly don't know how to answer. It could have been before I was born, when Mama decided to name me after a musician. It could have been listening to Stuart Hamblen's gospel radio program before I could talk plain enough to make Mama understand what I was saying. It could have been when Darrel Epps' mother told me I sounded "just like that guy on the radio." It was always there, I suppose; it just took me awhile to recognize it—and admit it.

SING ME BACK HOME

By the time the little box with fuzzy pictures came along in the early 1950's, I began paying more attention to the local talent. One of the first popular TV shows around Bakersfield was *The Billy Mize Show* on Channel 29, the first TV station in the San Joaquin Valley. Besides television there was quite a bit of local club activity. There were places like The Lucky Spot, the Barrel House, Doc's Club, Green Door, Club 409, The Blackboard, and High-Pockets—all featuring live country music. Hangin' out at some of these places got me thinking about playing in a band myself. Singing? Hell, I wasn't out to be no star, I just wanted to pick.

To me, the word "star" meant a man like Lewis Talley. He had his own TV show. He was a cross between Hank Williams and Ernest Tubb. He also owned a record company and a publishing company along with his cousin, Fuzzy Owen. Fuzzy was also a musician. If someone had told me when I was about sixteen years old that I would ever be as big a star as Lewis Talley, I would have laughed.

It's not difficult to remember the first time I met Louie and Fuzzy. I didn't know much about the "business," but I did know that a person had to have something that would show what he could do. I must have been about seventeen when I went to a studio in Bakersfield and had a couple of discs made. They weren't tapes back then, they were flimsy little discs. Then, real quick before I lost my nerve, I went over to Louie's studio on Hazel Street to play them for anybody who would listen.

To say I was impressed was an understatement. Louie, who was the biggest thing in Bakersfield, treated me just like I was as important as he was. He says he remembers me as just a green kid off the streets with hardly enough courage to get inside the studio door. He had me pegged right.

Louie took the discs into the studio and listened to them. Then he called his partner in so they could listen together.

It was a good thing my conversation wasn't needed because I couldn't say nothin'.

"Well, what do you think, Fuzz?" Louie asked when the disc stopped turning. When Fuzzy didn't answer right away Louie came back with, "I think he's pretty damn good."

God, I thought, they're talking about me like I wasn't even there.

"Well, he sounds an awful lot like Wynn Stewart and Lefty Frizzell," Fuzzy said, again as though I wasn't in the room. "We've already got them, don't think we need any more. I like his songs pretty good, but I just don't think . . ."

That was all I heard. I slipped out of the studio and waited outside.

As I stood outside leaning up against the wall, Louie came out and laid his hand on my shoulder.

"The way things are right now," he said, "Fuzzy is probably right." You learn early how to pick up on that old "don't call us, we'll call you" routine.

Still, there was something else about that first meeting. Even though I felt rejected, I didn't feel stripped of hope. I believed Louie was sincere when he had told me there was a possibility that we could do business later.

Looking back it's strange to see that the people who would later become so important in my life were beginning to put in their first appearances. It was almost like they were coming by, all through the early and mid-1950's, and signing in.

Music was taking off in all kinds of directions during those days. There were rumblings about a new age, a new kind of beat. Some said it was just another version of black music mixed with gospel and sometimes sung by far-out hillbillies who were shocking the older generation out of their socks. It was called rock 'n' roll, by those who did it. Some folks were more convinced it was the "devil's doings."

SING ME BACK HOME

Even though a lot of people were listening to Bill Haley and the Comets, me and my bunch stuck to basic country. And you couldn't get more basic than a guy named Buck Owens, one of Bakersfield's own.

"Who's the dude in overalls?" I asked Deanrow, as we sat in front of the little black and white TV.

"Somebody named Buck Owens," he said.

"Who's the pretty woman?" I wanted to know.

"That's his wife, or she *was* his wife. Her name is Bonnie Owens."

That was the way I first saw Buck and Bonnie. Somebody told me Buck came right out of the cotton fields and he was still wearing his bib overalls. The people seemed to like him. In fact they still do. I see him on TV every now and then, and damn if he ain't still wearing them bib overalls.

As for the pretty woman, I was told that she worked at The Blackboard as a singing cocktail waitress. I remember thinking first time I saw her that she would be a big star one day—provided she didn't get mixed up with the wrong people.

Across the screen came one face after another, people who would figure in one way or another in my future. But I had no way of knowing that then. I only watched, studied, and wondered. I saw people like Tommy Collins. I would sit glued to the set when he did a song called "High on a Hilltop." I never figured one day Tommy would be writing songs for me. I felt the same way when I saw Dallas Frazier and Leon Copeland.

When I saw Lefty Frizzell again in Bakersfield, I made it a point to watch his lead guitar player. His name was Roy Nichols. I'd heard of him before. I knew he had started out with The Maddox Brothers and Rose when he was just a kid. They were big back then. They wouldn't have nobody playin' for them who wasn't first rate. And the same was true for Lefty.

"Hey, Roy," I hollered out at him during the break. He mumbled some kind of a greeting.

"My name's Merle Haggard," I said. "I'm a picker and a singer." He didn't look impressed. He never does.

"How's it working for Lefty?" I asked him.

"Not worth a shit," he growled back at me. "In fact, this is my last night."

"Whatcha gonna do next?" I asked, like it was any of my business.

"Gonna work for Cousin Herb's TV show," he answered.

That had ended the conversation. Roy was never a guy to stand around and talk, but in a few days I was watching Herb's show and there he was just a pickin' away. Who'd believe he'd be pickin' for me one day.

Gradually, I worked my way into this band and that band, sitting in with first one and then another, playing guitar and getting my name known around the local clubs. I didn't even realize that I was laying down a foundation for my future.

It was about 1956 when I was approached by a man from Springfield, Missouri. I was playing in a club in Bakersfield when he asked if I'd consider working out of town. Said his name was Jack Tyree and he had a radio show in Springfield. He offered me fifty dollars a week to sing on it. I thought this might be the break I was looking for since Springfield was the home of the Ozark Jubilee, where stars were being discovered almost overnight on national TV. I figured once I was there I might get to see Red Foley, the star and emcee of the Jubilee.

Being on *The Smilin' Jack Tyree Radio Show* wasn't all it was cracked up to be. I'd been there three weeks, and hell, I hadn't even got paid. What was worse, nobody at the Jubilee had any time to see me.

I decided to go home, so I went in to get my money from Smilin' Jack. He was on the phone when I went in. He had his big fancy boots propped up on his desk and was leaning way back in his chair. I sat down to wait for him to finish his conversation.

Son of a bitch, he was talking to Audrey Williams, Hank's wife. From the drift of the conversation, I took it she was Tyree's source of income for some damn reason. From the talk I also learned where he kept his ready cash.

When he got off the phone, I walked over to his desk and asked if I could have my hundred and fifty bucks.

"I just ain't got it, son," he said. "If I had it, I'd pay you, but the truth is, I just ain't got it."

I knew then that my radio career in Springfield had come to an end.

I walked over to the desk, lifted his pant leg, and pulled a roll of bills out of his sock. I peeled off my hundred and fifty and jammed the rest back where I'd found it.

I didn't say any formal goodbye to Smilin' Jack when I left. Fact is, I don't think he was smilin' at all when I left. On my way to the bus station, I gave the Ozark Jubilee the old Bakersfield salute. To hell with all of you, I thought to myself as I boarded the bus. All except Red Foley, I couldn't blame him. He never even got the chance to meet me. As the bus pulled out of the station, I told myself that Red woulda liked me—if he coulda heard me.

By the time I got home, I was beginning to wonder if the music business was right for me. I still loved the music, but I sure was hatin' the business.

Back in the Bakersfield barrooms, I still listened, picked, and sang every chance I got. I hung around places like the Barrel House, which had been one of the first places I worked. Tex Franklin, the owner, took a chance on an unknown back when not too many people would. He says I paid him back by taking all his good musicians with me when I left. He's never forgiven me. He still owns the Barrel

House, and when we see each other, we trade bad names and insults—then we go fishing.

By the end of 1956, one thing had become very clear. I knew that no matter what happened to me, and God knows, plenty did, music was not going to be something I could put away no matter what the business did to me.

The dream, thank God, had taken root. And at the risk of sounding like the Twenty-third Psalm, I hoped that surely the lyric and the melody would follow me all the days of my life, and I would, in due time, dwell on the stages of packed houses and auditoriums forever.

Eight

Leona Hobbs

*You can't love me and still love
to hurt me so,
If you're tryin' to break my heart,
You don't have very far to go.*

"*You Don't Have Very Far to Go*"
by Merle Haggard & Red Simpson

IT SHOULD BE LISTED along with the great battles in history, but it ain't. I've checked several sources and it's not there. How they could have overlooked it, I'll never know. It belongs there, all right, alongside Bunker Hill, Waterloo, The Alamo, and Gettysburg. Any complete listing of famous battlefields should, after all, include my marriage to Leona Hobbs.

If this were fiction instead of fact, I'd give the women in my life different names so it wouldn't be so damn confusing. Since this is not the case, I'll have to explain. Leona Hobbs was my first wife, mother of my four children, Dana, Marty, Kelli, and Noel. Leona Williams, the singer, is my third wife, and came along much later. Imagine the odds against a guy marryin' two women named Leona.

No matter what else I can say about the women who have shared my life, I'll tell you that none of them have been boring. Sometimes they were crazy and mean, sometimes loving and good, other times all those things—but goddammit, they never were, in any shape or form, dull.

My youngest daughter, Kelli, who is now eighteen, has a theory about me and her mother. She says God must have wanted to punish us both for some terrible event, so He gave us each other.

More like He sicced us on one another.

Actually, I'm probably making it sound like me and Leona had a lot of fights. Truth is, we didn't. We had one really serious fight. It started the day I met her and ended nine years, four kids, and countless external and internal scars later. We've also had a few disagreements since our divorce. Seems that endin' a marriage don't always end the arguments.

Maybe fighting was all we had in common, I don't know. We didn't like each other the first time we met and maybe we never did. It's hard for me to admit that I loved her, but surely that's what it must have been. I will say this. There was a lot of feeling there and it sure as hell was intense.

Let's blame it all on our youth. That'll do for starters. I'd done pretty much as I pleased since I was about ten. Leona had grown up in a very large family, just about as poor as they come. By the time we met, she was fifteen and I was seventeen. Neither of us was very innocent.

Even though Leona and I fought we always seemed to be on equal ground. There were times when I can honestly say it was a matter of self-defense on my part, and I guess she can say the same thing. She did seem to like a physical fight. She was a lot like a man in that respect, and hell, she could outfight a lot of 'em. That included me more than once. I remember one time we took one of our more lively arguments out of a club into the parking lot and some gallant soul came over to help *Leona*. She turned on him and in the end we both beat the hell out of him.

Everything about Leona was not negative, though. First of all, when I met her she was a really pretty girl. Her features were sharp, showing her Indian heritage to its best advantage. She is not totally unlike my last Leona when it comes to good looks. She used to have beautiful black hair and was always very slim. Besides, she was, and still is, a very outspoken person. Honest to a fault, I believe they say. Some things are just better left unsaid, but Leona could never do that. If she thought it, she said it. In the beginning, I liked this honesty. In time I would grow to hate it.

I met Leona after I got out of Preston the second time. Deanrow and I were cruising around Bakersfield one summer night, about 1954 I believe it was, and we saw two girls walking down the sidewalk near the drive-in. We stopped.

"You girls like to go get a hamburger and a Coke?" Dean asked, leaning out the window, hoping I guess to look cool.

Both girls gave us a quick once-over and decided we weren't too bad. They crawled in the back seat, and Deanrow wheeled the car into the drive-in and brought it to a sliding stop. I reached over and turned the radio down. I didn't know if these girls would appreciate Hank and Lefty, or whether they'd rather hear something a little more uptown like Patti Page.

By this time, I'd got to where I could look the girls over without being obvious. Hell, I had *some* class. I decided I liked Alice better than her sister, Leona.

When the girl came out to the car, I played the big shot and ordered everybody a hamburger and a Coke.

Leona practically leaped into the front seat.

"What do you mean, just ordering me *one* hamburger, you cheap son of a bitch?" she screamed in my ear. "I want two!"

I held up two fingers to the carhop, and Leona settled back in the corner of the back seat. I didn't turn around and look at her, but for some crazy reason I just knew she was grinning. Who did she think she was anyway, demanding two hamburgers like that? Sure did have a lot of spirit. I hated to admit to myself how much I was attracted to her. I decided though that when I asked one of the Hobbs sisters out for a date, it was not going to be "Miss Smartass," it would be Alice. And for awhile, it was Alice.

I knew from the beginning I'd have to have Leona, at least once. I was pretty sure she felt the same way about me. I guess what we didn't know was that this bond, whatever it was, would just about strangle us to death. I was never able to explain it, understand it, or control it. Love still seems like a strange word when it came to me and Leona. The sexual attraction was so strong that there wasn't much reason to talk about love. And I believe we were afraid of the word. Seems like I didn't want her to get the best of me, and she didn't want me to get the best of her. When we were together, hell, there wasn't any best in either of us.

In spite of our rough beginning, we started "going steady," just like everybody did in the 1950's. Actually, we decided to live together. Since we didn't have a place of our own, we went to stay with Lowell and his wife, Fran.

Even though Lowell didn't really approve, and Fran, as good as she always was to me, didn't care for our living arrangements, they didn't say too much to us. Then they started getting a lot of flak from the family about the sinful way we were living.

"Mama's gonna kill you, Bud," Lowell said one evening at supper. "Fact is, she's probably gonna kill me too." I didn't have to ask why. I knew all the hassle we were causing and this seemed like as good a time as any to take care of it.

"Will you take us down to Reno, then?" I asked, and I didn't look at Leona. But I thought that was a nice proposal. Lowell thought about it for a minute and then looked at Fran.

"Want to take a drive down to Reno tonight, Fran?" Lowell said. Fran agreed it was a fine idea.

I finally looked at Leona then and was relieved—well actually, happy to see that she was smiling.

"You ready to go?" I asked, and she nodded. There were not too many times when there was a real tenderness about Leona. This was one of them, and even though I don't recall too much about the actual trip, I remember her attitude was one of sweetness. She seemed happy. What had started out to be something to stop the tongues from wagging had turned into something real nice.

As we stood up together in the little chapel in Reno, I'm sure I was as much a believer in the state of matrimony as anybody. Of course, my definition of matrimony might have been a little different from most people's.

I'm not trying to make myself sound less guilty when I say I was good to her at first. I really was. I worked hard. I got a job in the damned cotton fields, which I hated, and I brought the money home to her. I helped support her eleven brothers and sisters, and it wasn't easy for either of us. We were only kids ourselves. In time, I stole for her too. She wasn't my excuse for stealing—just another reason I thought I needed. If I hadn't used her as an excuse, I would have found another one. That's not something I can blame on Leona.

Before we were married I'd had a job with a geophysical company—that's oil exploration. I'd been working on this particular job for about nine months when it moved to Utah, and I decided not to go. I liked that kind of work and kept looking for another job like it. It was several months before I found one down in Santa Paula. In the meantime, I worked odd jobs, whatever I could do to make a little money.

At night I'd take my guitar and make the rounds of the local clubs. Sometimes I'd play for free and other times I'd get a paying job for a week or so.

Leona, after awhile, was mean to me. Now, I know that sounds like a little kid, but hell, she was mean to me. I wasn't exactly a prince, but I didn't go out of my way to hurt her like she did me.

She knew the things I liked, and she made sure she put them down every chance she got. It used to drive me crazy wondering what she'd do next and why.

One of the things that hurt me most, I guess, was her reaction to my music, my singing in particular. She liked to hear me sing, or at least that's what people said she said behind my back. To my face, it was a different story. She was always making fun. Even after I was getting some recognition and had Roy Nichols working for me on guitar, she never missed an opportunity to zap me one. I overheard Roy ask her once why she hadn't been down to the club to hear me sing. She just laughed and told him she had better things to do.

"I don't wanna sit around all night in some smokey club," she said, "and listen to that son of a bitch beller."

She was a real expert at hurting my feelings about my friends too. She knew Dean had a bad complex about being thin. He'd drive up in the alley in back of our house, and she'd say, "Here comes that skinny son of a bitch again." Those kind of remarks made me madder than the insults she directed at me. One of the worst incidents happened when I got a chance to work with one of my idols, Tommy Duncan.

From my early days on, I'd followed Tommy's career. By now, I was working hard on starting my own career. It was about 1955, and I had never worked on stage with anyone of national prominence. Even though Tommy's popularity had faded some and he was booking out as a single in some small places, to me he was still that voice from the past that had come through my radio when I was a kid.

I got a call from Will Ray, a man who had seen me play in one of the Bakersfield clubs, and he asked if I'd work a dance over in Hanford, about a hundred miles away. He had Tommy booked in for the show, and I couldn't say yes fast enough.

Me and Leona got together with Leon and Mildred Copeland, who were friends of ours. We all drove over to Hanford in their '51 Ford. When we got there we could see the crowd was kinda puny. By the time the show started, there might have been seventy-five people in a hall that held about eight or nine hundred. I felt terrible because it was sad to see somebody of Tommy's stature having to come down like that. I was almost sick about it, but Tommy didn't let on that it bothered him at all. Maybe it didn't.

We got through the first set before I was even introduced to him. It was probably the worst goddamned band I've ever heard in my whole life. There were about four or five mandolins and three or four guitars—just a bunch of instruments that made no sense at all. Must have been about thirteen or fourteen *bad* musicians on that stage.

All during the first set I knew Tommy was watching me, and I kept thinking how lucky I was to be on the same stage with him. I still remember how he looked. He was wearing a blue-jean outfit with a white shirt and hat. He looked like a man oughta look—kinda like Robert Mitchum playing a ranch foreman.

During intermission he told me I should move over next to him for the second half of the show since I was the only good musician on stage. God, I was ten feet tall. I had been complimented by one of my all-time favorites.

As high as I was on the music that night though, I hit rock bottom as soon as I got outside the dance hall.

"I'll drive back home," I told Leon as we walked across the parking lot. He said that was fine, and him and Mildred got in the back seat.

As I headed back toward Bakersfield I kept thinking about how terrible it was that Tommy didn't have a big crowd, and how humiliating it must have been for him to work with such a bunch of tag-assed musicians. I felt so bad I didn't want to talk at all.

"What in the hell is wrong with you, Merle?" Leona asked. I just shook my head and kept driving.

"I asked what in the hell is wrong," she repeated, but I still couldn't say nothing. Hell, I was afraid I'd start crying. I actually had a lump in my throat. It made me mad that she wasn't more tuned in to my feelings.

"Merle!" This time, I knew she wouldn't shut up until I gave her some kind of an answer.

"I feel bad," I said then, "because Tommy didn't have no people hardly at the show."

"Well, hell," she said, and she started laughing. "If the son of a bitch could *sing*, maybe he'd get a crowd."

I was doing about sixty miles an hour. I never did even slow down or look at her as I back-handed in her general direction. She ducked and I swung again. All of a sudden she shoved the door open and goddamn . . . jumped out!

I couldn't believe it. I looked in the rear-view mirror, and my God, I could see her outline bumping and bouncing all over the highway. I thought for sure she'd killed herself. I hit the brakes and slid to a stop, throwing Leon and Mildred up against the front seat. Jumping out of the car, I ran back to where she was. Thank God it was a moonlit night and there was no other traffic on the road. By the time I got to her, she was on her feet—hell, maybe she landed on her feet—I dunno. She was that *durable*.

"See what you've done, you goddamned bastard!" she screamed out at me as she held up the edge of her skirt. "You've ruined my new dress!"

"Are you *all right*?" I asked. I was genuinely concerned.

"Of course I'm all right," she answered as though I was some kind of fool for asking. She hadn't even skinned her knees, but she bitched all the way home about her new dress. Truth was, she didn't get many new dresses, and maybe that particular dress was as important to her as Tommy had been to me.

Leona always knew how to liven up an evening, I'll say that for her. Not too long after we were married something took place that will give you an idea how she could turn an ordinary evening into a hell of a night.

It was a Saturday night and some of us had been asked to play music at the American Legion Hall in Bakersfield. There wasn't any money involved. We were just doing it for fun. I don't recall who all played in our slapped-together band, but I do remember Sonny Barton played drums and Leon Copeland played guitar. We all got a table together. Sonny's wife, Joan, sat with Mildred and Leona while we worked on stage.

While we were doing the show, I looked out and there was Leona with a plate, passing it around—looked like she was taking up a collection. What'd she think this was, the Norse Road Church of Christ? Hell, she *was* taking up a collection. As she passed by the stage I could hear her telling everybody that her husband was up there playing guitar and wasn't getting paid. She explained that we were very poor—which we were—and asked if they would kindly put something in the plate for us, *please.* I couldn't help laughing 'cause Leona could be funny as hell when she felt like it. She had a great sense of humor but sometimes a strange way of showing it. By the time we finished the first set, she had a plate full of money.

Me, Sonny, and Leon took our break and sat down at the table. Everybody was having drinks except Leona, she was busy counting the money. She straightened each bill out, stacked the coins, and proudly pushed it to the center of the table. We all talked about how well we'd eat the next week.

Suddenly out of the blue Leona nudged me with her elbow.

"There's an old boy over there," she said then, "who run his hand up my dress when I was passin' the plate."

Merle Haggard's first birthday.

"Now ain't that a fine lookin' cowboy on that little colt? That's my uncle, Olis Harp, holding the little animal and my daddy with his steady hand on me."

The old boxcar house, a refrigerator car, 1936—as it was when Merle was born.

"Wearing my own kind of hat—even then!"

James and Flossie Haggard and Merle.

James, Flossie, Lowell, and Lillian with Merle, 1941.

"Here are two pictures of my dog, Jack."

"This is me and another one of the 'special people' in my life—Tuffy!" *(Photograph by Troy Russell)*

"I want to make sure nobody accuses me of 'telling all' when it comes to the women in my life. Here is a picture taken of me about 1943, with my first girl friend, Betty Donevan. There's not one wild and lustful story about me and Betty in this book."

Merle with his father and Jack, 1944.

"This is Daddy and Lowell when Lowell was about fourteen."

"And here I am in 1953, looking very cool with a girl named Lillian Burke, and I didn't tell no bad stories about Lillian either."

"This picture was taken about 1952 of me and a couple of my favorite people, my brother-in-law, Bill Rea, and Mama."

REGISTER OF ACTIONS—YOUTH AUTHORITY, STATE OF CALIFORNIA

Y. A. **15595**	NAME HAGGARD, Merle					
DATE CASE RECEIVED 1/14/52	COURT Juvenile	COUNTY Kern		JUDGE Warren Stockton		
DATE REFERRED 1/7/52	COURT NUMBER 12691	AGE 14	BIRTH DATE 4/6/37	Y. A. ACTION Accepted	DATE 1/17/52
CHARGE Sub. I, Incorrigible		JURISDICTION EXPIRES 4-6-58	ACTION TAKEN BY WLT & OHC		

FACILITY ASSIGNED

Nelles

DATE	ACTIONS	DATE	ACTIONS
1-22-52	Commitment Received		
1-28-52	Verdat Myles	9-25-53	Revoke par. Ret'n to Clinic. (In Kern Co. Jail)
3-31-52	Contd to July for prog rept	10-29	Rec'd at clinic
4-30-52	Graded	11-19-53	Trans. Preston
5-3-52	Out'd to Nelles for Escape	11-24-53	Rec'd at Preston.
6-2-52	Contd to Act for Prog sept	12-X-53	Escaped - Preston.
8-11-52	Escaped - Returned 8-14-52	11-54	Ret from Escape - Preston
7-2-52	Appd trans to PSI. Cont	1-8-54	Cont 7 mos. prog. rept
	to 2nd December calendar	6-73	Refg to parole. Cont 3 mos.
	for progress report.	9-2	Appd release + Pars 4/2/54.
9-12	Rec'd at Preston.		Cont 3 mos.
12-17-52	Refg to par for placement plans.	9-7	Paroled.
	Cont 2 months.	4-9-55	Cont. on TIP.
3-16-53	Appwe rel on par. eva 2-16-53 on pls	4-22	Susp. T.P. Await Court action
	prepared by the par. dept.	5-13	Cont on susp. par. Individually held to
5-18	Rel on par.		permit to be fee Kern Co. Jail Farm
8-20-53	No action on reported incident.		out to act as trusty.

FACILITY ASSIGNED

15595 - pg. 2 Merle Haggard

DATE	ACTIONS	DATE	ACTIONS
	Commitment Received		
8-5	Par. rev. pending comp. 180 da jail		
	sent. Cont to Feb, 1956 Sent. adv.		
	180 da in Kern Co. Jail.		
9-30-55	Appd rel from Kern cg ooa 10/3.		
11-25	Parole susp. await ct. action		
12-9	Cont on susp. par. await ct. act.		
3/9/56	Restored to parole eff 3/18/56		
12/2/56	Parole suspended. Await Court action		
2-1-57	Parole revoked. Comm. Ventura Co. Jail Cont'd to July, 1957		
7-26-57	Cond. rel. on par. from the Ventura Co. Jail on 7/16/57		
12-30-57	Parole susp.		
2-21-58	Discg. Failure on parole. Committed to Corrections - A-45200		

Flossie Haggard surrounded by Merle's children, clockwise from upper left, Marty, Dana, Kelli, and Noel.

Flossie Haggard Scott (*Photograph by Terry Moore*).

"I remember the weather was real nice the day Merle was born, and the child was everything I'd hoped for—prayed for. He began talking before he was a year old, and did he love music, especially gospel music. He loved to play preacher. He'd get his little apple crate out, crawl up on it, and just preach his little head off. I said to some of the family, 'Oh, he's gonna be a minister.' I always hoped that he would. Still, it was the music that seemed to affect him more than anything. The radio would be on when he was hardly big enough to understand words and you could just see his little old feet a movin' under the covers. I'd say, 'Looky there, Jim, his little feet are just a dancin' . . . he's gonna be musical.'

"When he was just learning to talk he kept saying something about stewed ham. I kept thinking he was hungry and I'd fix him something to eat. Well, one day he kept on saying 'stew ham' over and over and I noticed he was pointing to the radio. At that time Stuart Hamblen had a gospel program, and that's what Merle had been trying to tell me about all along.

"People often ask me about Merle, how I feel about his success now and everything. That's easy to answer because I have all the pride in the world in him and in his talent. When he first wrote 'Mama Tried,' I would cry every time I'd hear it. I still do sometimes.

"Someone asked me recently to describe Merle in one sentence but l can do it in one word. Unpredictable. Was when he was little. Still is. Unpredictable . . ."

—Flossie Haggard Scott

"There are so many things that have not been told about Merle's life and so many more things that have been told in error. One often repeated error is how Merle's troubles began. He wasn't a bad kid at all. In fact, quite the contrary. He was very strong-willed of course. Still is. But as a small child he was very ill for some time. He had what was called valley fever back then, and yes, we spoiled him. It was hard not to. Everybody loved him and he was such a charmer that nobody could stay mad at him for any length of time.

"When our father died and Mother had to go to work, Merle just couldn't handle the self-discipline, and he began misbehaving at school because quite simply it bored him. When the school officials suggested a weekend at Juvenile Hall might scare him into behaving and staying in school, we agreed because it seemed like a good idea.

"It wasn't a good idea. It backfired. He knew he hadn't done anything bad enough to merit being put there, and it didn't scare him at all. It made him mad. In addition, I don't think any of us realized how devastated he was by our father's death. Actually, we all were because he was such a special man. None of us were ever the same after that.

"As a result of his visit to Juvenile Hall, Merle began to rebel more and more against all forms of authority. There was no keeping him in either. Anyplace they put him he'd find a way to escape. He got very good at it.

"I remember so well visiting him at Nelles that first time and feeling such an overwhelming guilt that I had ever agreed that a weekend in Juvenile Hall would serve as an effective form of discipline.

"Merle grew up too young. He went from nine years old to eighteen in a matter of six months. Both my brothers have inherited very strong traits from our father. Lowell has that ability to do anything with his hands that can be done. Merle got his innate charm directly from my father. I don't think he realizes that all those good qualities of his, and there are many, are very much like my father. That's where the musical ability comes from, too.

"There's something else I've always wanted to clear up, too. We were not paper-shack poor. My father was a farmer and a rancher in Oklahoma when he met my mother. They moved to Chicago after they were married, where he worked for Hill and Hubble Steel Company as a foreman. They were transferred around the midwest, Indiana, Pennsylvania, and Ohio, where they might have stayed if it hadn't been for my mother's health. When a doctor suggested a warmer climate we moved to California in 1929. We returned to Oklahoma because the climate change was too drastic. And we were doing very well in Oklahoma until we lost so much in that fire. It was then that we moved back to California for good.

"Shortly after we came to California my father began working for the Santa Fe Railroad. He had worked for a short time on a dairy farm, and several stories have my mother milking cows to make a living, which was never true. After my father's death she went to work as a bookkeeper. She was a very educated woman for those days and her job was very good.

"There has always been something special about the youngest child in our family. Our mother began to make plans for him long before he was born. She prayed that he would love music, and she got everything she ask for in Merle—maybe more than she asked for.

"My mother was and still is a woman of great strength and character and she was also very caring and gentle. I remember when Merle's dog Jack had to be put to sleep, it was Mother who took him to the vet. She had always been the kind of person who would never allow a dog in the house, and yet that little animal managed to get around her. I always thought it was sad to think about her bundling Jack up in a blanket like a baby and getting on a bus to take him to be put to sleep. I know that had to be so hard on her, especially since she knew how much Merle loved that dog and the fact that he was away—in San Quentin, I believe.

"I hope, if nothing else, this book shows Merle Haggard the person, not just the entertainer, not just the so-called bad boy, the ex-con, but the warm and sensitive human side of him as well. There is an awful lot more to him than the surface things you read in the magazines and newspapers. More than you'll ever see on stage. I guess it's this man I'd like people to know more about. This is the man I like. In fact, I like him a lot." —*Lillian Haggard Rea*

Bill and Lillian Rea.

Lillian and Lowell Haggard, 1942.

"It was Christmas Eve and I was working as an electrician for J.C. Penney. We'd knocked off work about noon and some of us guys had been celebrating quite a bit. I called home and Fran told me Merle had been picked up and this time it was real serious.

"I decided I'd go down to the jail and—well, I don't know what I was gonna do—but they almost threw me in, too. That would have been a first for me.

"Sometimes people ask if things couldn't have been different for Merle and I guess they could. There's always a way to avoid a problem, although there were a lot of circumstances working against Merle back in the early days. After Dad died, I wasn't around maybe like I should have been. Of course, it might not have made any difference, but I probably could have been a little more help to him in that terrible period when he was about fifteen years old.

"It's always hard for the family or anybody else to understand what really goes on in the jails and institutions. I only saw the visiting rooms, except when I went back years later, when Merle did a tape in San Quentin for the Merv Griffin Show, then again when he did the live album.

"If one thing stands out in my mind it would have to be when I went to pick him up at the bus station when he came home from Quentin. I remember exactly how he looked as he stepped down off the bus carrying his guitar. He looked like a little whipped pup. He looked just terrible. His clothes, which were bad enough to begin with, looked like he'd slept in them, which he probably had. I don't think either one of us knew what to say to each other. I asked him where he wanted me to take him, and he said he wanted to go to Mama's house.

"He'd only been home a little while and he called Leon Copeland to come over. The two of them were sitting there singing songs and playing guitar when I left. I don't know how long they kept at it.

"Anytime Merle didn't know what else to do, he turned to his music."

—*Lowell Haggard*

State of California
GOVERNOR'S OFFICE
SACRAMENTO 95814

RECEIVED MAR 2 1 1972

March 14, 1972

Mr. Merle Ronald Haggard
P. O. Box 842
Bakersfield, California 93302

Dear Mr. Haggard:

After careful investigation of your case it has
been recommended to me that you be granted a
full and unconditional pardon.

I have considered the record and am satisfied
that yours is an appropriate case for executive
clemency. It is a great personal satisfaction
to me as Governor to make this acknowledgement
that you are deserving of favorable consideration.

Accordingly, I am enclosing the formal document
granting to you a full and unconditional pardon,
and with it I extend to you my best wishes for
your success and happiness.

Sincerely,

RONALD REAGAN
Governor

Enclosure

CERTIFIED - RETURN RECEIPT REQUESTED

Executive Department
State of California

PARDON

MERLE RONALD HAGGARD

Merle Ronald Haggard, of Bakersfield, California, has submitted to this office an application for executive clemency.

He was convicted on or about January 30, 1958, in the Superior Court of the State of California in and for the County of Kern, of the crimes of burglary in the second degree (Section 459 of the Penal Code), and escape without force (Section 4532a of the Penal Code), and was sentenced to serve terms of 6 months to 15 years and 6 months to 5 years in the state prison, such terms to run concurrently. He served 2 years, 9 months in prison and 2 years, 3 months on parole. He was discharged on February 3, 1963, having completed his sentence.

On July 7, 1971, the Adult Authority recommended that applicant be granted a pardon on grounds of rehabilitation.

Because the applicant had been convicted of more than a single felony, his case was referred to the Supreme Court of the State of California for the written recommendation of the Justices pursuant to Article V, Section 8 of the California Constitution. On October 8, 1971, Chief Justice Donald R. Wright advised me that the Justices recommended that a pardon be granted to the applicant.

THEREFORE, in view of the foregoing favorable recommendations and indications that the applicant is now a fully rehabilitated member of society and entitled to a pardon, I, Ronald Reagan, Governor of the State of California, pursuant to the authority vested in me by the Consitution and statutes of the State of California, do hereby grant to Merle Ronald Haggard, Prison No. A-45200, a full and unconditional pardon for the offenses set forth above.

IN WITNESS WHEREOF, I have hereunto set my hand and caused the Great Seal of the State of California to be affixed this first day of March, A.D. nineteen hundred and seventy-two.

Governor of California

ATTEST

Secretary of State

by

"When my mom and dad split up, it was him that I hated. I believed everything that was wrong was all his fault. I didn't even know him really, and like Kelli says, he was a stranger to all of us. I can remember hiding when the fights would start, and we were all scared to death as we listened to the terrible things they said and did to each other.

"Later, it made no sense to me at all when we were taken away to live at Grandma Haggard's house. I remember her and Aunt Lil coming to get us and my mother crying and saying how she couldn't take care of us the way we ought to be taken care of. Us kids were in the back seat of the car and I was kicking and screaming.

"I looked out the window at my mother as she watched us leave. She was crying. 'Things will be better,' she said, and I just couldn't see how that could be.

"I loved my mother. It was her we'd spent so much time with, and she wasn't much more than a child herself when she had us.

"Living at Grandma Haggard's house was so different from what we'd been used to—like going from a hot bath to a cold shower. She was very strict, and I know we gave her such a hard time for awhile even though we really loved her. Dad would come around now and then, stay awhile, sometimes overnight, but I couldn't even bring myself to call him Dad until I was thirteen, then it was the hardest thing I ever did. I wasn't comfortable calling him Dad until I was about eighteen.

"I remember the day they told us he was gonna marry Bonnie Owens. I just died. I hated to even hear about it. I felt betrayed. When they came to take us to the house they got for all of us, I was determined to hate everything, especially Bonnie. I guess for more than a year we gave her and Dad pure hell. Then we grew to love her. How she ever stood us until we began to understand how hard both her and Dad were trying to make a better life for us, I'll never know. She became—and is—one of the most loved and important people in my life.

"If there was a time when things were almost ideal for us, I'll have to say it was when we lived out at the ranch. I remember Dad coming in off the road, happy to be home and ready to take off on a fishing trip with the whole troupe of us. He seemed very happy and I know us kids sure were. Then he started coming home less and less and I saw him get very sad and restless. I didn't know why and back then we didn't talk about our feelings much.

"We all understand each other a little better now that we're older. I'm married and have two children of my own, which is what Dad wants for me, I think. I tell him he is a chauvinist when it comes to women in the entertainment field, because I love music and he's done everything in the world to discourage me. Told me I was awful and everything. Gave me a real bad complex for awhile. I know he was trying to spare me some of the pain and disappointment that comes along with the business, but I've had a lot of that in my life anyway and I've survived. It could be, if he'll just stop and think about it, that somewhere in my heritage there is quite a bit of strength and determination. After all, I have some pretty amazing relatives. . . .".

—*Dana Haggard Stevens*

"It's never easy growing up with a famous parent, but I guess it's not easy growing up, period. I'm beginning to understand now how hard it is to give enough time to people who are important to you and still work at your music. If I have any wishes about the past, it would be that we could have all had more time together.

"I can't pick out any one incident that stands out from all the rest when I was a kid, but a couple or three years ago something happened that really turned me around. I had always known, or believed, that my dad was a good musician and a fine singer, even when I was very little, but I always had a feeling that maybe I thought that just because he was my dad. The thing that happened later convinced me I wasn't alone in the way I saw him and his music. Dad and Willie Nelson were doing a concert together, and like a lot of guys my age, we all loved Willie, too. It was always easier to admire someone outside your family or friends.

"On this particular night I remember watching Willie on stage and thinking how good he was and one look at the audience showed that he really had them in his hands. Then my dad came out. He sang 'Amazing Grace' and just stopped the show. That audience just came unglued. I've never seen anything like it. I knew then that Merle Haggard wasn't just another singer. I knew he was great.

"As my dad, and a human being, he is, like the rest of us, subject to mistakes. On stage, nobody can touch him."

—*Marty Haggard*

Noel Haggard at his seventeenth birthday party.

Dana and Marty Haggard.

Dana at her wedding, with her father and Kelli.

"Most of the time we called him 'hey.' We really didn't know what to call this man who had come to take us to live in a new home with a new mother who was also a stranger.

"I think we kinda huddled together like orphans of the storm wondering what was next. I must have been about seven or eight when my father and Bonnie brought us together to establish what would become one of the more stable periods in our lives. It seems like it didn't take much to confuse me anyway, and we'd lived with my grandmother most of the time. Before that, memories of my parents together were better forgotten. My solution to almost any problem back then was to cry. It seemed to be what I did best, followed by a run to my room and a quick slam of the door. All of this tended to make Dad understand me even less.

"I don't think any of us kids were aware of how important our father was becoming in the entertainment field, but little by little he became more important to us. It didn't take Bonnie long to win us, especially me, over. She was constantly reassuring us that 'everything was going to be all right.' It was something I liked hearing since I'd been through a lot of times when nothing was all right.

"I loved my dad's music, but I honestly didn't know how many other people did until the year he won so many awards. The show had been taped earlier, and Bonnie called us from Los Angeles to make sure we all watched. Well, I was absolutely and completely amazed. The next day at school everybody was talking about Merle Haggard, *my father*. He was a celebrity. I couldn't handle all that at once, so I promptly got sick and cried. My teacher took me to the principal's office and they let me lay down on a cot. In a few minutes the principal came in, sat down next to me, and began to talk. He was so kind and he took time to tell me things about my dad. Hearing all those great things from somebody outside the family really made an impression on me.

"He told me I ought to be proud of my father, and I said I was. Saying it out loud for the first time made me realize how much pride I did have in the man who had once seemed like such a stranger to me.

"I think I started to understand him better then—and know why we'd been left without him so much. Maybe I started to love him then—not because I realized how important he was to all those people out there, but because I knew what it cost to follow his dreams.

"When I think of the good times I remember Lake Shasta when I was about twelve. All us kids swimming and splashing, scaring the fish away from Daddy's line. He'd yell and laugh at the same time, blaming us because he couldn't catch that 'big one.' I think he loved those times too.

"There were a lot of times in our lives when we didn't see eye to eye, and we've argued a lot, but I really believe I have a friend now as well as a dad.

"He'd better know he's got one too."

—*Kelli Haggard*

Deanrow, Bonnie, and Merle, 1965.

The Strangers in Reno at Harrah's. Left to right: Ronnie Reno, Norm Hamlet, Roy Nichols, Biff Adams, Eldon Shamblin, Tracy Barton, Gordon Terry, Bobby Galardo (drums), Tiny Moore, Don Markum, Mark Yeary.

Merle Haggard and Bonnie Owens, early years.

"When I first heard Merle Haggard I truly believed there wasn't a better singer anywhere. I haven't changed my mind in all this time except now I believe he is just as good a writer as he is a singer and that's a very rare thing in this business.

"I was once part of his personal life and now I am part of his family—his musical family, and that's the way I want it to be. It's strange now, looking back, even when I was married to Merle, I felt more like a member of his musical family than his home family. We're all members, the band and I, and we care about each other, even though our personal lives are separate. We've all gone through periods of change, and when I think of me and Merle back in those early days I see two other people because, really, that's what we were.

"When I met Merle I'd been single for about thirteen years and I'd always made it on my own. Hadn't lived with nobody but my two boys, Buddy and Mike, and when I finally realized Merle was thinking of me as more than a friend it was a shock. I'm still not sure he was ever in love with me, but I've never doubted that he loved me. I was a phase in his life, an important phase I hope, but I thought of it as a partnership. I remember thinking to myself, well, if it lasts three weeks, it lasts three weeks. If it doesn't, then we can enjoy what time we have.

"With me and Merle, it was never a 'bells ringing' or a possessive kind of love. There was a period of time though, probably about the first three years we were married, when I believe I was number one in his life. The rest of the time there were probably at least fifteen others who may have been ahead of me. It was something I tried to understand. He says I was always able to read him pretty well, and I could. I knew the two of us were ending long before it actually happened. I could feel the difference and see him going through so many things, personal and professional, that he couldn't talk about. I knew in the early 70's that things were becoming more and more difficult for him. Success is not an easy hat to wear, especially if it is as heavy as his was.

"When I decided to quit the road in '74, it was as much for Merle as it was for me. It was something we both needed. I was going through a bad period, too, not from him, just from life in general. I was feeling a little like I did when my boys grew away from me. I felt like Merle had outgrown me. I did feel the kids needed me at home and I needed them. That's why I left the road when I did and became a typical housewife, putting my mind totally on the home and children. I didn't know what was happening out there on the road and I didn't try to find out.

"By the middle of 1975, I filed for legal separation, but I wasn't ready for divorce then. I wanted to make sure I could close the door on that part of my life totally before I went through it. On November 10, 1976, I reached that point and I filed for divorce. I knew then I was ready to let go of the past. When I closed the door it was like cutting off my arm in a sense, but it had to be done. Once it was done, I was sure it had been the right thing to do. That's why I can work with him today without problems. I waited until I was sure there was no possible way we could be together as man and wife anymore. From that point on I was much more of an individual and more in charge of my own life and career.

"Merle has a great capacity for love, but I honestly believe he was never really in love until he met Leona Williams. He knew only the joys, the fun, and the disagreements that go along with sharing somebody's life. With Leona, he has learned it all—including that pain of loving completely. I don't think he knew about that before like the rest of us.

"When I was asked to be a bridesmaid at their wedding, it wasn't the big thing people all made it out to be. Someone kidded me not too long ago saying there could have been an extra line in the ceremony that asks who giveth this husband, and I could have said 'I do.' And, I would have.

"Then I was asked to describe Merle. I had to laugh. There is no describing him. He is different things to different people. His mother said he is unpredictable and that's true. There is also a very complicated simplicity about him. If I described him in one word it would be 'alive.' He sure is that."

—*Bonnie Owens*

To my good friend
Merle Haggard — Jimmy Carter
2-80

Merle Haggard and Tex Whitson at Bakersfield Park with one of Merle's collection of antique cars.

Merle and Leona, *Hee Haw* taping, 1980 (*Photograph by Jim Miller*).

"Look at that grin—I think I must have been losing and trying to pretend I was winning."

Porter Wagoner, Lewis Talley, Fuzzy Owen, Merle Haggard.

"Don't ask me to sum him up because Merle Haggard is one hard dude to figure out. Anybody who tells you they have him figured out don't know him very well. I can't actually remember the first time I met him, but I do remember Louie playing me a tape of his. I wish I could say I predicted then he'd be a star, but I didn't. I did tell him later that if he found a song I'd record him on Talley Records. He did—and I did. The rest is history.

"There is no way I can put into words what a lifetime of friendship and work with Merle has meant to me personally and professionally. Talentwise he is the best. Even more important, I think he gets better with age and experience. It shows in his work, on stage and on records. We disagree about a lot of things, lord knows, and nobody can ever accuse me of being a 'yes' man. In fact, I think Merle will tell you I'm a 'no' man. As his personal manager I sometimes have to take the opposite side just to get all sides of an issue out in the open, because whatever is best for him in the long run is best for everybody concerned.

"On the negative side, I've never seen anybody who can take a light load and make it a major burden the way Merle can. As for life around him, I'm only surprised when there are no surprises. It's when things level off and begin to get kinda normal that I really start to get worried."

—*Fuzzy Owen*

"It was no surprise to me that Merle Haggard became the star he is today. I knew it the first time I saw him get up before a crowd at the Rainbow Gardens in Bakersfield. I can even remember what he was wearing—had on khaki pants and a real heavily starched white shirt. In fact, if I'm not mistaken, it was *my* shirt.

"He was just a kid and Lefty Frizzell was appearing there. When Merle got up on stage he just turned those people up, over, and around. Some of them actually thought he *was* Lefty.

"We had a lot of great times. I remember playing for five dollars and all the beer we could drink. I remember the fights I could never seem to get out of. Once we even signed up for the Marines. Told them we were brothers and wanted to go on the buddy system or some such thing. Hey, it was serious. The FBI came looking for us. The Marines didn't take kindly at all to somebody signing up and not showing up.

"Then we went through our 'cowboy days' when we toured Texas. We really thought we were something, and I guess we were.

"I love him like a brother. It hurts me sometimes when he don't have enough time for me 'cause somehow I feel like I helped raise him. I hate that I don't get to see him much anymore, but I live in Arizona and he's on the road. I still pick a little guitar and sing a little now and then.

"Sometimes I get to thinking about all those old times and I get a terrible urge just to take off again the way we did back then. You know, just hop a freight with a loaf of bread and a stick of baloney . . ."

—*Bob Teague*

Merle with Gordon Terry *(Photograph by Jim Miller)*.

Sandra Palumbo (secretary at HAG, Inc.) with her husband Neil.

"There's been a lot of crazy times since that first day I met Merle in that little studio on Hazel Street. Looking back though, I can honestly say there is little basic difference in the man. He's living a little better now and a little faster. He talks a little more and he's got a few more problems. Not too long ago he said he wished we could go back to the way it was when we were working up in Tehachapi at Paul's Lounge—not having any more problems than we had then. Still, we had problems then, too. He just don't remember them all. I know we worked so many hours I'd have to drink a fifth of whiskey, which we stole from the bar, just to be able to drive back to Bakersfield. Merle would have to have a few belts just to be able to face my driving. I guess in all the years I've known him, I've seen him in every kind of situation, most of which I can't even repeat. We've argued about every damned thing in the world and even settled some of our disagreements with our fists. One time we even fought on the streets of Belfast, as if they didn't have enough fighting over there already.

"We're both gamblers. I've seen him lose big, both money and other things, and I've seen him win big. Once I saw him lose $104,000 in cold cash at Harrah's in Reno, and then $62,000 at the Sahara. Then I saw him hit three $25,000 Keno tickets during a three-month period.

"The only difference in his gambling and my gambling is that I've lost every goddamned thing I've made in the last twenty years. Overall, Merle has pretty much broken even. Not too many people can say that about their money—or their life either for that matter."

—*Lewis Talley*

Leona Williams

Tex Whitson

"When I first got to know Merle he was just out of the joint and down on his luck. A friend of mine, Freddie McMillon, told me about him—said he didn't have a car and even had to walk to town to play music at the Barrel House. Well, I could sure identify with all that and I loaned him an old Plymouth I usually kept out at the airport.

"When we went over the prison part of the book it became a little too real. At one point both of us just sat there and looked at each other. We couldn't help crying. I don't think we cried for each other or even for ourselves. We cried for the millions of people who will never understand what we're trying to tell them. It's impossible to put into words that feeling a man gets locked away, watching the best years of his life slip away from him, and knowing that society honestly intended to teach right from wrong. God only knows what they could learn from us if they'd only listen, just a little bit. It's so frustrating to try to explain to our overeducated and well informed civilization that a very young man might have a hundred years of living locked up inside his head because of the things that happen behind those walls.

"We've talked about it so many times and have come to the conclusion that maybe the only ones who even come close to understanding humanity are the children. They aren't confused with all this prepackaged wisdom, so the truth, pure and simple, comes easy.

"The Merle Haggard who stands on stage and sings to the people from his heart is as real as rain, but the other man who talks and sometimes agonizes about the problems of the world is real, too. It is that man who gazes out the bus windows as we roll across this country and talks about all the things that keep him awake way into those early morning hours. That's the man the public never sees and except for certain passages of this book, probably never will see.

"That's the Merle Haggard I know."   —Tex Whitson

"Don't ask what it's like to be Mrs. Merle Haggard, I would have to ask you what day you're talking about. It's always different—and like he said about the women in his life—it's never boring.

"It hasn't been all hearts and flowers, and at the risk of sounding like a line from a song, it's either heaven or hell or a combination of both.

"I've left him, swearing I won't be back.

"I've come back.

"He's told me he never wants to see me again and called me the next day. I've screamed at him one minute and whispered to him the next. I guess I've loved him so much at times I've hated him and hated him so bad I loved him. If that makes no sense, then remember I told you not to ask what it's like to be Mrs. Merle Haggard.

"Being the wife of an entertainer is not exactly easy, and when you have a career of your own it doubles all the problems and cuts down on the happiness. But my music means the same to me that his does to him and it seems that neither of us can exist with any kind of peace without being what we were meant to be. It's very difficult to rest easy in a marriage that is celebrated wherever we happen to meet—Nashville, Austin, Reno, or Atlanta—wedged in between telephone calls, knocks at the door, business, fans, greasy fried chicken, cold coffee in foam cups, and motel rooms that all look alike. Still, it is our life and we made our choices long ago. I can't help but wonder if we could exist under normal circumstances.

"Once we tried to get away from it all. We took off to Hawaii for a few days vacation. There we were in the most romantic place in the world, way up at the top of a beautiful hotel overlooking Diamond Head and the ocean. Merle got restless and wanted to go for a drive so we rented a car. He wasn't too impressed with the scenery either, and we stopped at a place where they sold souvenirs and junk. He bought a bunch of those little balsa wood airplanes that you snap together.

"We went back to the room and started putting the planes together, and Merle stood on the balcony and sailed them out toward the ocean. He was hoping the wind would catch them and they'd fly right out to sea. Well, he never could get them to go more than a few feet but he kept trying, and when he'd run out of planes I'd go get more and put them together. The ones he sailed fell down to a big ledge about six floors down, and it looked like a little airport below us. I often wondered what the next people thought when they looked down at that miniature landing strip.

"Maybe they went out and bought some planes themselves and tried their luck. Maybe the wind was right for them and they watched their planes fly away. It could be that maybe that's what life is all about—being able to get the right current of wind to lift you up enough to fly right out to sea. Sometimes you can do it—other times you just end up on the ledge.

"But you never stop trying, and you never stop learning—and you never stop trying and learning to love. Together we've learned that much and God help us if we forget it. . . ."

—*Leona Williams*

Merle and Leona's wedding, October 1978. Dean Halloway; Lewis Talley; Merle; Leona's sons Ron and Brady Lee; Leona; Bonnie Owens.

"Over where?" I asked. She leaned over and pointed across the room to one of the biggest bruisers I'd ever seen. Looked like one of them big sun-bleached tanned dudes who works on a road crew—usually on the cement mixer or the jack hammer. He had on a sweatshirt with his sleeves rolled up. He had arms big as my legs.

"Aw, Leona," I said, "why don't you just forget it? That old boy's probably drunk. He don't mean no harm, and I don't imagine he'll cause no more trouble. Just forget it."

For a minute she didn't say nothin'. Then turning to the others at the table she said, "Did you all hear that?" They hadn't and she repeated it. I tried to laugh it off, but she wasn't gonna let it go at that. The more I tried to ignore her the louder she got. Then she turned to the tables nearby and began telling her story to them.

"That guy over there run his big old hairy hand up my dress, and Merle—my husband here—won't do a damn thing about it. Now what do you think of a man like that?"

"Come on Leona," I said. It was getting a little too serious to laugh off. "Just drop it, okay?"

Finally, she stood up and made her announcement.

"Anybody else want to run their hand up my dress?" she asked. "Merle—my husband here—he don't care none." She leaned down to the surprised looking man at the next table and said very sweetly, "How 'bout you mister, wanna run your hand up my dress?"

"Leona, for God's sake, stop it and sit down." I tugged at her dress. She knew where my breaking point was and she was already well past it. Everybody around us was looking and laughing. Leona just kept standing there with her hands on her hips, defying me to "defend her honor."

"Okay, okay, just sit down, dammit . . .," I said. "I'll go over and talk to the guy. . . ."

As I walked toward the table the guy got bigger and bigger.

"Pardon me," I said, as politely as I could, "but I would

like to settle my wife down a little bit. I don't really give a damn what happened awhile ago, and just between two gentlemen, I'll tell you I don't want no trouble. However, if you could see your way clear to go over and sorta apologize . . . to my uh . . . wife, then . . ."

I had my hand extended out in the direction of Leona on the other side of the room. Cement Mixer just looked up at me like I was crazy. Well, hell, I was, or I wouldn't have been standing there.

He turned to his friends and said, "Now, what did that little son of a bitch say?" He started to get up. There was no way I was gonna whip that one in a fair fight, so with my hand already out, I closed it into a fist and got in that first punch before he was ready. He went back across the table and landed up against the wall. Somebody came running with a wet rag and started trying to wake him up. By this time all the smart people were looking for the doors. I just stood there looking at him and Leon came running up beside me.

"Need any help?" he asked, then went on over to where Cement Mixer was laying. Leon leaned down next to him as he was rubbing his jaw and asked him if he was the guy Merle Haggard hit.

"Hell, I don't know who hit me," he said, shaking his head, and Leon, who wasn't exactly playing by the rules either, hit him again.

In the meantime, everybody else got in on the action, including the ladies. It turned out to be one of the wildest free-for-alls I was ever in.

In the middle of all this madness this very meek looking little guy with round glasses, who'd been in charge of getting the entertainment together for the evening, got up to the mike. He tapped it a couple of times, looked around the room like a scared rabbit, and made an announcement.

"Ladies and gentlemen," he began. "Would you kindly return to your . . . ah . . . tables . . . and would you . . . the musicians who are here . . . and fighting . . . please just *leave."*

Of course, it would seem that Leona would be extremely proud of me for coming to her defense, for standing up to Cement Mixer and living to tell about it.

She never mentioned it. But all the way home every time I'd look in her direction, I'd see the trace of a strange little grin around the corners of her mouth. In spite of all the bruises and the pain, I was fighting back a little bit of a smile myself.

She was something back then, my Leona.

By 1956, Mama had built the new house on Yosemite Street in front of the old boxcar house. Leona and I moved into the boxcar, and considering some of the places we'd lived, it was quite a step up.

Other things were looking up as well. I had found me another job with an oil company. It was all the way down in Santa Paula, but I felt like, for the first time, I might have a future.

Something else was happening to us too. Leona was going to have a baby. I was going to be a father. I was a little bit afraid of that. I knew that, compared to my own father, I'd come up short. I liked kids, but I really didn't understand them. Leona was happy, seemed like, and didn't appear to be worried or concerned. There was really no reason why she would though since she'd been surrounded by kids and babies all her life. Her family loved kids. Guess that's why they had so many of them.

Don't ask me why I did what I did next. Lord only knows, and He musta been ready to give up on me after the deal I pulled down in Santa Paula.

It all began innocently enough. Most of the trouble I've been into started from some insignificant thing. There were four or five of us guys from Bakersfield who worked down in Santa Paula, and we took turns driving every day. One Friday night we were asked to come back for a half-day on

SING ME BACK HOME

Saturday and we agreed. Everybody went home that night except me and Dennis Myers. We didn't see no point in drivin' all the way back just to come back in the morning.

Although I'd known Dennis most of my life, I was never very close friends with him until we began working together. To pass the time that evening we went downtown to walk around. We passed a used car lot and I started telling Dennis how me and Deanrow had borrowed some cars a couple of summers before and how we'd never got caught—even once. The more we talked the more exciting the whole thing got until the temptation seemed to get the upper hand of what better judgment I had.

"We'll just borrow one for tonight," I said, "and run up to Bakersfield. We'll surprise our old ladies, get a piece of ass, and have the car back by six in the morning."

Great idea.

There was no problem picking out a car. The '52 Olds had a set of keys under the mat. That old invitation again. Yep, thank you, we believe we'll take it.

We drove off the car lot, went to a gas station, and topped the tank. Bought a case of beer, some wine, and pointed the machine down the Ridge Route.

"There can't be no more than six of them bastards, Dennis," I said. "Looky there. They're all there at that restaurant. There ain't never been no more highway patrol on this grapevine than that. We've got this fuckin' road all to ourselves."

The Olds felt like it was gonna lift right off the ground. I looked over at Dennis and he was smiling. We were rolling down that five-thousand-foot mountain, that well-known suicide slide between Los Angeles and Bakersfield. Hell, we were feeling great.

As the speedometer needle moved to the right I felt like we'd cheated death every time we took a curve. Down close to the bottom we could see two big semis.

"Look at them mothers, Dennis," I said. "I bet they're

doin' seventy-five. Let's make 'em think they're backin' up."

I pulled out in the fast lane. As we cleared the first truck, I looked over at Dennis. His face had gone totally white. It didn't take long to understand why. Looking out the right window, I saw it too—that damned black and white. That dirty, sneaking son of a bitch was running between the trucks, waiting for some fool to do just what we'd done. Why in the hell wasn't *he* back at the restaurant drinkin' coffee like the other cops?

The flash of red lights caught our back glass. My first thought was to outrun him. But by now he'd probably radioed ahead. There would be a road block if I tried that. We'd bought it. We were caught.

I started feeling sick, physically sick. I knew I was pushing for hard time. Speeding ticket? Naw, I wasn't afraid of no speeding charge. I was dreading those four chilling words I knew I'd hear as soon as I pulled off to the side.

"Let's see your registration."

How stupid could one man be? One more cheap thrill— another kick. One more time to prove I could steal a car and get away with it. I'd proven just the opposite.

The cop leaned down and looked inside the car. Of course he wanted to see the registration.

"I don't have one."

There was no good reason why I did it. It was a dumb, fool thing to do and even at the time I did it, I knew that. I did it anyway.

"This guy doesn't have a registration."

Stolen car. Well, *technically*, it was, but hell, we were gonna put it back in the morning. They were not impressed. The Ventura County Jail had a space all reserved for us.

In view of my past record, or records, the authorities didn't take to my "car borrowing" too lightly. Dennis didn't have a prior record so he got off. I was sentenced to one year in the Ventura County Jail. I did nine months, working as a fry cook, which was a little better than some of the things I'd done.

During that time I missed a lot of things, but the most important was the birth of my first child on April 1, 1957.

I remember the first time I saw Dana. Leona brought her to the jail on visiting day. She was such a pretty little black-haired baby girl. All I could do was stare at her. Me, a father. God, that seemed strange, but it didn't seem bad—actually it seemed very good. Being in jail, it didn't quite seem real. I'm sure it was all real enough for Leona though.

It was always hard to tell what Leona was thinking, but as she stood there in the visitor's room of the jail that day I thought she looked very proud. I wanted to ask her if she was happy but was almost afraid to. I wasn't too worried about her because if there was one thing Leona was, it was a survivor. She'd been brought up to manage on *nothing*—and that's what I gave her a lot of the time. Other people might have given up, but Leona kept on keepin' on. Sometimes she'd go back and live with her folks, or she'd go stay with Mama for awhile, but she always managed. I never saw anybody who could do more with less than Leona Hobbs Haggard.

By the time I got out of jail, Leona had done so well without me, she didn't seem to care much if I was home or not. I'm sure she resented being left alone to have a baby like that, and I'm sure she blamed me for a lot of things that went wrong, and she was right. We almost called it quits then, but decided to try a little longer. We may have even used that old "for the sake of the baby" excuse.

The baby, though, was really something special in spite of its mama and papa.

In addition to the new baby, I soon found myself a business venture. Me and a couple of other guys got us a scrap iron business going. We were making good money picking up people's old jalopies and junk and selling the stuff to the scrap iron companies. Only problem was some of the junk we picked up belonged to a guy who was also in the scrap iron business. He interpreted our operation as stealing. The law took his side.

I got ninety days in a road camp. That shouldn't have seemed so bad after all I'd been through but it might as well have been ninety years. Five days was all I could stand. I just walked away when the guard wasn't looking.

The walk turned into a run and the run into flight from the law. It didn't really matter which direction I took, as long as it was away from Bakersfield, home, family, responsibility, *everything*.

Before I knew it I was in Utah, looking for Dean. He wasn't there, or if he was I couldn't find him. I moved from one place to another, working odd jobs and never staying in one place too long. I remember a lot about that particular time though. I went through the giant redwood forest for the first time and I couldn't believe how beautiful it was. Don't stop. Keep moving. Don't look behind. They may be gaining. Sleep light. Listen for noises. Move on again.

During that time I felt like I was passing through life on fast forward. I'd see flashes of towns on sign posts before my eyes—Burnt Ranch, Whiskeytown, Willow Creek, Hayfork, and Peanut. Next town. More strangers. Now and then a helping hand with no questions. Only one name remains— Olgar Flowers—a good and deeply religious man who practiced his faith by helping strangers. Time always seemed to be my enemy and darkness my only friend.

Sometimes I found a place I wanted to stay. Sometimes I almost felt like I could begin a whole new life.

"How do you like being a fry cook in a roadside diner?"

"I've done worse—and in worse places."

"I need somebody at the front counter. Think you could handle it?"

"I'll think about it."

The next morning I'd be gone.

Once I stayed too long. The long arm of the law got me

when I was working at a plywood factory in Eureka. Old warrants never fade away—they just reach out and get you, no matter where you run.

Being behind bars was almost becoming a way of life. I didn't like it, but I didn't like life on the outside either.

Back in jail this time I decided to play the "good guy" and it worked. I only served a few months and they gave me my release—for good behavior. A man can do almost anything if he puts his mind to it.

Being out, as usual, didn't mean the end of my problems. One of them picked me up at the jail and drove me home.

"Well, what's next?" Leona asked, as we drove up to the house.

"You tell me," I said, as I got out of the car.

"Nobody can tell you nothin'."

At least the baby was glad to see me.

We had no trouble picking up where we left off. It was still the same old fight—me against her and vice versa. During one of the lulls in the battles though, Leona got pregnant again.

In no time I got the itch to run again—not from the law, but from my life in general.

Then Bob Teague and Deanrow showed up. They were out of work too. When someone mentioned an oil boom in New Mexico, we considered it worthwhile to look into the deal. Only trouble was, we didn't have no travelin' money.

"Leave it to me, boys," I told 'em. For some reason they both looked worried.

There was a Shell station where I used to work. I only worked there for a couple of weeks, but I knew they usually left some money in the cash register overnight. I also knew they locked the door with one of them big old Yale padlocks. I bought one just like it, dirtied it up, and went over to the station. While the guy was putting gas in my car I switched locks. Then, that night, I put on my old Shell uniform and went down and grabbed the money. Even waved at one of the cops who always went by checking on the place. I knew he'd say he saw somebody—one of the guys who worked there, cause he didn't know my name—and they'd think it was an inside job. I switched the locks back, and I suppose, until now, they thought it was one of the regular employees.

I don't remember how much money I got but it was enough to make a payment on Dean's new '57 Pontiac and finance our trip to Farmington, New Mexico. We even tried to fill up at Shell stations when we could.

The money didn't last long, and the weather in Farmington was so goddanged cold they'd almost closed the whole town. Even worse, there were no jobs, and no prospects of any.

Deanrow and Bob decided to head for Texas. I told them I wanted to get back to California where I'd at least see the sun shine now and then. God, it was cold.

We divided up what money we had left. With my twelve dollars I bought a bus ticket to Flagstaff, Arizona, and had a whole quarter left. The bus station was on the east side, and I found out the only all-night truck stop was on the west side.

I walked into the dingy looking old diner at the bus station, and I saw a big picture of a steaming cup of hot chocolate up over the back counter. God, it looked good. It had marshmallows on top with a little bit of hot steam circling up from it. I could almost taste it. The counter was short, only six or eight stools, best I remember. The waitress kept watching the clock, waiting, I guessed, for her shift to end.

"How much is your hot chocolate?" I asked. She told me it was fifteen cents. God, that was highway robbery. I thought for a minute. I saw a sign saying coffee was a dime and I kept trying to decide if I should or shouldn't spend the extra nickel. I really wanted that hot chocolate.

"I'll have the hot chocolate," I said, as I sat down on one

of the stools. "And how far is it out to the truck stop?"

"I dunno," she said, slapping the cup down in front of me, spilling about a third of my expensive drink.

"It's probably two or three miles," she said then, dabbing at the chocolate with a dirty rag.

It seemed a hell of a lot farther. It was late November or early December of '57. I'd heard somebody say it was fourteen below zero with a hard wind blowing. I could sure as hell vouch for that.

I didn't have no luck at all at the truck stop, and besides, the guy there suggested I move on since he was alone and there had been a few gas station stick-ups. I was a little offended. Did he think I looked like a guy who would hold up a service station?

Once on the road, I tried to tell myself I wasn't freezing to death—but I wasn't very convincing. I turned up my collar and buttoned my coat. I knew I was in for one hell of a night. Walking west out on old Highway 40, I found myself wondering again how I got myself into such situations. I was cold, with no place to get warm. I was hungry and down to my last damn dime.

Leona was probably sleeping, and Dana must be curled up next to her. The picture of them flashed through my mind as I looked down that cold, deserted road. I had to admit that I was homesick.

Think positive, I told myself. Pretend you ain't cold. Pretend your damn blue jeans ain't frozen to your numb legs. Ignore the fact that the snot is froze in your nose and every time one of the fuckin' semis come by, it turns your cold ass around. Pretend you ain't freezin' to death, you fool. Yeah, do that.

I'd left the truck stop about two that morning and was on the road thumbin' till about eight. I was really happy when I saw a truck pull over up ahead of me. He had a big load of Christmas trees.

"I'm going to Kingman," he said, as I managed to climb

into the cab. "That okay with you?" I forced my head up and down. It was heaven. Kingman is about sixty miles from Needles, which is supposed to be one of the warmest places in the country even though it's only two hundred and fifty miles from Flagstaff.

The truck began to move. All at once I felt something cold hit my face. Right down at my feet was a dang hole about the size of a saucer, lettin' all that cold air and road slush come right up in my face. The truck wasn't exactly a speed demon either. It took us the best part of that day to get to Kingman.

When I got back on the road again, I was a mess, but thank God, I was *warm*. It made no difference that I was starving and pissed-off. At least I wasn't shaking anymore. I was beginning to get the feeling back in my blue fingers. My feet hurt, but even that felt good. At least I knew I still had toes.

When a pickup truck stopped just outside of Kingman, I didn't even look at the passengers as I crawled inside. Then I realized I was in the company of three full-blooded Apache Indians. They were all smashed. Now, I don't like to admit that I'm afraid of too many things, but I've always been a little scared of Indians. Leona, after all, had enough Indian in her to give me good cause. Their customs were different from ours and a lot of them just flat out didn't like white people—something to do with broken treaties and speaking with forked tongues, I would guess.

When they offered me a drink, they just handed the bottle in my direction and said, "You drink." Bygawd, I did like they said. And when they suggested we all sing, I didn't argue. I was glad Indians loved Lefty too.

It was about five-thirty in the afternoon before I said goodbye to a "great bunch of guys." Then I started walking in the direction of Bakersfield. Just outside of Needles I put my thumb out again, but before anyone came along I changed my mind.

SING ME BACK HOME

"Enough hitchhiking," I said aloud. Then I noticed the old Santa Fe line that ran into Barstow, and behind me I could hear a train coming. I made a run for it and caught a gondola car, the only open car on the whole train.

The trip on the train was no better than the Christmas tree truck or the Indians. By the time I got to Barstow, I was covered with coal dust or something. It was hard to tell who or what I was. I musta looked like death warmed over.

In Barstow, I found a restroom with a mirror. I had still had a dime in my pocket. I knew there was no need to call Leona. She didn't have no money. But, as usual, I had either left some money with Mama, or she owed me some. I knew she'd send it one way or another. I dialed Mama's number.

We'd had the same conversation before.

"No, I didn't find a job."

"No, I'm not in trouble."

"Yes, I do need you to send me some money."

"No, I don't want to hear about it, Mama."

When the money came, I took part of it and rented me a room in a small motel. I took a long shower and got the first good night's sleep I'd had in a week and a half. I needed all the strength I could get when I faced the home front, or so I believed.

As usual, Leona didn't seem to care whether I was home or not. She cared even less that I'd gone in the first place.

"Didn't get a job, huh?" she asked. I told her I hadn't. She shrugged and went ahead with whatever she'd been doing.

It was a few days later that *I* got a collect call from Texas. Seems like there were these two ol' boys callin' home broke. Wanted *me* to send them money?

"I'm broke," I said.

"Did you get home all right?"

"I sure did."

"Everything okay there?"

"Couldn't be better," I said.

Why should I tell them about the damn train ride, the hitchhiking in subzero weather, the frostbitten fingers, the

Christmas tree truck, and the wild ride with three drunken Apaches.

"I'll see you boys when you get home," I said. "Bye."

Three days later they drove up in the alley in back of my house. There was a door missing on Deanrow's new Pontiac and the two of them looked like hell.

"Ya'll had a little trouble, did you?" I said, trying to keep a straight face.

"You don't have to be so damn smart about it," Dean snapped, "just because you had such an easy time of it."

It was one of the few laughs I had during that time.

Things in general were coming down all around me. I had a premonition that the worst was yet to come. Leona and I were getting along so bad—we were hardly fighting. When we did, it was cruel and vicious. Neither of us cared how much we hurt each other anymore.

With this sense of doom all around me, I was even more depressed. I watched 1957 coming to an end. It was almost as though every hope I had was dying. Around me I could see and hear the sounds of another Christmas. I'd look at Dana and think about how this should be a happy time. A baby in the house at Christmas oughta be the greatest thing in the world. Why did I feel so damned awful?

Where was the peace on Earth? Where was the good will toward men? Where was the Christmas spirit? I didn't feel anything but doom.

Somehow I knew I was on a downhill run and I couldn't stop. I was moving fast toward something, but didn't know what. I was powerless. It was almost like I could see that rough whitewater up ahead of me, and hell, I was afraid. But I didn't know why. What scared me even more was that I was already in rougher waters than I could handle. About the only thing I could do was ride it out through the rapids and hope I could survive.

Had I known how rough the ride would get—hell, I might have just gone over the side.

Nine

Christmas Eve in Bakersfield Jail

Keep me from cryin' today
Help me forget
in your own special way.
Let's save our goodbyes for tomorrow,
And keep me from cryin' today.

"Keep Me From Cryin' Today"

by Merle Haggard

CRIME HAD FINALLY WON. Hands down, or was it
hands up? I had to face the fact that I had no control over
the direction I was taking.

All my friends were crooks. My family had all but given
up on me because they considered me a criminal. And, I
was. There were no more excuses I could offer, no claims of
innocence or putting the blame on somebody else. Worse
yet, I didn't really want to change.

My criminal way of life was taking over. That became
very clear when I teamed up with two men who were

142

"professionals" in their field. One was an older man in his late fifties, and his specialty was cracking safes. The younger guy was in his late twenties, a burglar, plain and simple.

Just like big business, they used a local person to help coordinate their efforts. I pointed out the places of interest and they took care of business. It was from them that I learned that crime not only paid, but it paid damn well. In the past my crimes had been just another kick. From Burglar and Safeman I learned it was a business.

We'd go in, look over a grocery store, which was their specialty, find out where the office was located, and what kind of safe they had. When the store was closed, Burglar and I would come back, put up a ladder, and climb on the roof where we'd cut a hole over the office for Safeman. That was called "topping the joint." Then we'd go back to their place while he went in and emptied the safe. I worked as an apprentice, you might say, and did very well for a little while. After a couple or three weeks they moved on to a new place. I didn't feel much of a need to practice my new profession—except once. As it turned out, once was more than enough.

Micky Gorham had always been living on the edge just like me. He was a hard-luck guy, and even when he tried to do right, it went wrong. There was even a look on his face that spelled out loser. At that time I probably had it too.

Me and Micky had a lot to complain about that December in 1957. Everything was coming down ugly. Although we'd never been real close friends I'd run into him one evening, and he'd come by the house for awhile.

I remember that evening so well. There were four of us sitting around the table at my house—me, Micky, Leona, and a cheap bottle of wine. Mine and Leona's relationship wasn't any better and it was hard to see how it could be any worse, but there were times when we could carry on a civil conversation.

"This country is in terrible shape, Micky," I said looking at my glass.

"I know it," he agreed, "and I don't see no chance of it gettin' any better, do you?"

"Sure as hell don't."

We talked about things that were going on in the world like the school mess down in Little Rock and old Khrushchev sayin' we had his damn Sputnik.

"Ain't no jobs to be had, Merle," he said then after a few more drinks. "A workin' man just can't make it no more and that's the God's truth."

"I know it . . . I know it," I said, "an honest man might's well quit tryin'."

"I know where there's a bunch of money," I said. "It wouldn't be no trouble to get it."

Leona, as I recall, got up to see about Dana or something, and even though she heard us, didn't take us seriously. When we started to leave she wasn't even sure where we were going. She just bundled up the baby and came along with us, probably as much to get out of the house as anything. Nobody looked at the clock, but we figured it to be around three in the morning.

We drove around in back of a little restaurant out on old Highway 99. By that time Leona was getting worried.

"Merle, I don't think you ought to . . . ," she began. I lifted my finger to my mouth. "Hush, woman," I said. For some reason she obeyed. I dragged my crowbar out of the trunk and staggered around to the back door. Micky was right behind me. After ripping off the screen I began prying on the lock. The door came open.

"What are you boys doing?" I heard this voice from inside. It was one of Deanrow's cousins who owned the place, and he knew me real well.

"Why don't you boys come around to the front door like everybody else?"

I looked at Micky and he looked sick. What we hadn't

realized was that it wasn't three A.M. at all. Hell, it was barely ten and the place was still open with several customers inside. Drunk as I was I figured right away we'd made a *slight* miscalculation. If we'd had any sense at all, we would have just laughed and walked around to the front like it was some big joke.

Like fools, we ran.

Once inside the car, I could tell Leona was scared, and to tell the truth I was too. As we pulled out into the street I remembered that I still had a set of burglary tools and a check protector from one of the supermarket jobs.

And, just when we didn't need them—there were the cops.

They got Micky out of the car first, and both the doors were open as we sat there on the street. The headlights from the police car shining against our car made a big shadow down the street. I knew if I was gonna run, it had to be quick. With the tools and the check protector, it would not be easy to talk myself out of this deal. They had us cold.

"I'm gonna run, Leona," I said, slipping off my boots and leaning down below the door of the car. "They won't do nothin' to you. They won't put no pregnant woman and a baby in jail. But if I get caught this time, it's hard time for sure. I gotta run."

Leona wasn't afraid of too many things, but I could see the fear on her face as she held on tight to Dana. I wanted to think she was concerned for me. I was touched. I wanted to tell her, but there wasn't time. Besides, it was hardly the time or place for setting anything right. I pulled the blanket back, took a quick look at Dana, then at Leona. She motioned for me to go and I hit the pavement running.

Over the hill and down to the railroad track. Where was a goddamned train?

It didn't take them long to pick me up. They knew me well at the Bakersfield police station. Jail, this time, took on a different complexion. This time I figured I'd be sent to

Chino or Tehachapi. At least, thank God, I wouldn't have to go to Quentin or Folsom.

As I lay down on my bunk that first night in jail, I couldn't help but worry. Everything that could be wrong in my life was wrong. On top of everything else I'd heard that Deanrow got his hand cut off out in the oil fields. After our New Mexico trip he'd managed to land a job and was doing real well. He'd stuck his hand under a full length of pipe and it had come down on him like a cookie cutter. There was some fear he might lose his whole arm. Every time I thought about it, I could feel the pain shoot up my own arm.

I couldn't get Leona off my mind either. I thought of all the ways I'd let her down. I'd been so used to blamin' her for stuff, I hadn't took time to admit that a lot of things were my fault. We hadn't exactly complemented each other. I felt a terrible need to talk to her, be with her for just a little while. I was going to be leaving her for a long time, I thought, and there she was, with a little girl and another baby on the way. God, I needed twenty-four hours—a measly twenty-four hours. I didn't have no lawyer and I figured this caper had cost me what few friends I had.

I turned over on my stomach and lay on that jail bunk way into the night. Somewhere in the early morning hours I began to pray. There had only been a few times in my life when I'd sincerely prayed. This was one of them. I didn't just pray though, I *begged*. From somewhere deep inside of me, I begged Him for just a little time to get some stuff done. I didn't ask to get out of the trouble I was in. I just wanted a little time on the outside.

"Lord, I know I'm going to have to do some hard time," I told Him, "and I ain't got no right to ask, but I would really like to have about twenty-four hours to straighten up some of the mess in my life, just a little time—twenty-four hours—I need it so bad."

I was so sincere that I didn't realize I was beating my fists on the iron that holds up the bunk. Then I talked to Him about Deanrow. The last thing I remember before drifting off to sleep was saying, "Please . . ."

The next morning they called my name and took me downstairs. The man who'd been my probation officer from the Youth Authority had come to see me. He said he wanted to tell me how sorry he was about my trouble and offered to help me in any way he could—which he said was probably very little. He was a good man, a big red-headed guy who really cared about what happened to the boys he worked with. As I stood there in front of him I couldn't help thinking how I'd disappointed another nice person. I wanted to tell him how much I appreciated him coming by but the words just choked me. All I could do was watch him walk through the door and into the main hall that led to the street.

The street—outside—freedom.

I stood in front of the sergeant's desk for a few minutes waiting for him to say something. I looked back toward the door and it was still open. I could see the cars going by. Freedom was just a few steps away, but I couldn't move.

I was beginning to wonder if Sergeant Matlock knew I was standing there. He hadn't even said anything to me, and I'd spent so much time around the jail we knew each other pretty well. He was a good honest cop and always seemed upset to see me back in trouble. In a little while then he got up from his desk, walked around behind me, and kinda directed me toward the door that led to the hall. I thought we were going to talk to one of the other detectives, but that wasn't the case. As I turned around, I saw the strangest look on his face. His eyes seemed almost glazed over, and he wasn't really looking at me at all. As we walked on through the main hall, I saw other officers I knew but none of them even turned around to look in my direction. I couldn't feel the sergeant's hand at my back any longer so I just kept walking toward the door. Nobody said a word, and I didn't dare look back.

I was out the door and on the street. God as my witness, and I'm sure He was—it happened that way.

The Pontiac garage was just a few blocks down from the jail. I headed in that direction. Leon Copeland worked in the paint shop. I thought he could help me get away. He took me out to a motel on Route 99 and checked me in. Then I called Leona.

I stood by the window waiting for her to come. Outside I could see the flashing sign, LAME DUCK MOTEL. What a hell of a name for a motel.

Then she was there and I was holding her again, something I hadn't done for quite a while. No matter how rough the times had been for us, there was still *that* feeling between us. For most of the day we were together. We talked some, argued a little, and made love a lot. This time I can call it that. Mostly with us, it was just sex. This time it was more.

Even though it hurt like hell to leave, I was almost happy with the strange, uneasy truce we'd reached. We both knew I couldn't stay in one place too long so we said goodbye as quick as we could.

I honestly don't remember how I got out to Flora and George Newton's house in Lamont. Lamont, which was about twenty-five miles out of Bakersfield, was one of our family gathering places. It was where we had those after-church picnics, the holiday get-togethers, and all the to-dos that I hated and bitched about. Yet, there I was, back at the old gathering place like I was trying to relive it all before I had to go away.

But, of course, there was no family gathered there that night. As I looked around I realized how much everything had changed. How much I'd changed. Uncle George and Aunt Flora seemed glad to see me but it's hard to be sociable when you're expecting the cops to show up any minute.

My cousin Bob came in then. Him and his sister, Sylvia, had always seemed more like brother and sister to me than cousins. Sylvia was married to Lomar Boatman, another person who had been so important to me during those awful days right after Daddy died. They were part of the reasons I'd come to Lamont. It was almost like I needed to say goodbye to everybody.

"Merle," Bob said, as he walked into his mama's living room. "You shouldn't stay here." He was right.

"Mom's gotta live in this town," he went on, "and if the police pick you up here, it'll be real embarrassing for her. You know she won't send you away." That was true. Flora had been one of those relatives who had always treated me well, even during the worst times.

"Will you take me to find Lomar?" I asked Bob. He said he would. Then Lomar pulled up in the driveway. He told us he'd just come through the canyon.

"There's a roadblock up there, Merle," he said, "and I just heard on the radio that they've got an APB and a shoot-on-sight order out on you."

God, who did they think I was, "Mad-Dog Haggard"?

"A freight train is your only chance outta here," Lomar said.

"Would somebody take me to Lowell's house?" I asked.

"Bad idea, Merle," Bob said. "You know they're waiting for you to show up there. They're watching your mama's too."

"I want to go anyway."

By the time I walked into Lowell's house on Panama Lane, about halfway between Lamont and Bakersfield, I had taken care of most of my plans. I had started feeling better as soon as I'd settled things with Leona and found out Dean wasn't gonna lose his arm. Things were falling into place. Me, I was just falling.

SING ME BACK HOME

All up and down Panama Lane there were Christmas lights and I supposed that inside the homes there was that certain warmth and good feeling that comes with special times of the year.

It was Christmas Eve.

Outside Lowell's window, I caught a glimpse of a light. I knew it wasn't old Santy and his sleigh. There was a knock at the front door, followed by one at the back. My time was up. Somehow I felt almost relieved.

Through the front door came the same guy who had arrested me the night before. Strangely enough his name was Tommy Overstreet, same as the country singer.

"Here we are again," he said, holding a shotgun in his hand.

"Yeah," I said, "here we are. Merry Christmas."

"Merry Christmas to you too, Merle," he said, reaching for the handcuffs. There was a fifth of Jim Beame on the table and I nodded toward it.

"Before you put them cuffs on me, Overstreet," I said, "do you think I might have one little drink? I ain't had my Christmas drink yet, been kinda on the move you might say."

Overstreet shook his head. "I shouldn't let you have that kind of privilege, Merle," he said, "seein' as how slick you've been gettin' away and how much trouble you've been to me the last thirty-some hours."

Thirty-some hours. It was then that I realized I'd got the twenty-four hours I'd asked for, then some. I reached out and took the bottle. I turned it up and downed the biggest drink of whiskey I ever took in my life. It hit bottom, then I took a shot of water, another big swig, and more water.

"Me trouble to you, Overstreet," I grumbled as he snapped on the cuffs. "Think how much trouble you are to me—'bout five years' worth probably."

By the time I hit the jailhouse door, I was half drunk and glad I was.

Christmas Eve in Bakersfield Jail

Christmas Eve ain't no time to be behind bars. Peace on Earth. Soon it would be a new year, and God knows what I'd have to face then. Still, I was glad to see '57 fade outta sight. It had been such a bastard.

The next time I walked out of Bakersfield Jail I was escorted by "the law" and on my way to the Chino Guidance Center where I would receive my assignment. What a nice sounding word for such a goddamned thing.

Chino, the guidance center. That great walk-through to the big time. It was everything I'd expected it to be, but I'd seen much worse. I decided maybe I'd make it okay if that turned out to be my assignment. The judge had sentenced me to "what the law prescribed," and Chino would tell me what that was.

Chino has a dual function as a penal institution. It is a guiding center and a minimum security prison, one side separated from the other. The minimum side doesn't have much security of course and it houses the guys who are just in for small offenses. The maximum side though serves as a kind of boot camp where all prisoners are sent to be evaluated. Some are only sentenced to the minimum side, some to Tehachapi or state camps. Others are sent to San Quentin or Folsom. Again, I was assured by those who knew that I would not have to go to San Quentin or Folsom. Those places were for the real hard cases.

I began to look upon Chino with appreciation. The cells were clean and pretty good sized. Maybe I wouldn't have too long a stretch, I thought, and if Chino was to be my home for a few months then I'd make it just fine.

Then the tests began. They gave me every possible test in the world, trying to find out who and what I was. At the end of about four weeks I felt like I was walking around wrongside out. They'd prodded and questioned me till I felt like a guinea pig. Then I had to wait three weeks for the results of the tests.

On the day the evaluation report comes, there is a lot of

anxiety. It don't even come in the regular mail. So, instead of getting the news at four in the afternoon when they clip the regular mail on the bars, you have to wait until sometime during the night. It's a hell of a way to start a new day.

I couldn't sleep on the night I was supposed to get my results. I waited up all night, and it wasn't until about three-thirty when I heard footsteps coming down the hall. They stopped at different cells, and I could hear the rustle of paper. My cell was dark, and I pushed my back against the corner so the guard couldn't see me sitting there.

Then the footsteps stopped at my cell. I sat totally still. I don't think I even breathed. After a few seconds, the footsteps moved on down the cellblock. For some damn reason then, I couldn't get up and go get the piece of paper I'd waited for all night.

Instead, I sat there trying to think of something else. The day before some guy had told me about a hit song somebody inside Chino had written. I asked how he knew it was a hit, and he said 'cause some singer named Roy Hamilton was gonna record it. It was too good not to be a hit, he assured me.

"You say some guy in here wrote it?" I asked again. He told me all I had to do was listen to it and I'd know it was by somebody in the slammer.

"What's the name of it?" I asked. "I wanna remember it just in case I do hear it."

"Oh, you'll remember it all right," he said. "It's called 'Unchained Melody,' and buddy, it flat out says it all." Then he started singing it.

> *"Oh my love . . . my darlin' . . .*
> *I've hungered for your touch . . .*
> *these long lonely nights . . .*
> *Time goes by so slowly . . .*
> *And time can mean so much . . ."*

I had to admit that it did say it all. And I not only remembered it, I *lived* it, every damn line of it. Still, I couldn't help wonder about the guy who wrote it and think how great it would be to express yourself in a song like that. What a way to communicate . . . goddamn!

I eased over to the door and pulled the paper free from the clothespin on the bars. At first I couldn't see the words clear enough to read it. My hand was shaking so bad when I held it through the bars and into the hall light that nothing registered. I had to wait till I could hold it still.

The words began to form. Oh my God—it was so plain.

I could feel a knot forming in my stomach, a knot that would, in time, grow into a full-blown rage.

I held the paper up again, surprised that my hand was steady. I couldn't believe I was calm. There had to be a mistake. It couldn't say *that*. It's wrong. But I looked again.

"San Quentin."

That son of a bitchin' paper actually said San Quentin.

I wanted to scream but I couldn't make a sound. I wasn't going. I wasn't going to no San Quentin no matter what "they" said. That was a place for criminals fergawdssake! No way was I gonna do time there. No, goddammit, no.

"You're wrong," I whispered down at the damn piece of paper. "There's been a mistake. I ain't going."

I let the paper fall to the floor and went back to my corner. Sitting there in the dark I still couldn't make a goddamned sound. Hell, I couldn't even swallow. I put my head back against the cold cement and began to mouth the words over and over.

I ain't goin'.

Ten

San Quentin

The warden led a pris'ner
down a hallway to his doom,
And I stood up to say goodbye
like all the rest.
And I heard him tell the warden
just before he reached my cell
Let my guitar playing friend play my request.

"Sing Me Back Home"   by Merle Haggard

YOU MAY HAVE seen me that day. That could have been you in that restaurant with your family. You might have been a little bit scared as the armed guards filed the shackled men through the door.

Outside the bus that had brought us down Highway 99 told the world that we were guests of the State of California. Written underneath the barred windows were the words CALIFORNIA CORRECTIONAL TRANSPORTATION, and we were being transported to the end of the line—San Quentin.

We'd left Chino around seven o'clock that January morning. I think I was still in some kind of shock from reading that piece of paper.

The goddamned bus driver was wearing white coveralls.

Even today I wonder why that seems to be so clear in my memory. I can't even remember the face of the man they had me chained to. I can still feel the leg irons. I sat still so I wouldn't feel the cold steel against my legs. Nothing helped. When they clamp them around your wrists and ankles, they clamp them around your mind as well. Even when your arms and legs are freed, you still feel the clamps around your mind.

The bus ride from Chino to San Quentin took all day. Went right up old Highway 99 through Bakersfield. No point in asking to stop here for some of Mama's cooking. It seemed strange moving over streets I'd raced across in those fast little cars. All those good times now seemed like they'd happened ages ago. But we did stop somewhere around Madera for lunch. I couldn't eat. I doubt if anybody did.

We could see the building long before we got there. The roads were winding. It was beginning to get dark. The lights from San Quentin showed for miles. If you drove by there after dark you might even have remarked how impressive it looked. But for a human being about to be swallowed up inside, it looks like some kind of an electronic monster. It brought to life all those childhood fears. No waking up from this nightmare. This is for real.

As the bus pulled up in front of the gates, I noticed it was raining. I don't know how long the rain had been coming down, but in my mind it began when I saw San Quentin. The way the rain was coming down, I knew that whoever was in charge was not happy with me at all.

For what seemed like hours—though I know it wasn't— we sat outside the gates. The only humorous thought I had that day was that maybe they were all filled up, and we couldn't get a room. But, hell, we already had reservations.

Later, I figured out that they didn't want to take in any new prisoners until the others were in their cells for the night. It was about ten o'clock when they finally filed us out of the bus and into the joint.

SING ME BACK HOME

We were being marched across the yard. From the cells above us came the catcalls and whistles. I tried to shut them out, but it was impossible. Even though they had us waiting underneath a shelter, it was no protection. We were still getting soaked.

Standing there, wet and cold, wondering what was next, I began to make that first mistake a prisoner makes. I wondered what was going on outside. I felt like everything else had stopped. Maybe I hoped it had. There was such a strange feeling that maybe this place was all there was in the world. Nothing else existed but *this* time and *this* place.

I was put in the south block, fourth tier, B-section, cell 13. Hell of a thing. Glad I wasn't superstitious.

I couldn't believe how damn little that cell was. How did they think I was gonna exist in that? I got a chill all over when they opened the door and shoved me inside—it was only nine foot long and five foot wide—hardly room for one man, much less two.

You'd think I'd remember the other man in the cell that night but I don't. I just kept thinking—ain't no way in hell I can stand this. Nobody could help me, nobody. I was totally alone. No way possible I can describe the helpless feeling I had. It was, I would think, a little like being kidnapped.

What is worse and so inhumane about California prisons is that you never know how much time you have to do. They don't actually set a time you can count off. They just give you what "the law prescribes," and let you wonder what the hell that is. God, that does something to a man's mind that never heals up right.

It must have been the little kid in me that wondered how it would be if I ever got sick in San Quentin. Who would care? Back in Bakersfield Jail I always knew they'd take me across town to the hospital and I'd be close to my family. In Quentin I had no idea what they did with the sick and the lame.

In a short time I learned. I got a case of the Asian flu

when we had the first outbreak in the States. It reached the epidemic stages inside the prison, and everybody who had it just had to stay in their cells and suffer. There wasn't enough room in the prison infirmary and there wasn't much they could do anyway except give you aspirin. Sometimes it seemed like a toss-up as to who would last the longest, the flu or me.

I did learn something though from that ordeal. As sick as I was, I found out that the men behind bars are not the uncaring monsters some make them out to be. Time and again I'd be aware of someone stopping by my cell just long enough to ask how I felt. I began to realize I had become a member of a rather strange and select brotherhood of people.

"How ya doin' in there?" somebody would ask.

"I'm dyin', I believe," I'd answer, trying to keep it as light as I could. Sometimes I thought I might not be kidding.

But I survived the Asian flu—and I survived San Quentin. I believe I survived prison not because it taught me a lesson—though I learned a lot—but because I had to prove I could survive. I believe I got my life together in spite of prison, maybe even in defiance of it. I will say this now, and it'll sound strange, but prison was an experience I'm glad I had. I could have done without it, for damn sure, but for all it gave me and all it took away, I believe the score was higher on the plus side. One thing I know—if a guy goes into prison and he sets his mind to better himself, he can do it. If he wants to learn a trade, he can do it inside those walls. When I was in Quentin the facilities for most basic education were available. Of course a man could learn about safe-cracking, bank robbing, and things like that too, if he chose. A lot of good teachers were in there.

There is no way, though, that I can ignore the bad side. There was a lot more of that than the good. There was the goon-squad that walked the yard with their cocked 30-30 rifles, hoping somebody would get outta line. And there were horrors too terrible to think about, much less talk about. The public don't want to hear things like that but until they do listen, and do something about them, prison will always be a bad sore festering in our society, ready to spread its infection more and more throughout the human race.

I will say that Quentin, unlike some of the prisons I've heard about, gave you a choice. You could either apply for a job, work hard, and build up a good record, or you could lay around in the yard all day. I voted for layin' around in the yard all day. We could make our time count—or just count our time. I did some of both.

While I was doing my time, I became educated. I learned that sometimes one mistake can be your last error. There is no such thing as a petty quarrel inside those walls. When two prisoners hook it up, one of them will not make it. I learned to make quick decisions and decide whether something was worth putting my life on the line.

I learned the house rules right away. Not only does a prisoner have to follow the authority rule, he's under the prisoner's code as well. The main rule among the inmates is simple straight-on honesty. When you tell a man something in the joint, it goddamn better be that way, or hell, he'll kill you. That's about as basic as life can get. It's hard to give the other man as much space as you can in a place where there ain't no space to give.

It's also a good idea not to get too friendly too quick. You learn not to accept gifts or favors, or to borrow anything from anybody, because if you can't make payment on demand, it could be all over for you. Even worse, there are other ways of making payments. I made up my mind right away that I didn't want to be nobody's "old lady."

Most of all, you learn to ignore. You don't mention the roach or rat shit you find floatin' in your soup. You pretend the free tobacco, or duffy as they call it, don't taste like crap. You try to hide any weakness you have because somebody will take advantage of it at every opportunity. For once I was grateful for my pre-San Quentin education. I was a little more prepared for prison life than some of those first-timers. I saw new guys coming into prison for the first time, and before they knew what happened they were forced into homosexual situations they couldn't avoid. There are so many humiliations and degradations inside those walls, I can't put 'em down here. And, hell, you don't really want to know. You'll sleep better if I skip 'em.

That first night in my cell I thought of so many damned things. I was scared to death by what I'd heard, and by things I already knew. I'd been scared before but on this night it was different. I was afraid of Merle Haggard. I was afraid he didn't have what it took to stand up to the reality of that place.

That night I couldn't sleep at all. I held on to my damn scratchy blanket like a baby, and I fought against all the old memories that marched through my head like a fuckin' parade. I closed my eyes and I was back in Bakersfield. I would ride my new Schwinn bicycle down Yosemite Street just so I could zip by pretty Janet Issac's house. What was she doing this night I wondered?

I could see the church down by the railroad tracks with a hand-lettered sign over the door—NORSE ROAD CHURCH OF CHRIST. I could even hear the singing and the music. This was one of the Churches of Christ that allowed music.

I could hear people talking from my past, all their voices messed up in my head like radio stations cutting in on each other.

"We ain't goin' back to Oklahoma. . . . I'm really settin' my foot down on that. . . ."

"Look what you've done, you goddamned son of a bitch, you've ruined my new dress."

"Ain't no use in people like us tryin' to think about a music career, Bud, you gotta have a degree. . . ."

"You *will* run. . . ."

"I'll take this one upstairs girls. . . . This one is special."

"Pick out whichever one of the puppies you like, son. . . ."

"Why Merle, you sound just like that guy on the radio. . . ."

"If it was up to me, I'd sign you, but Fuzzy ain't for it. . . . I gotta go along with what he says. . . ."

"Could you send us some money, Merle? We're kinda stuck in Amarillo. . . ."

"You're making too much of this Merle. . . . Sherman is a nice person. I like him. . . ."

"Gimme a can of them green beans, boy. . . ."

With my eyes closed I could also see the little store where I bought my first pack of Camels, the cement porch Daddy built on the boxcar house, and the grape arbor in the back. Oh God, I could see it—*feel* it all. Was I going to spend the next fourteen years seeing all the old reruns of my life?

There were almost six thousand men inside those walls and I wondered about them. How many of them felt the same way I did? All of them, I would guess. I knew they must think about their women and their kids on the outside. I sure as hell thought about mine. I began to wonder if my new baby would be a boy or a girl. I'd missed the birth of my first one and I'd miss the birth of my second one too. How would they feel, I wondered, about their old man being in the joint? Would they ever forgive me? Would *anybody*?

There were about thirteen or fourteen men in Quentin I'd known on the outside. Some I knew pretty well, others just slightly. The one I knew best was a friend from Oildale, Delbert Smart—the one who'd taught me so much about guitar pickin'. I had no idea where he was. It wasn't like I was at a Holiday Inn where I could call down to the desk and ask what room old so-and-so was in. And now that I think about it, the room service wouldn't exactly get a four-star rating either.

I thought that first morning would never come. I discovered during the first night that there was only one thing to look forward to in the joint, with the exception of getting out. Tomorrow. And there was one thing to dread. Also tomorrow.

When I was "let out" in the yard with the other unassigned prisoners the next day I was more scared than ever. There must have been about four hundred of us scattered between the lower yard and the big yard. We had nothing to do but stand around. Everybody else was working, or in their cells.

I found me a place to stand, out of the way, and I looked around at what was gonna be my new home. The only thing missing was the flames. It was hell. I leaned up against the inner wall by the mess hall, and I couldn't believe the next sound I heard.

"Merle Haggard!" My name never sounded so good. And there he was. Delbert Smart. He had two guys with him and they both had guitars. Delbert grabbed one of the guitars and ran to me with it. I hadn't even touched a guitar in three months, and I had a hard time deciding which one I was the happiest to see, the guitar or Delbert.

"This is the som'bitch I been tellin' you about," he said, slapping me on the back and talking to the other two men.

"He sounds just like Lefty Frizzell . . . sing for 'em Merle . . . let 'em see I ain't been lyin'."

"Hell, Delbert, I can't sing *now*," I said. Several guys had turned to look at us. "I can't hardly talk, much less sing."

"We heard you were comin' Merle," he said, almost like he hadn't heard me. "I want you to sing for these guys. . . . Oh shit, I forgot to introduce you."

I don't remember one of them, but the other one became a good friend. Because of one of the stories I'll tell later, I won't use his real name. I'll just call him "Sam."

By the time I finally convinced Delbert I was in no condition to sing, the crowd had moved away. Then he began talking about getting me on the Warden's show.

"What's your custody?" he asked then.

"My what?"

"Your custody, man," he repeated. "What classification are you in?" I knew what he meant then. There were five classifications or custodies, ranging from minimum to maximum.

"Well, you won't get the worst two, close or maximum," Delbert said when I told him I hadn't got mine yet.

"Only people who get those are the old-timers and the escape artists."

"Well, Delbert, if you remember," I said, "I got a few escapes under my belt."

"Naw," he laughed, "that won't count. That was kid stuff. They ain't worried about that in here. They probably won't pay too much attention to what you did back in them boys' schools. Don't worry about it. Hell, it's the least of your problems."

Sure.

When I got my assignment, it was close security. It seems they did take my escape record very seriously. It had also been one of the reasons I'd been sent to Quentin. On close custody I had to be in my cell at four in the afternoon, which meant I not only couldn't play music on the Warden's show, I couldn't attend any evening functions or even go to the prison library.

Delbert tried every way he could to get my custody changed. He wrote letters and told anybody who would listen how much I'd add to the Warden's show, but nothing worked. It seems the only talent of mine they were concerned about was that of an escape artist. They didn't want me puttin' on no show like that in Quentin.

Nobody had escaped from those walls in thirteen years. I was almost amused, and yeah, a little flattered, that they would even consider me a threat. As it turned out, their fears were justified. I could have escaped. I had the opportunity and I could have made it.

By the time my chance came, I had reached the bitterness stage and I was very close to doing something desperate. I'd tried working several jobs but had been fired from most of them. We got graded on the jobs—just like damn school. A number five was the worst grade—four was not that good. Three was average, two better than average, and number one was excellent. I got straight fives. The pay was quite a laugh too. It started at three dollars a month, went to six and nine dollars, with a grand high of eighteen dollars. It just seemed to make more sense to me to lay around in the yard and play the guitar. The future was laughable. I didn't have one.

I was seeing things I didn't want to believe or remember. I watched one man kill another over a simple insult—a disagreement. I saw another scalded to death in the laundry. As one incident followed another I began to wonder if I'd ever get out alive. It was not only the life and death matters that ate away at you either, it was the little things that just drove you right to the brink.

On one of my jobs, I began to think more and more about escaping. At first it was just a thought everybody has. Then I actually tried to form a plan. Nothing made any sense. As I sorted dirty socks in the laundry I could see myself flyin' right out over the walls, diggin' me a tunnel to freedom, or walkin' out disguised as a guard. Between these fantasies, I'd sort more dirty socks until my hands began to get sore with some sort of fungus I picked up. When I complained about it, the guards just laughed. Every day it got worse until it began to eat little holes right through my fingernails. It was like a bad science fiction movie. Little by little I felt like I was being eaten alive by some little invisible germs. I wanted out so bad I began to think all kinds of crazy thoughts.

SING ME BACK HOME

By this time I was celling with the man I called Sam. He was working in the furniture factory with another prisoner named Jimmy Hendricks. Jimmy—we all called him Rabbit—was in for bank robbery. He had two five-to-life sentences running end to end. He had no chance for parole for at least eight years and that was only if he didn't make no mistakes. His chances were next to nothing. I liked Rabbit and it didn't matter to me what he'd done. He was in his late twenties, a nice-looking man, the kind you might see every day in your neighborhood out mowing his lawn or playing baseball with his kids. He sure didn't fit the movie image of a tough guy or hardened criminal.

I'd been in the joint then for some time when I learned about the escape plan Rabbit and Sam had worked out. Because there was room for one more, I was offered the opportunity.

It seemed foolproof. I know people always say that, but hell, it was. And it did work. The plan had room for two escapees and one helper back in the prison. As Sam was going to help, they told me about the space for a second passenger.

I had one night to make up my mind.

I really wanted to go. I didn't sleep. I tossed and turned all night, both in mind and body. I went over the plan they'd outlined. It was *perfect,* a once-in-a-lifetime opportunity.

The plan was simple. In the furniture factory there was a large desk being built for a judge's chamber in San Francisco. It weighed about fifteen hundred pounds and would be picked up by a truck and delivered to the courthouse as soon as it was finished. It was even a kick thinking about how it was a *judge's* desk—poetic justice, maybe. God, I wanted to go so bad. Rabbit and Sam both tried to discourage me.

"Don't do it, Merle," Rabbit finally said that last afternoon. I knew he was worried about my going, but until then he hadn't said anything.

"I want you to know you're welcome," he said, "but I think in your case it might be a big mistake. You've got talent, and no matter what you think right now, you've got a future. You can sing and write songs and play the guitar real good. You can be *somebody* someday. After all, you're only lookin' at two or three years. I ain't got no hope but to escape. I'm almost thirty years old and this is *it* for me." Then he got very serious and his voice was almost like a warning.

"I want you to understand," he said, "that if you go with me, there ain't gonna be nothin' I won't do to keep from comin' back. If they try to take me, I'm gonna hold court in the streets. If you're with me, understand how it's gonna be."

I understood. I still wanted to go. I listened while him and Sam went over the final plans. Sam was gonna wait till just before the truck came before he helped Rabbit inside the desk. Then he'd nail on that last piece of wood, leaving it loose enough for Rabbit to push off once he was inside the truck and *outside* the walls.

I had to fight that awful urge to prove again that I could do something almost impossible. Escape from San Quentin. I honestly believe the actual escape fascinated me more than the thought of being free.

Rabbit told me if I wasn't there at nine-thirty when Sam nailed on the last board, he'd know I took his good advice and stayed behind. I couldn't say nothin'. He reached out and shook my hand.

I'd probably only had about an hour's sleep when Sam touched my shoulder.

"Merle," he said. "What are you gonna do?"

I lay there on the bunk, wide awake even though I'd had no sleep hardly. The words stuck in my throat and I honestly didn't know what I was gonna say till they were out.

"I'm stayin'. . . ."

SING ME BACK HOME

"I'm glad to hear it," Sam said. "Rabbit'll be glad too."

"Tell him . . . ," I began, but I couldn't finish. I turned my face to the wall, and shortly after that I heard Sam leave.

Later, I watched the truck come in, back up to the loading dock, and wait while several men lifted the big desk off the platform and onto the truck.

It moved real slow toward the main gate. I was afraid everybody around me could hear my heart beating. Nobody was paying any attention. Of course nobody but the three of us knew about the thing that was taking place at that moment.

I watched it go through the gate and I doubted that anybody was gonna tear the judge's desk apart. At that time there were no X-ray machines to check outgoing shipments.

"Tell him I said good luck," I said quietly in the direction of the gate, finishing the sentence I'd started that morning. Then I felt a chill, like something wasn't quite right. Maybe that was the reason I'd turned down the offer to go along. Something was wrong. I just couldn't put my finger on it, but it was a premonition I couldn't shake.

In about an hour though, I began to relax. Maybe I'd been wrong. Looked like it had gone off without a hitch. Ol' Rabbit was on his way. Somebody was waiting for him near Oakland Bay Bridge, I believe, and once the truck crossed there, Rabbit was supposed to get out of the desk, lift the canvas on back of the truck, and jump free.

God, it must have worked. By noon I was kicking myself for not going. Premonition, hell, I'd just been too chicken.

Four o'clock came and the prison began to take on a strange atmosphere. It began with a whisper here and there. Something was wrong. You could feel it in the air.

"The count ain't right."

"That's happened before. Damn screws can't count."

"Is somebody missin'?"

"From Q? You gotta be kiddin'."

Everybody had to stay in their cell until the mistake could be straightened out. It had happened before, the count being wrong, and sometimes we'd end up having our chow thirty or forty minutes late. Somehow, it seemed different this time.

The tension and excitement kept mounting. Sam and I sat in our cell. We didn't discuss what only the two of us knew for sure.

"Hey, didja hear . . . they's somebody missin'?" one of the other inmates yelled down the cellblock to us.

"Are you sure?" I questioned him.

"Pretty sure," was the answer. "I hear they're runnin' around like crazy tryin' to find out who, what, and where."

The prison came to life with rumors, excitement, and occasional cheers. By seven o'clock when we finally got to eat, the mess hall was one big celebration.

"They're talkin' to the snitches . . ."

"Who *was* it?"

"How in hell did he do it?"

Nobody knew nothin'. They never questioned me or Sam, even though they knew we were friends of Rabbit. One thing about the prison authorities, they knew, to a man, who would and who wouldn't talk.

The radio told us all the details. That night on the news there was the name, description, and the amazing fact that Jimmy Hendricks was the first man to escape from inside the walls of San Quentin in thirteen years. As to how he escaped, the voice reported, "That is still a mystery."

Every day for a week there was something else about the escaped convict in the news. Then, as the days went on there was less and less. Finally, there was nothing. Life inside the prison went on as usual. Sam and I seldom discussed Rabbit, but we both thought about him a lot and wondered how he was doing. Some weeks later, a news bulletin told us exactly how he was doing:

SING ME BACK HOME

"A man believed to be Jimmy Hendricks, escapee from San Quentin, has shot and killed a highway patrolman in San Jose. Police have surrounded an old hotel where the suspect is believed to be hiding."

"Gonna hold court in the streets, Merle," he had said. Dear God, that's what he'd done. The cop had stopped Rabbit on the street in San Jose, and since he had no identification, he knew that was it for him. He had only been stopped for some minor traffic violation, but sometimes life hangs on the balance of one simple little thing. The cop had asked to see Rabbit's driver's license. He had shown him the barrel of his gun instead. Blew the cop away.

"Gonna hold court in the streets."

Then the police flushed Rabbit out of the old hotel with tear gas. His worst fears of being captured and sent back to Quentin had been realized after all.

Even though we hoped for the best, we knew better. When Rabbit's trial was over we knew he'd be coming back to San Quentin—but we knew he wouldn't be staying long.

It was a terrible thing he'd done, killing that cop. You can imagine how little sympathy was with him on the outside. But on the inside we all felt his pain. We knew the cop was the real victim, but he wasn't the only one. I'm not making excuses for Rabbit, but at that time I understood the panic of being cornered. I couldn't help but identify with him. I could have been *with* him.

He was sentenced to die in the gas chamber.

When they brought him back to the prison, me and Sam and some of the others were waiting there on the bench in front of the mess hall. It was the same place I'd stood the first day I came to San Quentin.

We waited—and Rabbit knew we'd be waiting.

It wasn't that we could talk to him, or offer him any kind of hope. We just wanted to pay our respects to a dead man who was still walking around. As we stood there waiting for him, I looked up, half expecting the rain to start pouring or a flash of lightning to cut across the sky—but nothing looked any different. Instead there seemed to be a strange kind of silence broken only by the sound of heavy footsteps as we watched the guards coming across the yard with Rabbit.

A condemned prisoner walks with a guard in front of him and one behind him. Both guards carry rifles cocked and ready to fire.

As they got closer to us, I wished with all my heart I could at least step out and say something to him. All I could do was sit there with my back pushed against the building. We knew they would take him to the top of the North Block—Death Row. We had known they'd have to pass this way. We were determined to show our support for him the only way we knew—by being there.

At first Rabbit looked straight ahead. He didn't let on he'd even seen us till he got almost even with where we all stood. Then, he just motioned with one hand in our direction. It was such a simple gesture. We all waved back like a bunch of kids at a train station. That was all we could do.

That day was nothing, though, compared to the day of his execution, and the night before his death. I went to bed thinking about him up there in that little box, and I felt like I knew exactly what he was thinking. I tried not to think of the actual mechanics of the execution, but it was impossible. I could see the buttons, or the way I thought they'd look. And I wondered about the faceless men who'd push them. There were three buttons, but only one released the strap that held that little sack. The little sack—they say it looks like a Bull Durham tobacco sack—holds the cyanide. When it falls into the bucket of acid under the chair where the prisoner sits, it releases the gas.

They say not to fight it. Goddamn. Can you believe that? Just inhale—exhale—relax. Now we're all *safer. Jesus Christ.*

SING ME BACK HOME

From the chimney outside a puff of smoke comes out when it happens. Everybody watches. Everybody dies a little right along with the one being executed.

"You've got talent," he'd said. "You can be somebody someday." Rabbit's words roared in my head. Years later when I wrote "Sing Me Back Home," it was because I believe I know exactly how he felt that night. Even now when I sing the song, it's still for Rabbit and all those like him.

Once the execution was over, things went back to the way they had been before. I need to point out here though that my protection of "Sam" might even include a misrepresentation of where he was celling and his actual part in the escape—just in case someone would like to make trouble for a good man who only tried to help make things easier for a brother in need of help.

The next event in my life was my date with the parole board. When eighteen months had passed, I was automatically up for parole. I was pretty sure they'd let me out. I hadn't been a model prisoner, but I hadn't been in any big trouble. Frankly, I hadn't done much of anything.

They noticed that.

"You must like this place," one of the men sitting at the table said.

"Why's that, sir?" I asked.

"Well, it says here on the record you worked five months down in the laundry and quit," he said, leafing through some papers. My life in San Quentin, I supposed.

I looked down at my hands. Goddamned fingernails. Had holes in 'em. Look at them fuckin' holes, you son of a bitch, I wanted to yell out at him. Got 'em from a dirty, filthy fungus down in the damn laundry handlin' everybody's stinkin' socks. I wanted to lay my hands on the table and show him how the fungus had eaten away at my nails. I wanted him to look and see how hard and thick they were. Would he care? I didn't think so. I didn't say nothin'.

". . . been lying around out on the football field playing guitar . . ." The words went on and on. I turned them off. What was wrong with these bastards? I wondered what they'd say if I stood up and told them about the *real* San Quentin. Maybe they already knew and didn't give a damn.

"Then you went into auto mechanics, stayed three months, and quit that, right?"

"Yes sir."

"You're currently working down on the construction crew, aren't you?"

"Yes sir." I hoped he couldn't tell I was choking on the word "sir." I hoped he couldn't read minds either. I ain't working anywhere, asshole, I'm just puttin' in my time.

"Do you know what you want to do yet?"

That question really threw me. I almost blew it for sure. I wanted to tell him I certainly did know what I wanted to do. I wanted out. I wanted out of that goddamned chamber of horrors. I wanted to walk out of those damn gates while I still had some sanity left. *That's* what I wanted. I wanted to see my wife and kids, my mama. Hellsfire, I've got a *son* now, you bastards. His name is Marty, and some of the family says he looks a little like me. He's over a year old already. Does anybody in this room care? Hell, no!

I didn't say any of those things. It wouldn't have made any difference anyway.

"We'll talk to you again sometime."

Yeah, in about a year they would. I went back to my cell. They don't tell you what they're going to do, but I knew. When I pulled that note off the bars that afternoon, their fuckin' message was no big surprise.

"Denied."

When you can't look forward to one thing, you look forward to something else. I still had visiting days and my mail to get me through.

Whenever somebody from the family came—Leona, Mama, Lillian, Bill, or Lowell—I'd try to put up a front, but

SING ME BACK HOME

I doubt if I fooled them much. We spent most of our time talking about how much the kids had grown, what this or that relative was doing, and sometimes we even talked about the weather.

I wasn't ready for the news about Escar and Willie. They had broken up. There was one of those great combinations, living proof that marriage was really *right* sometimes. Seems like somebody had convinced Willie that because she had an earlier brief marriage before Escar, she was now living in sin with him. When she had tried to discuss "church reasons" why their marriage was wrong, Escar had made good his promise.

"Don't bring the church home," he'd told her back years ago. She had, and that was it. Escar had gone back to Oklahoma, Mama said, and Willie was heartbroken.

Was everybody going crazy?

"I had to have Jack put to sleep," Mama told me during one visit. Poor little dog. I couldn't even cry for him. It seemed like that was somebody else who ran up and down the railroad tracks with him anyway. God, was there no good news?

At least when Leona visited I could hear all about the kids. And she was pretty good about visiting at first. Still, seeing her was not easy. There was no contact except a brief kiss hello and goodbye. It hurt like hell to sit there in that damn visitor's room and see her knowing I couldn't touch her. Sometimes I almost preferred letters.

Then her letters stopped. Her visits stopped too. I thought I'd go out of my cotton-pickin' mind. I wrote one letter after another to everybody, but got no answers to why Leona wasn't coming to see me.

Where was she? What was happening? Finally, I couldn't take it anymore. I wrote her a letter demanding to know what was going on.

I got my answer. I wished I hadn't.

I knew she wasn't gonna sit around on her ass and wait

for me. I honestly didn't expect her to. I knew she wouldn't stay home and keep a damn light in the window. Still, I was both surprised and hurt when she got herself pregnant. Even then I wasn't so mad about her foolin' around as I was that she was dumb enough to show everybody she had been by having somebody else's baby. I didn't want living proof of her unfaithfulness.

When I found out about it, I got more and more bitter. I didn't care about nothin' anymore. All the pep talks I'd give myself seemed stupid, and I knew I was crazy to believe anything could ever be any better for me. There was no more reason, I decided, to work on good behavior.

Me and Sam decided we'd start our own little business, a gambling operation with a beer concession on the side. The fact that beer companies didn't make deliveries inside San Quentin was no problem. Hell, we just made our own brew. We'd get all the stuff we needed out of the kitchen. We could run off a batch in eight days and it was danged good, if I do say so myself. We made it out of oranges, apples, yeast, and sugar. It was about four times as strong as beer on the outside. We packaged it in milk cartons, and since it was okay to walk around drinking milk, it was kind of a kick to stand right under the guards' noses and get drunk.

As it is in any business, we made a little mistake—at least I did. I took a batch off too early and it turned out to be a bit too grainy. That Saturday afternoon some of us sat down in the yard to drink our beer and make a little music. Sometime later, I sure don't remember how long, I got up to go to the canteen. I think I made it about halfway up the steps. As drunk as I was though, there was no way I could mistake the next sound I heard. A click from a 30-30 is like nothing else. I froze in my tracks. I hoped to God I wasn't staggering or they might claim I tried to run.

When the voice from up on the catwalk said, "Hold it!" I did just that.

I was under arrest. It seemed strange to me that I could be

under arrest in a place like that. I supposed I would be charged with public drunkenness. It was funny but I couldn't laugh. Stand still, you fool, the next sound you hear could be your last.

Up till then I hadn't given much thought to what they did with drunks. If I'd been sober, I might have worried, but of course if I'd been sober, I wouldn't have had to worry.

The next morning I did wake up sober—or reasonably so. But I wasn't as worried as I was sick. And alone. And, in isolation.

Isolation . . . day one.
Isolation . . . day two.
Isolation . . . day three.
Isolation . . . day four.
Isolation . . . day five.
Isolation . . . day six.
Isolation . . . day seven.

Sometimes it takes one more thing to tip the scales one way or the other. I don't know if it was the thing with Chessman, the seven days in isolation, the death of Jimmy Hendricks, or the combination of everything that made a difference.

Whatever it was, I came off isolation determined to do something positive for Merle Haggard.

My attitude improved. I decided not to try to prove anything to anybody. It was just me I had to convince and only me I needed approval from. Once I got that through my thick head, I was surprised at how things began to fall into place. I knew I didn't have all the puzzle pieces to my life, but I'd made up my mind I'd put the ones I had together.

The next thing I did was apply for the toughest job in the joint—the textile mill. The man over me was a civilian named Ramsey. He was a fair and honest man, a little red-headed guy who gave me due credit for what I did. I made con-boss in a short time because my grades were so good. Toward the end of my first six months I got "twos" every day and sometimes I even got "ones." I was so dedicated to my work I even stopped playing the guitar.

Some days though I thought I'd never make it.

In the meantime, Chessman did not.

On the morning of May 2, 1960, a day I'll never forget, we watched the stack for that little puff of smoke that told us Chessman's life, like Rabbit's, was over. His long struggle for freedom had finally ended.

I couldn't help but identify with Caryl Chessman. Hell, he'd been in Preston like me. He'd had many of the same charges brought against him that I had, and even the one that really did him in, he claimed even until the end, was a case of mistaken identity. I knew about that, too. Hadn't I almost been caught by a crazy posse because I had looked like the real rapist-killer?

By the time Chessman was executed, he'd been in that tiny stone and metal box on Death Row for more than a decade. He had filed over fifty separate appeals. Even if he'd been guilty of all the things they said, he'd paid for those crimes a thousand times over.

On the night before his execution, there was a strange feeling all over the prison. The men said very little. It was so quiet it was scary. Sometime after dark somebody down the cellblock called out for everybody to listen. What we heard sent chills down our backs. The sound seemed far away at first, but as we strained to listen, we could hear people singing hymns out on the hillside. Between the songs we could hear prayers.

"You think Chessman hears that?" somebody asked.

"Of course he does," came the answer.

On that Monday morning when he got up, we heard he'd finished the last of seven letters he'd written through the night. It was a little before eight o'clock, they said, when he handed them to the turnkey to be taken to Warden Dickson to be delivered.

We hung on to every word about those last few minutes.

SING ME BACK HOME

They said it was exactly 10:03 when the Warden nodded to the man standing next to him and the buttons were pushed. I remember reading that some of those at the execution said he tried to say something but they couldn't hear his words. A reporter from the *L.A. Examiner* read his lips.

"Tell Rosalie I said goodbye . . . it's all right. . . ." He was talking about Rosalie Asher, one of his defense lawyers. The reporter made a circle with her thumb and forefinger to let him know she understood. They said he smiled in her direction before his head fell forward.

There was a last minute call to the prison that would have delayed the execution, but it didn't get through on time.

That afternoon a hearse from a funeral home in San Rafael backed up to the prison morgue and hauled the body of Caryl Chessman away.

Life would never be the same for the rest of us.

All my memories of San Quentin were not so painful however. Some were even pleasant. The visit by Johnny Cash was probably the only real good time I had during my entire stay. But it was—really—a good time. Anybody who can actually make a group of men forget they're in San Quentin is some kind of a magician.

Cash wasn't nearly as famous as he is today, but it was easy to see the raw talent in that tall, hungry-looking dude from Arkansas.

On the same show there was Larry and Lorrie, "The Collins Kids," and a bunch of strippers. Johnny was by far the most popular, which should give you some idea how impressive he was. I remember he just looked *terrible*. He was hung over from the night before and his voice was almost gone—but hell, he came out on that stage and just blew everybody away.

It's funny, too, that was the first time I ever saw Stu Carnell, Johnny's booking agent at the time. Who would have believed that in a few years he'd be booking one of the inmates into places like Reno, Vegas, and Lake Tahoe?

I was never one to predict who will be what and when, but I remember sitting down there in front of the stage that day thinking I was surely watching what would some day be a country music legend. When the show was over the man had done what he'd set out to do. He'd ripped down the walls with his music and he'd touched us with his songs. For a little while he'd accomplished the impossible. He had replaced our misery with music. He'd made us *forget* where we were.

Leona came back on visiting day and made me remember.

I didn't know whether to be surprised, shocked, mad, or happy. I wanted to hate her. I wanted to tell her where she could go, what she could do, but I didn't. To tell the truth, I was glad to see her. She told me she was sorry. Since Leona was hardly ever sorry for anything, I found it impossible not to forgive her—or at least try.

Although I didn't want to talk to her about the new kid, she told me he was a boy and that she had named him James, after his father. She called him Jamsie. Just hearing about him was like a knife in the gut. It was so much worse being in *there* and having that happen.

"Do you think we can make our marriage work?" she asked. I thought about asking her when we ever did that. Instead, I told her I hoped we could. And I meant it.

"When you go before the parole board this time, they'll let you out, won't they?" she asked then. I told her I was pretty sure they would.

"I'll drive up and pick you up."

"I'd like that."

When Mama came to visit I asked her to take some of my songs over to Louie and Fuzzy. Told her to tell them I'd probably be out in six or eight months. She did, and they sent word back to me that I should come by and see them as soon as I got home. I was very encouraged.

My need to get out was stronger than ever. I couldn't help

but think about one ol' boy who'd been so anxious to get out he'd gone to what I felt was very extreme measures.

We called him "Shitty Fred" and with good reason. He'd smear hisself with his own shit, and nobody, including the guards, could stand to be around him. He didn't have no problem with homosexuals, and he never had to mess with crowds. He thinned out a bunch in no time flat. Sometimes he'd save up buckets and throw it on the guards when they'd walk by his cell. They decided he was crazy, of course, and one day a bunch of guards, dressed in their yellow raincoats, came and took "Shitty Fred" away. We all wondered just how "crazy" he was. He got out before we did.

My date with the parole board came up again, and as they leafed through my papers I couldn't help thinking how much hangs on a few printed words.

Does it say how I've sweated blood in the textile mill, old men? Does it say how I've tried to prove in every way possible I'm fit to be on the outside again? Does it say how my insides are turning over and over?

Look at me, you bastards! I'm the human being here—I'm not what it says on some goddamned report.

"Something must have occurred in your life, boy."

"Yessir, it did."

"Do you have a place to go when we let you out?"

"Yessir, I do."

"What do you plan to do?"

"Go to work, sir. Make a livin' for my family."

"Family, huh. You got a wife and kids?"

Read the records, bygawd. "Yessir," I said. "Wife and . . . uh . . . three kids." Two born while I been in this stinkin' prison. How about that?

"Are you serious about your work and getting out?" God, what a question. Did he think I was kidding?

They said they'd let me know. And they did. When I

opened the thin paper note later that day it was more than one word. I read it over real slow.

Time set at 2 years 9 months in. 2 years 3 months on parole. Time set at 5 years.

I started figuring as fast as I could. I had less than ninety days to go. Oh good God! *Ninety days.* You'll never know or understand what that means unless you've been there. I began yelling at the top of my voice. Then I couldn't help it. I started to cry. I told my friends. I told strangers. I told the guards. I even told the walls. That night I whispered it to myself over and over. I never heard such pretty words.

I was going home. I was a short-timer. In the yard my friends would yell out at me, "Hey, short-timer. How short are you?"

"Why I'm so short I could walk under a snake."

What I didn't realize though was that the ninety days would seem longer than the rest of the time I'd spent in Quentin. Even worse, the closer time got to going home, the more the time dragged.

My last night there was almost as bad as my first night. But at the same time it was really wonderful. I pictured how things would be when I got home. I tried to imagine what Leona would be wearing, what she'd say, what the weather would be like, everything. Oh hell, what did it matter, I'd be *free*.

But dear God, I thought the night would never end. I'd doze a little, jump and wake up, thinking every time it was morning. I'd check the time. First it was three o'clock, then four, four-thirty, five, five-fifteen, five-twenty, five-twenty-five. I ticked off the minutes until it was finally six-thirty, time for chow. I had no idea how long it would take me to get processed. Some guys told me I'd be out by nine. Others said it might be noon.

SING ME BACK HOME

I waited for my call ticket—a ducat as it's called in prison. It comes to you in the morning clasped to the clothespin on the bars. Just before chow it came.

Report to the Captain's office directly after chow.

For the first time I felt the strings begin to loosen up. They'd been pulled tight ever since I knew I'd be paroled. Only now with the ducat in my hand did I feel it was really happening. I was getting *out*.

Then, as I walked into the mess hall, I realized I'd be leaving my prison family. It scared me when I realized that these men might be the only friends I had. Was society "out there" going to be forgiving, or would I be trading one kind of a prison for another?

There were about eight or ten men there who had become what I considered my prison family. We all had breakfast together that last morning. They were glad I was leaving but talked about how much they'd miss my ugly face. We tried to laugh about everything and keep the conversation light. I told 'em not to worry, that one day I'd come back like Cash and put on a show for 'em. We all thought that was a big joke. Some of the men were still there when I went back years later with my show.

"I'll miss you guys," I finally said, not knowing what else to say. At the time I didn't know how true that was. We'd told each other our life stories over and over and knew each other pretty well. By the time breakfast was finished we'd passed the stage where we could kid about things. We were all crying.

I walked toward the main gates trying not to think about the ones I was leaving behind. Instead I tried to picture the other side of the gates. I wondered if Leona would be standing outside or waiting in the car. It was warm for November. Finally I reached the last of the three main gates.

God, in heaven—I had survived!

When they opened the main gates I could hear a radio playing in one of the guard shacks. It was Hank Snow singing "The Last Ride." I started to walk faster. I had an awful fear that the PA system would start to crackle and announce that it had all been a mistake.

Convict #45200 please report back to the Warden's office. There has been a mix-up. You have a lot more time to do.

Then I was almost running. I looked down at my clothes. My shoes were navy-colored and made out of paper I think. The pants were a bluish gabardine. My shirt was blue with some kind of flaps in front and my bad-fitting coat was tweed. I musta looked like one of the Dragnet thugs. What few belongings I had I carried in a beat-up canvas bag in one hand. I had the Martin guitar I'd won during my gambling enterprise in my other hand.

All at once, I was outside. I looked around me. I was free! Where was she? Dear God, where was Leona? I couldn't see anything familiar. There was no sign of her at all. I didn't know what to do. I felt almost like a kid lost in a big department store. Where *was* everybody? I stood there outside the gates with my knees about to give way on me, and I could feel that damn lump rising in my throat. Everything I'd dreamed about was a joke. I was alone.

Goddammit, Leona. Where are you?

I had fifteen dollars they'd given me. I figured that would get me a bus ticket to Bakersfield and leave me some change. As I started to walk away from the prison I could feel the cold ground through my damned paper shoes. My clothes hung on me like I was a coat hanger, and I was fighting an awful urge to look back. Hell, to turn and run back. What a crazy thought. Instead, I started running.

I didn't even turn around when a car pulled up to the curb

beside me. I didn't care who it was. I knew it wasn't Leona.

"Say there," a female voice called out. It was warm and friendly—and more important—it was talking to *me*. I turned around then to see a stranger leaning over to open her car door.

"Do you want a ride to the bus station?"

I leaned down and looked in the car. She wasn't a bad-looking woman, and when she smiled I got in.

If I had any fantasies about being "taken advantage of," they were soon gone.

"I'm not a streetwalker or anything like that," she said. I didn't know whether to be relieved or disappointed.

"I do this for some of the men who come out of San Quentin and don't know which way to go. When I see that nobody's there to meet them, I drive them to the bus station."

I thanked her. At least somebody was there, even if it was a stranger.

She let me out at the station. I had about an hour and a half before the bus left for Bakersfield so I called Lowell. When he found out Leona hadn't met me he wanted to drive up and get me. I told him I'd already bought my bus ticket.

"I'll meet you at the bus station in Bakersfield then," he said. I told him that would be fine.

Then I walked into the bar in my cheap suit and paper shoes, ordered two double shots of vodka, and poured them down. Before I got on the bus I bought a half-pint of Smirnoff to keep me company.

As the bus pulled out of the station, I leaned back in the bus seat and closed my eyes.

"I'm going home," I said out loud. I didn't care if the others on the bus heard me or not.

"I'm going home."

Eleven

Where's the Danged Yellow Ribbons?

"Hey, Merle, how are you, old buddy,
ain't seen you in about three years.
What in hell you been doin' . . . ?"
"About three years. . . ."

—A conversation

BAKERSFIELD HAD GONE AHEAD without me. My not being there hadn't left a hell of a gap in nothin'. Worst of all, my coming home probably wouldn't make much of an impact either.

I checked the Smirnoff bottle to make sure it was empty. It was. I looked out the window of the Greyhound bus and nothing looked familiar. Nothing looked quite right. I checked my own appearance. Hell, I didn't look quite right either. I was sure anybody could look at me and tell right away I was fresh from the joint.

Why wasn't I drunk? I had killed a whole half-pint of vodka and I didn't feel much of anything. Why in the hell wasn't I feeling any of that courage I thought I'd find in the bottle? Why was I scared? Hell, this was my home town. This was *Bakersfield*. I was finally home. Why did I feel so damned terrible?

The bus slowed down, and I looked out the window again. Still nobody. I might as well have been in a foreign country. I really didn't expect a brass band and banners across the street, but I sure thought Lowell would be there. He said he would.

Who gives a damn, I told myself as I stepped down off the bus. I didn't want nobody to meet me anyway. I was glad nobody was waiting for me at the prison, I told myself. Myself knew I was lying. I wanted Leona to be there. I wanted her to be there so damned bad.

Freedom was a bad dream—just like prison had been.

I was a little unsteady on my feet as I walked into the bus station. At least there were no 30-30's aimed in my direction, no eyes watching me from the catwalks. How come I still felt like there was?

Over by the door then, I saw Lowell. I wanted to run up to him and tell him how good it was to see him—how glad I was that he was there. Instead, I walked over to where he was, shuffling along like a scared kid.

"How ya doin'?" I asked.

"Fine, and you?"

"Real good."

It occurred to me then that it must be hard for him to see me like this too. I could tell he was trying not to say the wrong thing to me or upset me in any way. We hadn't always seen eye to eye—still don't—but there's always been a strong tie between us, even during the worst times.

My homecoming wasn't the way I hoped it would be, but by the time I got to Mama's table with all that good food in front of me I realized how great it was to be a free man.

At first I wasn't even going to ask about Leona, much less

to see her, but she was still my wife. She told somebody that on the day I got out of prison she'd had car trouble or some such shit. I didn't, *couldn't* buy that story. I was hurt.

It was probably three or four days before I decided I might forgive her long enough to get a piece of ass. Well, hell, I'd been in the joint three years and I'd thought about her a lot—mostly how it was in the sack. Whatever else I thought about her didn't change the fact that she was great in bed. Besides I really wanted to see the kids—all three of them.

Best I remember I wasn't so crude that I just walked into the house and said, "Hello, I'm here for a piece of ass," but I probably might as well have. I remember being mad even before I got there because Lowell wouldn't let me borrow his car. It's true I didn't have a driver's license, but considering all I'd been through, another rule or two bent wasn't gonna hurt nobody. It really ticked me off to be a free man and not have no way to get from one place to another.

When I walked through the door Leona didn't even look surprised—which didn't surprise me.

The kids all looked great. I couldn't stop staring at Marty and Dana but couldn't hardly stand to look at Jamsie. It was just too painful. I know now it was stupid of me to put any blame on the little kid. If I had it to do over, I believe I would accept him as my own and love him as much, maybe even more, than the others, because he was not to blame. To know you've caused pain to an innocent child is not an easy thing to live with.

In any case, Leona and I tried again. Don't ask me why. I didn't know then and I don't know now. I believe I needed her and I wanted to believe that she needed me.

And, I needed something more. Rabbit's words had not faded from my mind. Sometimes I'd wake up in the night and I could hear him just as clear as the day he'd said it.

"You can be somebody, someday, Merle."

SING ME BACK HOME

But in the meantime I also had to support my family. And, my family would be increasing. Leona got pregnant again right away.

I went to work for Lowell, digging ditches and wiring houses. I made eighty dollars a week doing that, but I figured it wouldn't hurt to earn a little extra playing music on the side.

It wasn't really hard to get a job pickin'. I felt lucky to go to work at a place called High-Pockets. I made ten bucks a night and got to work four nights a week. I felt rich. Compared to my eighteen dollars a week in San Quentin, a hundred twenty seemed like a fortune.

My job at the club lasted about a month. Foster Ward, the owner, fired the whole band one night. Then he called me in and asked if I'd work for him alone, or put together a new band.

"I can't do that," I said. "Those guys are my friends." I couldn't imagine telling Jack Collier and Sonny O'Brien that I was staying and they were leaving. I was beginning to build my circle of friends around the music people in Bakersfield. There was a fierce loyalty in those of us who were there in those days.

"The only way I'll work for you," I told Foster, "is if you'll let me hire the guys back." I told him I had several ideas about improving our sound. He agreed to let me have a go at it.

It felt great to have a band—my band—behind me. Jack played lead guitar, Sonny played drums, and some guy named Bob played upright bass. I remember Bob drove a potato chip truck in the daytime, and I'm sure he was better at that than playing bass else he would have thinned out half the population of Bakersfield.

All considered though, we had a damn good band, and people liked us. Hell, they kept comin' back, and they brought more people with them. I was feelin' great. I had no dreams about bein' in the "big time." Hell, I thought I was "big time."

It's funny how things happen and how you can look back later and realize that one little thing can set off a chain of events.

One Tuesday night when I wasn't working, me and Leona, on one of our rare nights out together, drove out to the Rainbow Gardens.

When we walked in we could see they had one of those talent deals going on. Leona told me I ought to get up and give it a shot. No way would I do something dumb like that, I told her. Hell, a man would have to be a damn fool to get up there and make an ass of himself in a silly amateur talent show.

I came in second.

As I started to walk offstage the head of the band, Jelly Sanders, a well-known musician in the area, called me off to the side.

"You play an instrument?" he asked.

"I play guitar a little," I said.

"How well do you play?"

"Well enough to work four nights a week over at High-Pockets."

"Oh yeah," he said, "I know who you are. You been hurtin' our crowds." Compliments like that made me feel so damn good.

Jelly asked me if I'd be interested in a relief job for Johnny Barnett at The Lucky Spot. I jumped at the chance. The Lucky Spot was the top place in town then, and Johnny Barnett was a very important name. He'd been working there for about ten or twelve years and had a big following. Jelly worked in Johnny's band along with Fuzzy Owen and Gene Moles. I was really glad to get the opportunity to work with Fuzzy because I hadn't forgot about him and Louie's record company. I hadn't given up the idea of going back to them about my songs.

I went to work at The Lucky Spot two nights a week, which was perfect for me. I was working Thursday through Sunday at High-Pockets and Tuesday and Wednesday at The Lucky Spot.

I quit my som'bitchin' ditch-diggin' job real quick.

Pretty soon Johnny, who wanted more time off, talked me into taking four nights a week at The Lucky Spot. That meant quitting my job at High-Pockets, which I did.

It must have been about this time that I got up the courage to make a call I'd been wanting to make for a long time. It would be the beginning of a friendship that would last through all the bad times, the good times, and the danged times I don't even remember.

"Louie, this is Merle Haggard," I said into the phone. "Whatcha' got goin'?"

"Not a goddamned thing," was the answer.

"Well, I need a job for Sunday."

"Hell, I can get you the whole week if that's what you want."

"Well, why don't we just get together, maybe drive around, and talk about it?"

"Fine with me, hoss."

It was a Saturday afternoon and I remember how great it was to be in the company of somebody as impressive as Mr. Lewis Talley. We drove up toward Ridgecrest in his white Eldorado. He had the top down, and as we were driving over the Tehachapi Mountains it seemed like all that cold concrete, those iron bars, and the red bricks were a million miles behind me.

For those not familiar with the legend of Lewis Talley, let me tell you that there ain't nobody like him. That's as plain as I can put it. He could have been one of the biggest stars in country music today if things had gone right. At one time he was very close to being right up there with the best of them, 'cause hell, he *was* one of them.

Louie had a lot going for him in 1960. He owned a restaurant in Bakersfield and the record company, appeared on a daily TV show, and ran a Saturday night dance in Fresno. He was doing real well and dressed like the star he was. He was making more than five hundred dollars a week and had more women than he knew what to do with—but he managed. He had that lean, hungry look that seemed to make the women think he needed them to take care of him. It was the same look that worked so well for Hank Williams and Johnny Cash in his early years.

At one point Louie was almost a movie star. When Hollywood was casting the role of Hank Williams in *Your Cheatin' Heart*, Louie was one of the top contenders. Everybody said he was the perfect choice since he looked somewhat like Hank and had a lot of the same qualities. Only trouble was, he missed the screen test. He was, like the original had been so many times, out drunk when the time came to show them what he could do.

So, they chose that good ol' country boy, George Hamilton, instead.

As a result of the drive me and Louie took that afternoon, we got a job in the little town of Tehachapi at Paul's Cocktail Lounge, working Friday and Saturday nights at twenty-five dollars a night *each*. Hell, I was beginnin' to think this music business was a gold mine.

What was even more satisfying, I was beginning to collect a following. I had *fans*, people who actually went from one place to another to hear me play and sing. I couldn't hardly keep my feet on the ground.

Some of those fans became my closest friends. Others have worked for or with me over the years. It was at Paul's Cocktail Lounge that I first remember seeing Tex Whitson, who is now my business manager. He'd come in and sit near the door in the back. He never said much, sometimes nothing. He'd just slip inside the door, listen awhile, then he'd be gone.

Tex Whitson has been part of my life—my other family—ever since those early days. He is the kind of man, who, if he'd been with the children of Israel, would not have been tacky enough to question Moses when he came down from the mountain with the Holy Tablets. However, before he Xeroxed the Commandments and distributed them among his people, he would have thoroughly checked the source and been totally satisfied with its origin.

Tex has always looked more like a football player than anything else—or maybe a classy bouncer. I spent a lot of time back then trying to figure out exactly what it was he did, but there was always something about him that nobody could quite put a finger on. Later I found out that was the way he wanted things to be. All I really needed to know back then was that he liked my music and he loaned me a car. That was very important to me then. He didn't ask no questions, didn't care whether I had a driver's license or not, just said to use it till I got my own car. Granted, it was a bad-looking old Plymouth, but it really meant a lot to me.

Over the years Tex has moved in and out of my life. Sometimes he'd drop out for several months, then I'd look up in the middle of a song and there he'd be again. From the first I got the feeling that if I ever needed help, all I'd have to do was call. That's the way it's been.

My music life was getting better. It wasn't long before I got an offer to work five days a week on Cousin Herb Henson's television show. Herb was the Ralph Emery of Bakersfield, and it was quite an honor to be called up by the top guy in town.

Back then, if you showed up on the tube people believed you had it made. Hell, you were a star. The show paid only about nine dollars a shot but that added another forty-five dollars a week to my pay. For the next two or three months I worked seven nights a week in the clubs and spent Monday at the television studio.

Me and Leona? How were things with us? Just fine, as long as I didn't go home. I do have to give her credit though. She was consistent. She didn't just dislike some of the things I was doing—hell, she hated them all.

The new baby was a girl and we named her Kelli. Kelli didn't seemed to be too thrilled with us. She cried a lot, and I didn't understand that. By this time I didn't understand much of anything at home, and I was getting restless to move on to something else. I'd been pretty straight for almost a year and a half. It was time something snapped. One night I was getting ready to go to the club when I heard a knock at the door.

I opened it and there he stood, lookin' like he had the answers to every question right in his hip pocket.

"Why you old son of a bitch," I hollered. "I've been thinkin' about you lately."

It was Deanrow, my old runnin' buddy. We'd hardly exchanged hellos when I ran to the phone. I asked Johnny for a few days off. He told me to enjoy myself, that I'd earned it. I didn't figure Leona would be that understanding, so I was glad I didn't have to be there when she read the note telling her I'd gone with Deanrow.

The next thing I knew I was leaning back in the front seat of Dean's brand new '62 Ford. It was like old times, except this car had not been "borrowed." We took off across the desert toward Las Vegas. Dean had got hold of some of them Dramamine inhalers, equal to about eighteen bennies. Back then you could buy 'em across the counter at the drug stores like Vicks Inhalers. God, you could fly for five days. My head began to buzz, and I felt all the old pressures of Bakersfield sliding away.

"Hey, let's go to the Nashville Nevada Club," I said to Deanrow. "That's where Wynn Stewart is. I've heard that club is the best anywhere, and hell, I'd like to see the man who keeps turning out hit record after hit record." Modesty prevented me from telling Dean how everybody had been comparing me to Wynn during that period.

By the time we got to Vegas, we were stoned out of our gourds and we couldn't wait to see a fancy club.

"God," I whispered, "this sure ain't no Barrel House, is it?"

"You can say that again," Deanrow answered. I could see he was as impressed as I was.

It was really something else. It had a half-moon bandstand down in the center of the room, and the sound just moved right through your danged body. It was the best sound system I'd ever heard. Of course I hadn't heard too damn many.

From where we stood I could see the band members real well, and the first person I spotted was Roy Nichols playing guitar. A man I recognized as Jim Pierce was playing piano, Bobby Austin was playing bass, and a woman named Helen Price was playing drums. I was even more impressed when I heard that great steel guitar cry—who else but Ralph Mooney could do that?

This was *it*, I decided. Who'd ever want any better than this?

As soon as I got a little closer to the bandstand, Roy spotted me. He hollered at me to come on up.

"Here," he said, shoving his guitar in my direction. "Play this son of a bitch while I take a break."

"I can't play with this band," I said, feeling my knees go weak.

"Aw, bullshit, Merle," he said, "come on up."

"Roy, I can't play alongside Ralph Mooney and them—in a place like this. What would Wynn say if he walked out here and found some half-assed guitar picker with his band?" Roy paid no attention to me, just pushed the guitar in my hands and went on his break.

Where's the Danged Yellow Ribbons?

I thought, well hell, why not? When they asked me to do a couple of songs, I didn't hesitate. Besides, Wynn evidently wasn't there anyway.

I did Marty Robbins' "Devil Woman" and was in the middle of "Cigarettes and Coffee Blues" when I spotted Wynn standing right in the middle of the dance floor. He was staring at me real hard. Scared the shit outta me. I felt like a kid who'd been caught with his hand in the cookie jar.

When intermission came, I started to walk away and Wynn stopped me.

"Let me buy you a drink," he said. I must have said okay.

"You workin' anywhere?" he asked then.

"Been workin' with Fuzzy Owen and Lewis Talley in Bakersfield," I said, "and some on Cousin Herb's TV show."

"You know I just got back from Nashville," he said, looking down at his drink, "and in fact, I've been all over the United States looking for somebody."

"To do what?" I was almost holding my breath.

"To take Bobby Austin's place," he answered. "Bobby's gonna be startin' a band of his own, and he's leavin' us in about a week or two. You can play bass, can't you?"

I think I nodded my head.

"Well, do you want the job?"

Did I want the job? Hell, it was a dream come true. I think I said something about not knowing much about the bass. He told me Roy'd show me what I needed to know.

"How much, uh, does it pay?" I managed to ask. He told me it was two hundred twenty-five dollars a week to start. I couldn't believe my good luck. I'd been at the right place at the right time, all because old Deanrow had come a knockin' at my door, just when I was comin' down with a bad case of ramblin' fever.

I sure hoped Vegas was ready for me. I aimed to flat out knock it on its ass.

As it turned out, Vegas *was* ready for me—really ready.

Twelve

"Sing a Sad Song"

"That was a new kid from
Bakersfield with 'Sing a Sad Song'
written by Wynn Stewart. . . . It's the
pick of the week here on
KRAK in Sacramento. . . ."

—Late night DJ

I WAS BY MYSELF fiddling with the radio dial on my '57 Chevy in the driveway of my forty-five-dollar-a-month house in Bakersfield. My life as a "big star" in Las Vegas was already a thing of the past.

Sitting there in the car in the early hours of the morning after putting in my time at The Blackboard Club, I finally found the sound I was searching for.

There he is, friends and neighbors, that "kid from Bakersfield" the DJ was talking about, singing his heart out. I laid my head back on the seat and closed my eyes. I could even see the record on the turntable, the color of the label, everything—round and round it goes—where it stops nobody knows.

"Sing a Sad Song"

Are you listening Lefty, Mama, Lowell? See, Lowell, they're playin' my record. That DJ didn't say nothin' about whether I'd studied music theory or not. Man, he was just playin' the record. Hot dang!

Where was the crowd to share this great fame with me? A man ought to have *somebody* with him at a time like this. If I'd been back in Vegas, maybe I'd be surrounded by a whole bunch of good-lookin' women.

I wasn't in Vegas though. I was in Bakersfield. I'd come home like a whipped dog, done in 'cause I couldn't control something that was threatening every dream I'd ever had.

I'd discovered gambling. I hadn't discovered a way to stop so I had to get away.

As the last chorus of "Sing a Sad Song" faded out, I wanted to run into the house and wake up Leona. At least she could hear the end, I thought. But I knew better. I could just imagine how that little scene would end. My musical career was not the most interesting thing in the world to Leona. Well, hell, who could blame her? Vegas hadn't been much of a good thing for her.

The song ended and even though it had been one of those "once in a lifetime" deals, it was over. The depression that had been so bad before the song now came back. I sat there in the car thinking about how I had screwed everything up.

I'd left the best job I'd ever had, working with the best band I'd ever heard, making the most money I'd ever made. I'd come home to Bakersfield to work in what now seemed like chicken-shit clubs that had no class, no heart, and held no interest for me. That's not meant to be a put-down, but it sure was a comedown. I knew who to blame for it all though.

Merle Haggard.

Another record was playing then and my big thrill was gone. I thought about the first time I'd heard the song and how excited I'd been. This was my *hit*. I knew it when I walked into the Nashville Nevada Club for work one evening, and heard Wynn singing it.

"That's a great song, Wynn," I said. "Did you write it?"

"Sure did," he answered. "It's gonna be my next single."

It took me two or three days to get up the courage to talk to him about it again. Finally, I walked over to a table where he was sitting in the club one day and pulled up a chair.

"Wynn," I said, "if it was in your power to make me a star, would you do it?" He looked at me and kinda grinned.

"Sure I would," he said.

"It *is* within your power."

"Name it," he came back.

"Give me that song. That 'Sing a Sad Song' you wrote. Let me record it."

Before he could answer me, I told him about the deal me and Fuzzy Owen had. "Fuzzy told me when I left Bakersfield to come here to work that if I found a song—that *right* song—he'd put me on Talley Records. I've talked to Louie about it on the phone and he says if you'll say the word then . . ."

"You've got it," Wynn said.

Just like that. I had my song. Although I knew it might be awhile before I could get to Los Angeles to record it, I knew I had that hit, I could feel it, taste it.

I called Fuzzy, who didn't even ask to hear it. He just told me he'd set up the session as soon as I could make the time. Then I went out to celebrate. What better place than the casinos? It never occurred to me that by the time I finally recorded "Sad Song" I wouldn't even be working in Vegas anymore.

Once I'd gone to Vegas, I couldn't get enough. There's no place like it in the world. I was going around in as many circles as the roulette wheels.

My home life was even worse. Leona and the kids had

moved to Vegas with me, and we were living in a three-bedroom apartment. It never occurred to me that *she* was having a rough time of it.

I was young and horny and there were great-lookin' broads everywhere I looked. And I must have been trying to make up for those three years I'd been in prison. I played music until it was comin' out my ears, and when I wasn't playin' music, I was gamblin' with the rent and grocery money. Whatever time I had left over from music and gamblin' was spent either fishin' or foolin' around. I had more luck with the second than the first.

Me and Leona were still fighting. One night I remember she wouldn't iron my white shirt before I went to work. She told me to do it myself. As I stood over the ironing board, she walked by me—leaned over and stuck her tongue out in my face.

I threw the danged iron at her and wore a wrinkled shirt to work.

I stood up on the bandstand that night, hatin' her 'cause I knew I looked like hell. Threw my whole show out of kilter.

There was really something great about those early days in Vegas—musically speaking at least. It was like one big roarin' party, with all the guests, some famous, some soon-to-be-famous, coming and going—sort of passing across the stage of the Nashville Nevada Club.

One night I looked out in the audience and there was none other than *the* Jim Reeves and with him was Patsy Cline. They were applauding *me*. That was strong stuff for the boy from Bakersfield.

Every night there'd be other faces in the crowd and people dropping by who were working other clubs. During this time I met Gordon Terry, who is the fiddle player in my band today. Now and then a fresh-faced boy from Delight, Arkansas, would come by and sit in with the band for a few numbers. Glen Campbell was a pretty good guitar player. Some of us thought the kid even had a chance to do pretty good someday.

There were wild times, good times, and times I don't remember too well. A lot of those took place in the company of a singer from Ohio, Donnie Young. A lot of people said he had talent but would never make it if he didn't straighten up. Actually, he was no different from most of us back then. We'd all stay up for days at a time with the help of the little yellers we used to order from a Doc Baker back in Ohio. He actually put ads in magazines for the "mini-bennies." They were a lot easier to swallow than them big old corn-fed, double-cross things we used to take. Grady Martin said one time that they set music back twenty years when they took the little yellers off the market. Dope was legal then and a hell of a lot better.

Incidentally, in case the name Donnie Young don't ring a bell, try the one he uses now—Johnny Paycheck.

It was not all good times and laughs, even though that's the way it seemed for awhile. I'm surprised I could hold together a crumbling marriage, balance a music career, and party around the clock without losing control. But there was one thing though that was beginning to take control of me.

Pull the handle. Watch the cherries line up. Listen for the bell that tells you you've hit the jackpot. Sing the songs. Have a run at the twenty-one table. Pick a little guitar. Grab a Keno card. Pick a little more. Listen to the clack of the ball rolling into the roulette wheel. Work an extra shift to make up for the money you lost during the break from the first set. Pull the handle. Drop in the money. Back to the bandstand. Then back to the tables.

The first thing to go was my money—then anybody else's money I could get my hands on, borrowed or begged. Then there went my '62 Olds, not just a car mind you, but almost a symbol of the success I'd had in Vegas.

Pull the handle. Spin the wheel. Next time I'll be a winner. It stands to reason I've got to win sometimes. Hell, it's the law of averages.

"Hello, Fuzzy. This is Merle. Could you send me some money. I got a lot of bills pilin' up."

"Ain't got no money to send you, Merle."

"Hello, Mama. Guess what? I got paid this morning and somebody robbed me."

Well, hell that was *almost* the truth. The Golden Nugget was *always* robbing me.

"If you could send me two hundred dollars, Mama, I can pay the rent and get the groceries. If I go home with no money, Leona is gonna kill me."

She wired the money.

Back to the Golden Nugget and the Horseshoe Club. All I had to do was double the money, send Mama back hers, and I'd be home free.

Las Vegas is awful when you're broke. It's even worse when you've borrowed all you can, lied to your mother, and lost that too. I walked up and down the strip, hands pushed down in my pockets, and I looked at the lights blinking off and on. What had once seemed exciting to me was now ugly. Vegas had turned on me—and after all we'd been to each other.

So I packed up my family and went back to Bakersfield. The only thing I had to look forward to when I came back home was the recording session Fuzzy had set up in Los Angeles.

Me, Leona, and the four kids moved into a little one-bedroom place—all we could afford. I went back to work at The Lucky Spot and the Barrel House, sometimes playing extra at The Blackboard and The Porthole in Ridgecrest. Leona, in the meantime, was pregnant again.

When the time came to go for my first recording session, I wasn't even excited. I was so let down. The session went real well anyway. I felt rather satisfied with the record we produced.

Fuzzy and me hit the promotion road with it—something I hated then and still do. I only agreed to go if he'd promise to visit radio stations where there was good fishing nearby.

The people at the radio stations weren't all that thrilled to see us—new singer, new song—it was nothing new to them. About the only promise came from radio station KEEN in San Jose. They said they'd play it. Fuzzy was really pleased. He said that was a big station and airplay on it would mean I'd be heard in the whole Bay area—which included San Quentin.

We also took copies over to Fresno, to L.A., and to KRAK in Sacramento, wherever there was good fishing. KRAK sounded like they might give it a spin, but they didn't promise.

And, son of a bitch, they *were* playing it. I'd heard it with my own ears over my car radio, sitting in the driveway there at about four in the morning.

I turned off the radio and almost ran into the house. I wanted to wake Leona and even the kids and tell 'em about what I'd just heard.

Instead, I sat down on the edge of the bed and took off my shoes and socks.

Hot damn! On the radio—the kid from Bakersfield, the DJ had said. I threw my socks into the air, and decided that would have to do for a celebration.

The changes in our lives were small at first, then things began to pick up. It was a little like hoppin' a slow freight in the yard and watching the people around you scramble to get on board too. You put out your hand to help 'em, but some just can't quite reach you. You know you could jump off and stay, but hell, you've tried so hard and so long to make the grab you just can't let go. Besides the wheels are turning faster and you're afraid that once you jump off this train you might never catch another one. Sometimes you turn your back and keep riding, hoping the ones who matter will come along. Some do. Others don't.

There was something else bothering me too. I was an ex-con. Some people didn't like ex-cons and they sure as hell didn't trust us. I couldn't help but wonder what would happen to my little growing public if they found out I was a San Quentin graduate. Mama even suggested I change my name.

"I can't do that, Mama," I told her. "I want the name Haggard right up there where it's supposed to be—where it should have been all along. It was my daddy's and it's mine."

I still couldn't help but think though that one day I'd get up on stage and look down into the face of an ex-con who'd recognize me. I had nightmares of fingers pointing in my direction and people hollering "imposter" and "liar." I started feeling like a phoney, pretending I was somebody I wasn't.

So, we announced to the public about my serving time in San Quentin. Some said it was a deal to get publicity. But it was a confession, and I was afraid it might end what little career I had going for myself. Folks back then didn't take well to news like that about their public performers. I knew it was a risk I'd have to take though if I ever wanted to stand up on stage again without being scared to death.

The public, God bless 'em, not only forgave me, they reached out their hands to me. I've never forgotten that, and there is no longer a fear I'll be recognized by one of the former residents. In fact, I welcome it.

By September, 1963, we had another baby in the house. The crowded home front was in such shambles by this time, I'm surprised Noel even let us bring him home from the hospital. We had quite a full house with five younguns.

Today I'm amazed how well they've turned out—no thanks to me. There've been tough times for them and hard going, but I guess, thanks to a lot of people, they've survived. Leona did love the kids but she didn't have an easy time in her life either.

It was mostly Mama who kept everybody from going under. Later, it was Bonnie Owens. Sometimes I think I can only take credit for the things they did wrong.

With the success of "Sad Song," though, I began to have more hope. I remember someone coming into The Blackboard one evening and asking if I knew my record was on the charts in *Billboard*.

"Hell, no," I said, and I sure didn't know how we'd missed it. Me and Fuzzy had watched that chart religiously. Every Monday morning we had driven down to L.A. to rub elbows with as many people in the music business as we could. We'd get a copy of *Billboard* and head for Cy's Coffee Shop where we'd search the country charts for that familiar song title, artist's name, and record label. We went around to the various record companies, knocking on such doors as Ken Nelson and Snuff Garrett. Both would produce me later.

After hearing we'd made *Billboard*, me and Fuzzy couldn't wait to get down to L.A. on the next Monday.

"There it is, Fuzzy," I said, pointing to a place about a third of the way from the top.

"Number twenty-three," he grinned. Fuzzy wasn't much on emotion, but it was easy to see how pleased he was.

"That's good," he said then, still smiling and looking at a bunch of little words that meant so goddamn much to both of us.

The following week it moved to number nineteen.

The next week it was gone.

It had done what we wanted it to do. It had put my name and my sound in front of a lot of DJ's. Even the B-side was a little self-serving number I'd written called "Hello, Mr. DJ."

All we needed now was a follow-up, something that would just knock everybody's socks off.

My next one, written by me and Red Simpson, "You Don't Have Very Far to Go," with a B-side called "Sam Hill" written by Tommy Collins, made the top twenty.

"We still need that monster—that blockbuster," Fuzzy said. "It's out there somewhere. All we have to do is find it."

I didn't expect to find it where I did. One night I let somebody talk me into going to some woman's house to listen to songs she'd written. I don't remember all the details, but Lowell was there at the club where I was working that night. A man named Curt Sapaugh, who booked talent into various clubs, kept on and on about this woman who had a bunch of *hit* songs. If there was anything I really didn't wanna do, it was sit around some danged woman's house and listen to her cute little songs. But I went anyway.

She was a pleasant enough lady, pretty, with a nice smile, but I was all set to be bored to death, even more so when she got out a whole bunch of songs and went over to an old pump organ. She began to play that damn thing and I was thinking what kinda deal is this? How did I get myself talked into *this* shit?

There they were. My God, one hit right after another. There must have been four or five number one songs there, and even though I was no expert in picking hits then, I knew a dynamite song when I heard it—and hell, I was hearin' it.

That's how I come to record my first major hit, written by Liz Anderson. "From Now On All My Friends Are Gonna Be Strangers" seemed to be tailor-made just for me. I believe she even played "Fugitive," too, that night. I forgot all the reasons I hadn't wanted to come that evening. I even forgot how terrible that old pump organ sounded.

When "Strangers" hit the airwaves and the charts, a lot of other people recognized the potential of the song. Carl Smith covered it. So did Roy Drusky.

SING ME BACK HOME

Everybody loved the song and *almost* everybody loved the way I did it.

"What do you think about 'Strangers,' Leona?" I asked her one night not too long after it had been released.

"What do I know about that stuff?" was her only comment. I sure as hell didn't ask her about nothin' else. Besides, there were a lot of people who really *liked* what I did and they didn't mind letting me know it.

"Strangers" gave us all confidence—me, Fuzzy, and Louie. We felt we were on to something when we did "Sad Song." But when we watched "Strangers" shoot up the charts, we were danged sure of it. Fuzzy was going with Bonnie Owens then, and she put in God knows how many hours promoting me and my career. She did it mostly to help Talley Records and Fuzzy, but I knew she also had a lot of confidence in my ability. That helped a great deal.

I liked Bonnie. She was a pretty woman. I'd never been able to be just friends with a woman before. It was nice.

It was only natural that when I found a song that would make a great duet, it was Bonnie I wanted with me. It had been her voice in the background for most of the other sessions. We had a good blend, and when "Just Between the Two of Us" hit, things really began to move for our little organization.

All at once, everybody began to notice, everybody from distant kinfolk who had hardly spoken to me before, to the big record executives in L.A. who no longer seemed to be tied up in business meetings.

I no longer had to search the radio dials late at night to hear my songs. It happened often—and it was still feeling great.

"Here is the latest from Merle Haggard . . . "

"Charlie Williams wants to book you on a tour with Hank Snow."

"There's a reporter on the phone from a newspaper in

L.A. wants to know about your signing with Capitol Records."

"It's Ken Nelson on the line . . . "

"Somebody from Nashville wants to talk to you about a TV special."

"It's Capitol Records."

"Hey, Merle, Buck Owens is on the phone—he wants to record your song 'Swinging Doors.'"

To hell with that, I'll record that myself. I didn't like the song even when I wrote it, but if Buck wants to record it, it must be good. It was my first number one.

I was now being booked on first-rate tours with major stars. I was in Phoenix on the last night of a big tour. Standing in the wings, I watched the headliner, Hank Snow, close the show, and the words he was singing seemed to describe what I was feeling.

"Last big eight wheel a rollin'
  down the track . . . means your true lovin'
    daddy ain't a comin' back . . . I'm movin' on . . .
  I'll soon be gone . . . "

Well, I thought, at least I know what country music's all about.

". . . I've told you baby from time to time . . .
    But you just wouldn't listen . . .
      or pay me no mind . . . I'm movin' on . . . "

"You tell 'em, Hank," I said, more to myself than to the man out on stage. "And bygawd, I'll tell 'em, too, and I'll keep on tellin' 'em just as long as I can string these damn words together and make the music fit 'em."

I looked over to the side of the stage and saw two other people watching Hank. I couldn't help wondering if they

SING ME BACK HOME

weren't thinking the same thing I'd been thinking. One of them, a young guy from Ohio, had been on stage earlier and it didn't take no genius to figure out he'd be heard from again. He was damned good. Bobby Bare, like me, was just then beginning to attract some attention here and there.

"Who's the skinny dude with the slicked-back hair?" I asked one of the people backstage.

"He's from Texas," came the answer. "I think his name's Jennings . . . Waylon Jennings."

"Well, the audience sure liked him," I said. "I got a feelin' we ain't heard the last of that boy either."

We sure ain't, and Jessi, I still like "I'm Not Lisa."

The tour had been a good one. On the plane back to L.A. I began to count up all the good things in my life. For the first time since I'd been a part of the music business, I felt like I was making real progress. I was even writing songs that made me happy just to hum them. I couldn't put them down on paper fast enough before another idea would come. I didn't fancy myself a star like Hank Snow, but like Bobby and Waylon, I'd got my share of applause. It felt real good.

Besides my music and my songwriting, I felt better about home. Not that Leona and I were the perfect couple, but at least I'd reached the place where I could give my family a nice place to live. Shortly before this tour, we'd moved into a mansion compared to places we'd lived before. The house was like a dream come true for us. I'd been poor all my life, and Lord knows, Leona had never had nothin'. The house we moved into belonged to a doctor and rented for two hundred seventy-five dollars a month. Same house would probably go for a thousand today. It was really nice, and it was like a gift we gave ourselves and the kids, to kinda make up for all those times when we couldn't afford nothin'.

Leona seemed really happy about the house. When she first saw it, she was like a kid—going from one room to another, looking at all that space. I kept thinking about how pleased she was with the house as my plane landed in L.A. I was almost glad to be getting home—something that was rather unusual for me. *I* had a nice home to go to, with a wife and five good-lookin' kids. Life didn't seem bad at all.

Bonnie and Fuzzy were waiting for me at the airport, and as we drove back to Bakersfield, the three of us talked all over each other about the great things that were happening with my career.

"I suppose you're still staying up nights shipping out records," I said to Bonnie.

"Everybody is doing everythin' they can to get your career up there where it oughta be, Merle," she said. "We believe everybody in the world oughta be able to hear Merle Haggard, and that's what we're out to do."

"What time she's not packin' up and shippin' out records," Fuzzy said, "she's writin' letters to DJ's and anybody she figures oughta know about our new discovery."

It was almost embarrassing to be the center of so much attention, but leaning back in the back seat, listening to Bonnie and Fuzzy, I felt real lucky to have friends like them. I knew it was more to them than a business. They cared about *me*, too. But then, Bonnie and Fuzzy were two very special people, not only to me, but to each other.

Bonnie had been divorced from Buck Owens, who was no relation to Fuzzy, for several years. Besides being a good singer, she managed to raise two fine boys. The only time I got uneasy was when I found myself getting pissed off at Fuzzy because he seemed to expect so much of Bonnie and often took her for granted.

In any case, the three of us—plus Louie—became quite a group.

As we pulled up in front of my new house, I noticed my '57 Chevy was not in the driveway. I didn't think too much about it, though. I figured Leona had gone shopping or something. We all got out of Fuzzy's car and I noticed the lawn. Something was all over it. To my surprise, I could see it was junk, all kinds of paper, toys, everything—looked like it'd been thrown out in the yard. Bonnie and Fuzzy looked as puzzled as I'm sure I did. I asked them to come into the house with me. I was a little scared. Something was wrong. I opened the front door and simply couldn't believe my eyes.

"My God . . . ," was all I could say at first.

It looked like a tornado had hit the place. There were thousands of scraps and bits of paper all over the house. Then there was a terrible stink—like ammonia. It was awful, and one look around told me it came from a bunch of dirty diapers all over the floor. Every room was totally wrecked, and as I began to walk from one to another, I felt such a rage boiling up in me.

"Why. . . ?" I kept asking over and over. Bonnie and Fuzzy had no answers. They could only stand and watch.

I kicked a dirty diaper across the floor in disgust. Little turds went everywhere.

"She *loved* this house." I couldn't say any more. I didn't know if I was gonna start throwin' things and wreckin' what was left—or if I was just gonna sit down and cry. It was so unexpected.

Then the strangest thing happened. It was so quick and so final. All those years—the bad years, even—I'd loved that woman. We'd survived almost everything. We'd screamed, fought, cheated on each other, hurt each other, lied, cried, and hell, yes, *loved*. Now, it was over, pure and simple.

I left that "dream house." Didn't even close the front door. I jumped into Fuzzy's car and told him to get me away from there as quick as he could. "Take me over to her mother's house," I said. I noticed the look on Bonnie's face. I told her there was nothin' to worry about.

"I just want to go pick up my car," I said. "There ain't gonna be no trouble. I'm too mad. I wouldn't dare start somethin' I might not be able to stop."

As we got in sight of her mother's house, I could see my car in the driveway. She always left the keys in it, except that day. Then I noticed something else that made me even madder. Somebody had kicked out the goddamn instrument panel. The glass was all smashed in the floorboard. The dash was bent up, and God, I was hot. I loved that car. It was such a pretty little vehicle. I'd always had such a thing about cars anyway. Still do.

Bonnie and Fuzzy had gotten out of the car, too. They could see I was in trouble. I couldn't even speak I was so mad.

"Merle, why don't . . . ," Bonnie began, but I assured her again that I wasn't gonna do nothin' 'cept get my car keys. That's all I meant to do.

Leona was standing there in the middle of her mama's living room with what I figured to be her latest boy friend. Some big Indian guy. I'd never seen him before, and I ain't seen him since.

"Where are my keys, Leona?" I said, surprised that my voice sounded that calm. "Give me the keys to the car and there won't be any trouble."

She threw them across the room.

"Where are the kids?" I asked then. She told me they were at some woman's house where she left 'em quite a bit.

I started to turn back toward the door. I'd like to think I would've walked through it without looking back.

"What's the matter?" she called out then, in that certain tone only Leona has. "You ain't gonna whip my ass this time 'cause my big boy friend is here?"

For several minutes I don't remember a thing. I was wild, I know that. I remember thinkin' I was gonna kill her ass. I meant to, God forgive me, I really meant to. I didn't even hit her. I just went straight for her throat and held her neck in a death grip. I felt Fuzzy pulling at me, begging me to let go, and Bonnie was crying and trying to help Fuzzy get me away from Leona.

SING ME BACK HOME

"It's not worth it, Merle," Fuzzy kept saying, "please stop . . . stop, please."

Leona was turning blue. I couldn't control what was happening. I couldn't stop the awful thing I was doing and so I kept telling myself she *deserved* this. There had been so many wounds, so much goddamned pain and humiliation. Somethin' musta snapped in my head. When I turned her loose, or maybe when Fuzzy tore me loose, everything went dead for a few minutes. I hadn't killed her, but I'd killed every feeling I'd ever had for her. The only thing left was the damn tattoo on my arm. It said, "Leona."

"Take me to get the kids, Fuzzy," I said, once we were in his car. I didn't even bother to get my car.

"I'm gonna take the kids to Mama's," I said. "Gonna be no more of this shit."

I don't remember what I said to the woman who was keeping the kids, but it didn't matter. I just gathered up four of them and took them to Mama's.

But I left Jamsie there—he wasn't mine to take.

Mama was used to keeping the kids, and she just figured it was another fight that would blow over in a few days. She was wrong.

As for what Leona would do next, I didn't know, but I figured she wouldn't forget what had happened—or let me forget.

The next day I needed to talk to a friend, somebody who would understand what I was going through. Besides I owed Bonnie twenty dollars, and that was as good an excuse as any to go to her house. Since I didn't have my car, I got out my old bicycle and took off down to her house.

By this time, Leona knew I'd taken the kids, and all I could do was wait for her next move. I hadn't expected her to come to Bonnie's house. That wasn't very smart on my part though, because she had made several little accusations since I'd been working with Bonnie. I had told her, truthfully, that there was nothing between me and Bonnie except friendship. I'd tried to tell her I respected Fuzzy too much, even if I'd had any of those feelings for Bonnie, which I did not. Leona was not convinced, and when she found out I was at Bonnie's house that evening, she was sure I'd been lying to her.

There was quite a commotion, but it was nothing compared to the day before. Just a lot of yelling and screaming and I do recall chasing her with a broom. The night before hadn't scared her at all.

After she'd gone, Bonnie got me to sit down and cool off before going back to Mama's. I guess that's when we first began to share our troubles. She told me that Fuzzy was seeing somebody else from time to time. Somebody, Bonnie said, who might become very important to him. Her name was Phyllis. She was very young and pretty. There was even a possibility she might be the one who could get Fuzzy to the altar if she wanted to. I told Bonnie not to worry, it was probably nothing. Phyllis is now Mrs. Fuzzy Owen.

After that I think I looked for things to be irritated at Fuzzy about. More and more I found myself getting in the middle of any disagreements they had. I often took Bonnie's side. She had a problem with her hearing and instead of being understanding, I thought Fuzzy was cruel about it. When he was mad about something he'd accuse Bonnie of not hearing because she didn't want to. One day she started crying when he said something like that.

"I hate for you to talk to her like that," I said to Fuzzy, realizing too late that I was butting in—again.

They both looked at me, but neither of them said anything. I suppose if we'd taken the time to analyze the situation, we'd have realized where we were heading.

Maybe Bonnie did. Not too long after that she took a job up in Alaska, one that would keep her away several weeks. If it was supposed to cool things off though, it worked out just the opposite. I began to realize how much I missed her. I was staying at Mama's with the kids, and even though things were happening with my career, I didn't have a full calendar booked. I couldn't accept steady work in the clubs anymore because I might get a tour date. That left me kinda in between. Boredom set in.

Bonnie probably hadn't been gone more than a week when I stopped by the Barrel House where Fuzzy was working.

"Where, in Alaska, is Bonnie?" I asked.

Old Fuzz reached in his pocket, pulled out a phone number, and handed it to me.

I went back to Mama's and called her. I could tell Bonnie was very surprised to hear from me. There was something else in her voice. It sounded a little like fear. I don't think she liked where all this was heading.

"I'm sittin' here at Mama's with nothin' to do," I told her in what I thought was my best "pore ol' Merle" voice. "I thought maybe you could get me a job pickin' up there. Wouldn't hurt my recordin' career to sell some Merle Haggard up in Alaska, would it?"

"I don't think Fuzzy would like that," she said.

"Well, hell, what's Fuzzy got to do with this?" I said. "We've traveled together before, we've done tours, and Fuzzy was all for it. What's all this about what Fuzzy likes?"

She wasn't going to buy my story, but I could tell she was having difficulty coming right out and telling me to buzz off.

"Look, Bon," I said, trying to change the mood. "I'll call you later, okay?" She sounded relieved.

Back I went to the Barrel House. I'd made up my mind what I was gonna do.

"I need some money, Fuzz," I told him. He asked me how much, then counted it out. I don't know if he knew what I was up to or not, but he didn't say anything.

By the time I called Bonnie the second time, I was already in Seattle.

"Hey, Bon," I said. "Why don't you see if you can drum me up a pickin' job? I'm on my way."

"I've been thinkin', Merle," she said, and she sounded very serious. "And I don't want you to come."

Before I could say anything else, she blurted out her reasons.

"I just want you to know, Merle," she said, "that there's no need for you to come up here if you're comin' up here for what I think you are—cause you ain't gonna get it."

There it was—out in the open. I didn't know what to say. I wasn't used to people calling my hand.

"I'm not in Bakersfield, Bonnie," I told her. "I'm in Seattle, waitin' for my flight to Fairbanks."

"Then I guess you've wasted your money on a trip to Seattle," she said calmly. "What I want you to do is buy yourself a ticket back to Bakersfield."

"I can't do that," I said. "I've got a one-way ticket to Fairbanks and I'll see you in a few hours." I hung up the phone.

There was only one airline to Fairbanks. It had trees in the motors I'm sure. I was scared to death. Had never been too brave on planes anyway, and this piece of tin and canvas didn't do nothin' to give me any confidence.

As I was going up the wobbly steps of the plane, I thought of turning around. But there was nothing back there for me. I got inside quick before I changed my mind.

On that long flight from Seattle to Fairbanks, I had a lot of time to think. I tried to keep my eyes off the damned wings. They looked like they would fall off any second. Serve me right, I thought, for what I'm doing.

What *am* I doing?

You know very well, you son of a bitch. Fuzzy is your best friend and he's loved Bonnie for years. Not only was I trying to get in his place, I'd borrowed his money to do it.

"You're an asshole Merle," I said to myself, "and Fuzzy ain't never gonna forgive you."

SING ME BACK HOME

I didn't know why I was arguing with myself. I'm only going to Alaska to see my good friend, Bonnie. That's all there is to it. Maybe she'll introduce me to a few people and I'll pick a little guitar, make a couple of bucks, get my name known around Fairbanks. Besides, I just needed to talk to my friend.

My good friend met me at the airport, but for some reason we didn't have too much to say. She took me to the club where she worked, introduced me to the man in charge, told him I was a good singer and a fine guitar player. He showed me to my room and assured me of some work while I was in town.

My good friend went to her room without another word. I went to bed alone.

Thirteen

Bonnie &
The Strangers

I'm goin' off the deep end
And, I'm slowly losing my mind
I don't approve of the way that I'm livin'
But I can't hold myself in line.

"I Can't Hold Myself in Line"
by Merle Haggard

"HOW COME YOU were lookin' at me like that during the ceremony, Bonnie?"

"I kept thinkin' you might change your mind any minute."

We were on our way home from Mexico when that conversation took place. It was June 28, 1965, and during that quick trip to Mexico, Bonnie Owens became Mrs. Merle Haggard.

To say all the loose ends had been tied up makes it sound a little cold, but actually that was the case. Much to my surprise Leona hadn't given me a problem about a divorce. There was no fight over my having custody of the children. She told them she loved them but that they'd be better off with me. At the time I don't think they shared that opinion. Mama had agreed to help take care of them. When the judge asked her what she thought about having four young children in her charge, she made it very clear. "I feel like I'd be savin' them from drownin'," she said.

We'd made our peace with Fuzzy, although it was very tough for everybody. I had taken the coward's way in the beginning by calling him from Alaska to break the news that Bonnie and I were no longer "just friends."

Although my first night in Alaska had been cold, things warmed up considerably as the days went by. Finally, even Bonnie had to admit there was something special between the two of us. We had to call Fuzzy and break the news to him.

"We're gettin' married," I said on the phone when he asked what was going on. "That's the reason we called, so you could hear it from us." Hell, I don't know why I thought that would be easier.

"What are you doin'?" he said over the bad connection. "Why are you doin' this to me?" He was asking questions I didn't have answers for.

"You're takin' somebody I've loved for years." I could hear the pain in his voice, and I knew there was nothing he could call me that I wasn't calling myself. I also knew I had better be serious about Bonnie or I'd have him to answer to. I felt like I was trying to explain something to a parent.

One look at Bonnie told me she was as miserable and confused as I was.

"Fuzzy," I said into the receiver. I was almost begging for his reassurance. "We love you, Bonnie and me. We love you and we want you to be our friend. We want to go on just like we have been if that's possible."

Well, *almost* like we had been. There was one minor

change. Bonnie was now *my* woman and *his* friend.

As I hung up the phone I knew it would take one hell of a big man to be able to go on working as a team with us. Fuzzy was one hell of a big man.

We stayed in Alaska for several weeks and even after we came back we didn't see Fuzzy for quite awhile. When we did, it was awkward, to say the least. Fuzzy never stopped working and promoting my career.

There has always been a lot of talk—then and now—about my marriage to Bonnie. I loved her. It was a simple and uncomplicated kind of relationship. Our marriage was built on mutual respect and honest friendship. I needed her very much when I married her and I believe she needed me. In the beginning she was not totally convinced that being married to me was the best thing for her. I sure understood that. She'd been on her own for a long time and had pretty much raised her boys by herself. She gave me the feeling then that there was nothing she and I couldn't accomplish together. And, for somebody who'd had more than his share of doubts, that was a great feeling. I needed the strength and security a woman like Bonnie represented. My children needed it too. God knows, I hadn't been much of a father to them. I'd been a pretty good provider, and even in the bad times the children had always come first. But as for being there when they needed me, I wasn't.

With Bonnie, I set about building a real home life. I'm still not saying I was the typical husband though. Our marriage wasn't exactly typical either. We had a little deal, Bonnie and me. To be frank, I had what some of my friends called a perfect situation. It may sound strange, but to us, certainly to me, it was ideal.

Make no mistake, I always loved Bonnie. I still love her as my friend, but nothing I suppose is ever perfect. To me the word "rules" was just something to rhyme with "fools."

Bonnie wasn't blind to my faults. She knew the business

and what went on offstage and on the road. She'd seen the women and the parties. She knew it was useless to try to get me to change a way of life I had come to consider quite normal.

"Merle, I know there'll be other women," she'd said in that hesitant voice of hers, "and I can deal with that. But I'm askin' you not to flaunt them in my face and make me look like some kind of a fool. Please don't embarrass me."

I tried not to, and I don't think I did it very often.

All the time we were together Bonnie was an easy person to be with—or not to be with. She had an uncanny way of knowing when to remove herself from a room, or from the front of the bus, when she didn't want to hear the conversation. She also made herself scarce when she knew—and she *always* knew—there was a woman around I wanted. In black and white that sounds bad, but hell, that's the way it was. Ain't no need to lie about it.

When it comes to the music business and songwriting, there was hardly a line I uttered she didn't copy down. There wasn't an idea I talked about that she didn't keep track of. A lot of my songs never would have seen the light of day if it hadn't been for Bonnie.

By 1965, it looked like the team of Bonnie and Merle could do no wrong. We won the Academy of Country Music Award for "Best Vocal Group." I got it for "Most Promising." And Bonnie won "Top Female Vocalist" that year.

In 1966 I was voted "Top Male Vocalist" and I got the top BMI (Broadcast Music Institute) award for the song "Swinging Doors." Me and Bonnie won again for "Best Vocal Group." We did it again in 1967.

When award time rolled around in 1969, we had "Okie From Muskogee," which took it for song, album, and single. I got "Top Male Vocalist" and The Strangers were named "Band of the Year."

When 1970 came, we hit the jackpot again. I was named

"Entertainer of the Year" by both the Academy of Country Music and the Country Music Association in Nashville. It seemed during that time period everything we touched turned to gold. Sure was a change from the old days when everything I touched got me arrested.

I think I've said this a lot of times, but I loved that climb up. I believe that's why I was unusually happy during this particular period. Whoever said getting there was half the fun was wrong—it's almost *all* of it.

Besides everything else, I had moved the family into a new home in Bakersfield, even fancier than the doctor's home I'd rented for Leona. I also had plans underway to build an even bigger home out in the canyon.

There was almost a normal family life for me, Bonnie, and the kids during this time too. The kids were finally beginning to believe I wasn't some kind of a monster, and Bonnie had done wonders to restore their sense of belonging somewhere. The first Christmas we spent in the new house in Bakersfield turned out to be one of the best ones we ever had, in spite of one incident.

Me and Bonnie had seen to it we weren't working during that holiday season. We told the kids they could skip school. We all went to pick out a Christmas tree and shop for presents. On our way back home I noticed a car in my rear-view mirror. It was weaving from side to side. I could see a woman behind the wheel.

There was no mistake about who it was.

As we pulled into the driveway, Leona brought her car to a sliding stop behind us. As she got out I could see that she was a bit unsteady.

"I've come to get the kids," she said, simple as that. By this time Bonnie was herding them toward the front door. Kelli had started to cry.

"Why don't you just go on home, Leona," I said, calm as I could. "It's Christmas. You don't want to upset the kids."

"What about me?" she asked. "What about my Christmas?"

She was too drunk to argue with so I asked her to come on in the house so we could talk. As best I could, I tried to convince her that it was a bad idea for her to take the kids since we had planned a very nice Christmas for them. Upstairs we could hear Kelli still crying and Bonnie telling her everything was gonna be all right.

Leona finally agreed to leave and I walked her to the door. I think I even wished her a Merry Christmas. Then I went upstairs to see if Bonnie had things under control. Marty, Dana, and Noel were quiet, but there was still the sound of crying coming from the bathroom.

I stood in the doorway and watched Bonnie wash Kelli's little back. She was gently rubbing the warm water over her as she kept telling her how everything really would be all right. I bent over Bonnie's shoulder and looked at Kelli's face.

"Your mama's gone," I said to her. "We didn't fight, and everythin' is all right." She sniffed a couple of times and managed a little grin in my direction.

Then I saw that Bonnie was crying too.

"Merry Christmas, Bon," I said.

"It will be," she promised. And it was.

Once it was over, though, it was back on the road again. I don't know who in the hell said "one for the road," but for me one was never enough. One drink, one gig, one lady, or one little yeller.

From 1965 to 1970, I felt like I was on a solid roll. I didn't have a "Tiger By the Tail," like old buddy Buck Owens sung about—hell, I was on its back and ridin' the beast full out. Most of the time I was in control.

When it came to money, I couldn't seem to keep up with it too well. It had a way of gettin' away from me real easy and I was still contributing heavily to the upkeep of the casinos every chance I got.

In some cases, I overextended myself. I figured it didn't matter though. I was choppin' in tall cotton and the money was rollin' in, both from concerts and from the songs.

When I found myself in trouble I took off to my publisher's office.

"Buck, I need money bad," I said, as I walked into Buck Owens' office at Blue Book Publishing. "I know 'Sing Me Back Home' is gonna make a lot of money, and I need some kind of an advance."

"What's the problem, Merle?" Buck asked.

"No problem at all, Buck," I answered, "if you'll just give me fifteen thousand dollars."

He started to laugh. He told me there was no way he could do that. I thought he might be lying to me because I knew people who had songs half the size of "Sing Me Back Home" who hadn't had any problem at all getting big advances.

"Buck, I ain't kiddin'. I need the money bad," I told him. "It's not just anybody I owe. I'm into Bennie Binion for five big ones, and gamblin' debts don't wait around for royalty checks."

"Maybe we can make a deal," he said then.

"What kind?"

"Sell me half of 'Sing Me Back Home' and I'll let you have the fifteen thousand today."

"Done," I told him. I was desperate.

It was later I found out he'd already received a check for more than I'd asked for—all mine. It had been in his desk when he was talking to me. I sued him and got my half of the song back. I had a hard time gettin' over that little deal and I wasn't real friendly with him for a hell of a long time.

Still, it was part of my "music-bizness-education" as everybody calls it. If I hadn't learned it from Buck I would've learned it from somebody else. Hell, I was learning something new every day.

The best thing I learned was how good it felt to pick out

my own band. By 1965 I felt like I had reached the place where I could hire a band and consider myself in the business to stay.

I knew where I wanted to go first. I took off straight to Vegas where Roy Nichols was still working for Wynn Stewart. I laid it out plain and simple.

"Roy, I can't pay what Wynn's payin' but I've got a feelin' I can make it now. If you'll come to work for me, you can work for me as long as I live."

"What *can* you pay?" he asked. I told him one hundred twenty-five dollars a week.

"Let me give my notice," he said.

Fuzzy agreed to play steel, and I got Helen Price to play drums. In those days we called her "Peaches," and I can tell you that Peaches was one hell of a drummer.

Then there was this danged crazy guy who had been livin' around my house off and on for some time. I couldn't run him off, and since he'd worked free for me, it was only right to hire him when I could afford to pay. So, Jerry Ward became my first bass player.

That was the first band of "Strangers." They were called The Strangers because of my first big hit, "From Now On All My Friends Are Gonna Be Strangers."

By 1980 The Strangers included Norm Hamlet on steel guitar; Don Markham with the horns; Tracy Barton on bass; Ronnie Reno, rhythm guitar and harmony; drummers, Biff Adams and Bobby Galardo; Mark Yeary on piano; Gordon Terry and Tiny Moore on fiddles; Eldon Shamblin on guitar; along with my only original Stranger, Roy Nichols.

It would take an entire book to tell about The Strangers, because it's sure a fact that these guys are all much more unusual than any fiction you'll ever read. That's not even mentioning the ones who've passed through the ranks from time to time—they've been really something—each and every one damn fine musicians.

Bonnie & The Strangers

The Strangers you see on stage today are accomplished men of music. Each man has his own personality and his own individual way of sharing his talents. Norm is our constant and dependable character. He's been able, all through the years, to maintain that mellow cool without the aid of any little helpers, and that's something in this business.

My horn player, Don, plays both trumpet and sax, which is unusual, because one is a reed instrument and one is not. He's the only horn man in the business I'd be satisfied with because he plays well in the "country chords" G-A-D-E. Most horn players can't find their ass in those chords.

Tracy Barton has been with The Strangers the shortest amount of time. I have a very hard time keeping bass players. Most of them are just passing the time till they can do what they really want to do—which is not playing bass.

Ronnie Reno came to The Strangers with a strong musical heritage. His father is Don Reno, the great bluegrass musician. Ronnie also plays harmonica and bass string mandolin—and makes fewer mistakes than any musician I've ever heard. I guess it's his bluegrass background that makes him sound so great singing harmony along with Bonnie, the only woman in our group.

Mark Yeary plays the keyboard with as much soul as you'll hear in any old-timer, yet he's the youngest member of The Strangers.

The drummers, Bobby with the fastest hands in the business, and Biff, who lays down a mood, give my band the foundation we can all build our music on.

Nobody likes a fiddle any better than I do. And there's nothing that sounds better than Gordon Terry when he gets on stage with Tiny Moore. Tiny is one of the original Texas Playboys and he is a true artist. Eldon Shamblin, another of Bob Wills' band, works with The Strangers on a lot of shows. Eldon's guitar work is so great that he can just stop everybody in their tracks. I've been so lucky to have people like those former Texas Playboys and great musicians like Roy and the others. It's been—and still is—a dream of a lifetime for me.

Of course there've been other Strangers. I can't name them all, but I've got to mention people like Leon Copeland, Ralph Mooney, Dennis Hromek, Bobby Wayne, George French, Dale Hampton, Gene Bolin, John McCormick, Jimmy Tap, Eddie Burris, Gene Wiggins, Jody Payne, Randy Ingram, and the Dixieland Express. And last, but not least, I have to mention a guitar picker by the name of Shorty Mullins who fainted dead away when I asked him if he'd like to go on the road as one of The Strangers.

And so it's been quite a trip, and the wheels are still rollin'. One thing I can say though, that during all the years of my career, I've never—even once—gone on what they call a "star trip." Never got the big head or nothin' like that.

Well, that's what I said till Tex Whitson asked me to repeat it. I couldn't, because it wasn't true. I did get very cocky for awhile—and yes, I was flyin' as high as I could. When I suspected I might be overstepping myself, I'd just say I deserved all the good times I could get. I'd been through enough bad times to last ten lifetimes. If I could live the life as a "star," hell, why not?

It was in Anaheim, I believe, when some of my star qualities began to show. I'd hired a very bright lady who had a lot of good ideas about how to run my show and how to keep "all those people" from crowding in on me. I didn't need to be bothered by this one and that one. Dorothy Johns knew how to handle things like that and people like them. Mostly, my friends.

I was in my dressing room when I heard a big commotion outside. Suddenly the door burst open and in walked Tex Whitson followed by a very upset Dorothy Johns. She had tried, unsuccessfully, to stop him from bothering the star. I hadn't seen him in several months and I was just about to get up to shake his hand when he almost hollered out at me.

"What in the hell's the matter with you?" he said. No "Hello, old buddy, how are ya?" Just a cold "What in the hell's the matter with you?" Tex always had a way of cutting right to the heart of things.

"Nothin's the matter with *me*," I said, and at first I was mad. What in the hell was the matter with *him*? Who did he think he was?

From behind Tex I could see Dorothy motioning me toward the door.

"The limo is waiting," she said. I just stood there looking at Tex, feeling a little like I'd been caught doing something nasty.

"Is all this shit true?" he asked.

"*What* shit?" I was on the defensive so I just pretended I didn't know what he was talking about.

"That woman out there," he said, half turning toward Dorothy. "She's directin' traffic. She's tellin' this one and that one to go this way and that way . . . and she's screenin' all the 'undesirables' away from you. *I* got in anyway."

"Well, hell, Tex. She's got a lot of good ideas about how to run my show and keep things movin'."

"Bullshit."

"Things are changin', Tex. Everything's gettin' bigger."

"You're changin', old friend," he said, "and, in my eyes, you're gettin' smaller."

Dorothy had the Security holding back the fans and was still trying to get me to run for the limo.

"I gotta do this Tex," I said. "You don't understand how it's gettin' to be."

He stepped aside, no longer trying to stop me. But there was something in the way he looked that made me realize something was very wrong—and it was most likely me.

As I walked by him he put his hand on my arm and I stopped.

"Are you removin' yourself from these people who made you a goddamn star?" I didn't have no answer.

"The next time I see you, I guess you'll be wearin' a full-length fur coat and surrounded by the *right* kind of people."

I looked him in the eye then for the first time. I could tell he wasn't accusing me, but trying to tell me something before it was too damned late.

"There's an auditorium full of people out there," he said. He was almost pleading with me. "You're their *man* . . . their *poet*. . . . They *made* you and now you're lookin' away from them."

He turned around before I could say a word and walked into the crowd. I didn't see him for quite awhile after that, but I took a lot of time to think about what he'd said. I decided to go back to my old disorganized way of doing things. I don't know if that was right or wrong, but I knew I never wanted to totally remove myself from my fans and friends. I can't give all they want me to, but I don't have to be a "king" way above his "subjects." I don't want to hurt nobody, and doin' the best I can I still do it time and again. Even today, I never go on tour that I don't see somebody on the sidelines that I wish I had time to talk to, but hell, I'm always in a hurry. Some people understand but are still hurt. Others just can't.

There's always that fear that someday you'll miss somebody or something real important. When that happens, it brings home all the warnings about the "high price of success." That was never more true than one night back in Oklahoma.

I'd just come off stage. There were about three hundred people crowding around backstage, and the management sent out six or eight cops to get me from the stage area to the bus. I was hot and tired and could only see a bunch of faces and hands reaching out for autographs. My feet were hardly touching the ground as the cops half dragged me through the path they'd made. All at once, one of the faces took on a familiar form.

"Lomar. . . !" I called out. "Hang on, Lomar." I couldn't tell if he heard me or not. He had the strangest look on his face. It seemed like he was saying that he'd come to see me—but knew he couldn't. I tried to turn my head to keep track of where he was but lost him in the crowd.

As soon as I got inside the bus I told Fuzzy to go see if he could find him. I watched from the window as the cops made everybody move back. I searched the crowd but I couldn't see no sign of Lomar Boatman.

Fuzzy came back shaking his head. "I don't know what happened to him," he said. "I never could find him."

"Maybe he'll come back in sight of the bus," I said, still looking out the window. "Hell, I didn't even know he was back in Oklahoma," I said. "I thought he was still in California." All that day I kept looking for him. I even tried to joke about how slick Indians can get away, since Lomar was almost a full-blooded Indian. Nothing was funny though, and I was getting more and more upset as the day went on.

We never saw him again.

Two weeks later I got word that Lomar had died of a heart attack. I felt awful. I'd had a feeling that day that it was important that we got to talk. Now it was too late. I believe he had a premonition about his death and had come to see me one last time. I knew he hadn't come because he wanted anything—only to say hello—and maybe goodbye. I know he knew he didn't have too long to live because we found out later he'd changed his will just a short time before he died. He had requested that his body be cremated and his ashes be scattered over Green Creek up on Lake Shasta near Redding, where I now live. And that's where he is today.

So, the road goes on—and if you're on the road, you do,

too. Now and then I catch myself searching through the crowds for faces hoping this kind of thing never happens again. Chances are, it will. Sometimes I'll see somebody who reminds me a little bit of Lomar and I'll sing a song in his direction.

> "Let him sing me back home. . .
>   with a song I used to hear,
>   Make my old mem'ries come alive,
>   Take me away, and turn back the years. . .
>   Sing me back home before I die."

It's the least I can do.

Fourteen

Here's to Success, the White House, and the Grand Ole Opry!

> I'd like to hold my head up,
>   and be proud of who I am,
> But they won't let my secret go un-told,
> I paid the debt I owed them,
>   but they're still not satisfied,
> Now I'm a branded man out in the cold.

"Branded Man"   by Merle Haggard

"HERE," HE SAID, pushing a kidney-shaped wine flask in my direction. "Have some of this." He was holding the container in his free hand as he stood by the urinal. I shook my head. He leaned down, pulled up a straw from the flask, and sucked up the wine.

As he walked over to the wash basin, he focused as best he could in my general direction.

"Don't I know you from someplace?" he asked.

"I'm on the show," I said.

"Oh, I know that Merle," he said, laughing, "and I know who you are. It's just that I've got the strangest feelin' this ain't the first time we've met. I just can't remember where I've seen you."

"I don't think you'd remember," I said. "But I do."

"Where was it then, San Quentin?" He started to laugh then stopped. He realized his joke hadn't been a joke after all.

"My God," he said then, totally embarrassed. "It *was* San Quentin, wasn't it?"

I nodded. Then I told him about the time he'd played Quentin when I was still a guest. He just kept on apologizing for what he felt had been a terrible thing to say. I kept telling him it was all right, and it was.

"Here," he said, fumbling in his pocket with a wet hand. "Maybe this'll help." He offered me a double-dot dexie. I took it. He'd made me so damn nervous by that time I really needed it. His hands shook and his arms moved in all directions. I just kept thinking about how this skinny dude, who was wilder'n a guinea, was on his way to becoming a country legend—if he could live that long.

His name, of course, was Johnny Cash.

After that meeting on a Chicago television program, Johnny and I worked several shows together. We were never what I consider close personal friends, but I believe we always liked each other's work. I'm not a dyed-in-the-wool fan of many people but I'm a true Cash fan. There's a certain magic that must have been born in him. He can grab an audience and hold them right till the last chorus.

During the lunch break in Chicago that day, Johnny and I got the chance to talk about his appearance in San Quentin.

I told him about the effect it had on the prisoners after he'd gone—and especially this one. We talked quite a bit that day, but I'm not sure how much registered with Johnny. This was during the time when he was heavily into drugs, but I've still never seen anybody more impressive, even at his worst. I'm very glad things straightened out for him later, because he's the kind of man who deserves to enjoy his success.

Success ain't the easiest pill to swallow though, no matter what you wash it down with. More than one entertainer has discovered this. Some of 'em too late. Elvis Presley was a good example of that.

I never knew Elvis as a friend. I would have liked to. The only time I met him was a disappointment. I almost wish I'd listened to Bonnie and turned down the invitation.

We were at the International Hotel in Vegas and James Burton, who played guitar for Elvis, was a good friend of mine. I don't even remember if Elvis sent word by James or whether James asked us to come to the suite after the show.

"I don't really want to go," Bonnie said, and that surprised me. I would have thought she'd be racing me to the door. We'd talked about him a lot of times and were like everybody else. We loved him.

"What do you mean, you don't want to go see Elvis— meet him in person?" I asked. "Don't you realize how many millions of people, women especially, would die for an opportunity like this?"

"I just don't want to go, Merle," she said again, "and I think, knowin' how you feel about Elvis, you'd be better off if you don't go either."

"Why, for gawdssake?"

"Don't you think it's better to keep this image we have of him, that fantastic entertainer on stage," she said, "than to go see him, meet him, and discover he isn't what we thought? People say . . . "

"Aw Bonnie," I interrupted her, "I don't care what people say. I don't care about the gossip, the rumors, all that talk about drugs. You know how that kind of stuff gets exaggerated. I mean, we know firsthand about talk like that. Come on . . ."

"No," she said. "I want to keep the image I have of Elvis—real or unreal. I like what I think and feel about him."

She'd been right. I came away disappointed and, for awhile, my Elvis image was tarnished. There was no big deal about the evening in general. I talked to Elvis only a little while. He seemed nervous and not too aware of his surroundings but nothing out of the ordinary happened. He introduced me to Priscilla, who didn't seem to know who I was.

"He's a country singer," Elvis told her in a voice I thought sounded a little irritated. I guess I was a little paranoid because I didn't like the way he said "country singer." I left his suite disappointed because Elvis didn't really seem "bigger than life" offstage. I guess I felt a little bit cheated to discover that he was just a human being like the rest of us. I guess that's why it bothers me so much to have fans put me up like some kind of an idol. That's wrong. We're all human. None of us can walk on water, even Elvis.

When I got back to the room Bonnie took one look at me and knew she'd been right.

"I wish I'd listened to you," I said, sitting down on the edge of the bed where she was laying. "I think my idol has fallen."

"What happened?" she asked, raising up on one elbow to look at me closer.

"Nothin'," I answered honestly. "Nothin' at all."

The strangest thing though, as let down as I was that night, it took only one show to wipe it all out. Elvis was that great, and whatever magic he had, it all came out when the spotlight was turned on him. He made the audience forget everything but his talent. And, after all, that's all he owed us anyway.

Before his death I'd been working on a tribute album to him. When he died, I didn't think I could finish it. I didn't want to be accused of hopping on the funeral bandwagon for profit. Then, after awhile, I didn't care what people thought, or what they said. I'd started out doing the album for Elvis, and his death made it even more important that I finish it. I don't even sing "From Graceland to the Promised Land" on stage anymore. That one never was for the fans— or even for me. It was for Elvis because, like everybody else, I loved him. Hell, we all loved him to death.

Success, with all its promise and glitter, had demanded the ultimate payment from Elvis Presley.

I guess we all handle success in different ways.

George Jones ignores it when he can. When he can't he tries to drink it away. When he can't do either one of those, he just walks out on it, even though he knows it'll still come looking for him.

I remember a time in Texas when somebody handed me a telephone saying George Jones wanted to talk to me.

"Yeah, George," I said, "what can I do for you?"

"It's all your fault, Merle," came the slurred voice on the other end.

"What's my fault, George?"

"You wrote that song . . . the one about throwin' away the rose. . . ."

"Yeah, George, I know the one," I said, "but I didn't know my songs would cause you problems. I'm sorry, George." It wasn't hard to see that ol' George was pretty wasted.

"I'm comin' to see you," he said.

"Sure," I said, laughing. "come on down to Texas, George."

I hung up the phone and some of the others in the room

said they wouldn't be surprised if he showed up. I told them I didn't think so, 'cause hell, he was supposed to be doing concerts all week.

The next day, who shows up, but the Old Possum himself—and he's still singin' my song.

We were at the motel, and he found out which room we were in. He didn't knock or nothin', just came right through the door. He actually kicked the damn door down, roared right into the room, and announced that George Jones had, indeed, *arrived.*

> *"I'm payin' for the days . . . of wine and roses . . .*
> *a victim of the drunken life I choose . . . "*

Fuzzy, who'd been sleeping on a roll-away bed on the other side of the room, raised up to see what kind of a wild man had come bustin' in the room singin' "I Threw Away the Rose."

"What's going on here?" he wanted to know.

> *"Now all my social friends . . . look down . . .*
> *their noses . . . "*

George may have been drunk, but he was in rare voice. I just sat there on the bed and laughed as I watched him cross over to Fuzzy's bed, fold the danged thing up, and roll it right out the door—with Fuzzy still in it.

> *"Cause I kept the wine . . . and threw away the rose . . . "*

"I didn't like the way things were, where I was," George said, sitting down next to me. It was as simple as that. Success had been crowding him. He had attacked the problem the only way he knew.

Even though George was supposed to be someplace else—

where he didn't like the way things were—he spent the next few days touring with us. That was probably the only time in my life I got a little tired of hearing George sing. Mostly because he kept singing the same song. Granted, I like to hear my songs sung, but there are just so many times you can listen to "I Threw Away the Rose."

Even though he was a lot of laughs on that trip, other times George really made me mad. One of those times started with a phone call I got while I was living in Nashville, about 1975, I think.

"George is down," the voice on the other end said. "We really need you to fill in for him. He can't make the show and it's really important. You've got to get him out of this spot. His career is sufferin' real bad."

"I can't help," I said. "My band's in California, and besides I just can't."

"The Jones Boys will back you up, Merle," the guy said. I think it was George's manager at the time. "We'll pay you under the table."

"I can't do it, man."

"You'll do it for George, won't you?"

"No, dammit, I won't do it for George."

"Think about it."

"I don't have to think about it." I was gettin' hot. Then I thought about that pore soul who was always gettin' his ass in trouble and if there was anything I could identify with, it was that.

"Tell you what," I said. "Have George call me himself, and I'll *consider* it."

Sure enough, the phone rang again in a few minutes.

"Hag, this is . . . the Old Possum. . . . "

He was talkin' so low I couldn't hardly hear him.

"Listen, old friend," I said. "I want to help you out but hell, you're gonna have to help too."

"I will, Merle, I will. Honest I will."

SING ME BACK HOME

"Well, if you'll get yourself together for the next date and give me your solemn promise," I said, "then I'll do the show for you *this one time.*"

From the other end I heard his very solemn promise.

I worked the job. The following night I checked to see if he had kept his solemn promise. He hadn't.

Shortly after that the Country Music Awards show came along. George and I were both up for awards so we were seated on the aisle—George right in the seat behind me. I decided to ignore him completely. I was still pissed off. When he sat down behind me I could feel his eyes on the back of my head but I wouldn't turn around. Finally, he leaned over my shoulder and said real close to my ear, "Hag, you still mad at ol' George?"

I didn't even answer. He tried again.

"Hag . . . " I was now trying to keep from laughing. His voice was pitiful. "Hag . . . are you really mad at pore ol' George . . . ?"

Well, what the hell. Of course not. What could I do? I broke up laughing. Nobody, not even Tammy Wynette, can stay mad at George very long.

Besides, George was just handling success the best way he knew. Everybody does it differently, I guess.

Some people, like Roger Miller, have learned that humor is the best way. He thinks it's funny to call people on his portable phone from just outside their motel room doors, then knock. Well, it is funny, but it's a hell of a shock.

Willie Nelson simply changed his image—both to achieve and handle success. Nobody can argue with the results.

Ernest Tubb never seemed to realize how successful he was, so he had no problem coping with it. It's people like him who make me very proud to be part of this business. Sometimes when I've just about had it with the backstabbing and the cheating, it's almost cleansing just to think about the old Texas Troubadour.

If Glen Campbell hadn't chosen to follow the commercial route, he could have, in my opinion, been a giant in country music—an all-time legend. Granted, he's very popular as he is, and in my opinion one of the finest singers of our time, but he's been exploited. He's also got lousy taste in song material. I guess what I would like to have seen Glen do was more songs like "By the Time I Get to Phoenix." I shipped that record out along with my "Today I Started Loving You Again," and eight weeks later, Glen's song was sitting at number one. Mine was number two. Still, no matter, Glen is a success, anyway you slice it. I just don't personally agree with the direction he's been taken in.

Success comes to us all in various ways—some we don't expect at all. Sometimes it's only a good sound on a guitar, the look on a fan's face, or the satisfaction of knowing you've written a good song.

Success is also holding a piece of paper that told me I'd been granted executive clemency from the state of California.

The pardon for my "past crimes" came on March 21, 1972. It was signed by Governor Ronald Reagan, and stated, among other things, that I was now a fully rehabilitated member of society, entitled to a full and unconditional pardon.

I was grateful to Governor Reagan for his efforts on my behalf. Once pardoned I guess they thought it was all right to invite me to perform at the White House. I even got there before ol' Ronnie did.

The invitation to play at Pat Nixon's birthday party in 1973 came as a big surprise. I had no idea until I was told that the First Lady was a fan of Merle Haggard. It was because of her request that I was asked to come to the nation's capital.

When the invitation came, I couldn't help staring at it and wondering what Rabbit would have thought of something like that. What would my daddy have said? I knew the answer to both of those things. They would have been very proud—just like I was.

The Washington show was the third day of one of the wildest tours of my life. We'd played for a huge crowd in the Houston Astrodome one night, then followed with a night in Dallas where we had very special guests in the front row.

As I stood up on stage in Dallas, I looked down into the face of one of my all-time heroes—Bob Wills. Although he was getting up in years and was in a wheel chair, he still looked great sitting there in his big old white hat and black suit. He looked like such a grand old man—and he was. His health was failing, and I kept thinking this might be the last time I'd ever have a chance to play for him. There were about eleven thousand people at the concert, and though I hope they enjoyed it, I was only playing for one person.

About halfway through the show I reached back and got my fiddle. Slowly I pulled the bow across the strings and began to play "Faded Love." I could see the tears just a rollin' down his tired old face. I dedicated the show to him that night. Hell, I'd dedicated most of my musical life to him, and I believe he knew that.

On our way to Washington, somebody asked me if I was worried about playing for the President.

"Hell, if I can play 'Faded Love' for the great Bob Wills," I said, "I can damn sure sing 'California Blues' for President Nixon."

I wish my memory of arriving at the White House was more dramatic and less muddled, but the truth is, we were all hung over, dead on our feet, and walking around in a daze. We were not, as you might guess, at our best after three days of shows and parties. I'm sure the people in charge of getting Mrs. Nixon's birthday party together must have been a bit upset when they saw this sorry-looking group come draggin' in.

"Boy, this place is really somethin'," somebody in the band said as we shuffled into the Gold Room.

"Beats the hell out of the Wheelin' Jamboree," somebody else added.

Sonny and Bob Osborne opened the show with their bluegrass group. Backstage we all waited for a response from the audience, which was made up of about three hundred dignitaries and top officials. For all they knew though, "Rocky Top" was a Senator from Iowa.

When it was my turn to go out, I found myself wishing I was anywhere else in the world, with a couple of exceptions. I felt like I was coming out for hand-to-hand combat with the enemy.

I don't know what they thought about me, but I couldn't believe what I saw. There they sat, with no expressions whatsoever, especially the President and the First Lady. I felt like I was playing to a bunch of department store mannequins. Notice how I didn't say dummies.

I did two songs. There was still no response. I don't remember what the songs were, because they sure as hell didn't work. What did they want, for cryin' out loud? What was I gonna have to do to get this bunch to look alive?

I searched the faces in the crowd, hoping to find just one that seemed at least interested in what I was doing. No luck.

Then I noticed how first one, then another, would ease out to the edge of his seat to see what their leader was doing. Hell, he wasn't doin' nothin'. Neither was the birthday lady, who'd asked for me in the first place.

Then I got mad. I kept telling myself to cool the Grandpa Harp temper. One outburst here would make the papers all over the world—and it might take me awhile to live it down. My damn head was busting from too little sleep and too much booze. My pride was taking an awful beating. I was getting more and more afraid of what I was liable to do next. I didn't *ask* to be here, dammit.

There *he* sat, the President of the United States, the most powerful man in the world. His face was a mask I couldn't read. It was blank. The least he could do, I thought, on behalf of simple politeness, was to lead his flock of sheep in some hint of appreciation. By the time I finished the third song, I didn't much give a damn.

"I've got a feelin'," I began, "that you people are not too sure what you wanted to do this evenin'." Not a sound. Then I directed my attention toward Mrs. Nixon.

"I'm not here to entertain anyone except this lady in front of me—the First Lady. She asked for me to sing at her birthday, and that's what I'm doin'."

From the time I'd come on stage, I hadn't looked Nixon right in the eye, even though I was standing only about three feet from him. I looked down at him then. I might as well have been looking at Rich Little doing his impression. There wasn't even a nod in my direction.

"I'd like to take time out though," I said, still looking at him, "to dedicate a song to the President. I know he's from California, like me, and we're both a long ways from home. I'd like to do 'California Blues' just for him."

> "Well, I'm goin' to California . . . where they
>   sleep out every night . . .
>   I'm goin' to California, where they
>   sleep out every night . . .
> Oh, I'm leavin' you Mama, 'cause you know
>   you don't treat me right . . . "

I got all the way into the second verse before I saw any change at all. I realized then that he'd never heard the old Jimmie Rodgers song. I suppose he hadn't hung out at the same places I did growing up in California. Slowly then, there was a change. Hell, there was even a little smile.

> "Let me tell you somethin' . . .
> Mama that you don't know . . .

Let me tell you somethin' now, good gal
that you don't know . . .
Oh, I'm a do-right Papa, I got a home
ev'rywhere I go . . . "

He looked at Pat, nudged her with his elbow, then began to applaud. All at once, everybody leaned out to look at their chief. Then they *all* applauded. Two sets of applause really, one from the Nixons, and the second—when they were sure it was all right—from the flock.

"I got the California Blues . . .
and I'm sure gonna leave you here . . .
I got the California blues . . .
and I'm sure gonna leave you here . . .
I can't ride the blinds . . .
Ain't got no railroad fare . . . "

After that everything went great. At the party later the President talked to me about his life and how it compared with mine. I was knocked out by the way he knew everybody in my group—last names, first names, Roy, Norm, Phyllis, Fuzzy, Bonnie, everybody. I couldn't believe how he was introducing everybody to everybody else. He'd sure done his homework on our bunch. It was really a sight though when Louie came strolling up to the President. Now anybody who knows Louie knows that he ain't no different talkin' to a man on the street or to royalty.

"And last, but not least," Nixon said, "here is Mister Lewis Talley."

I was struck by the whole unbelievable scene, the insanity of it all. There I was, in the danged White House watchin' old Louie standin' there in his normal slouch, shiftin' from one foot to the other, discussin' God-knows-what with our nation's leader. It was all I could do to keep

241

from bustin' out laughin', and I knew if I got started I'd never stop.

Everybody who did that show has their own stories to tell, each one more ridiculous than the other. Even today, none of us can discuss it without reliving some of the crazy episodes—everything from the Osborne Brothers' bass player, Dennis Digby, calling the press secretary "Hossfly," because he didn't know (or care) who in the hell he was, to a wild bus ride, courtesy of the U.S. government. I guess it scared the daylights out of some of my fearless band, and hell, they're used to riding with Louie. They said Dennis Hromek called that driver everything he could think of and came up with a few new vulgarities.

So, if your definition of "success" means being invited to perform at the White House, then, for one night, we were sure as hell successful.

For other people success could only be the Grand Ole Opry, or just being accepted in Nashville—two subjects *not* dear to my heart.

Now, before I go any farther I have to point out that it's neither Nashville nor the Grand Ole Opry I'm out to attack. It's the "system," and like everybody else I'm not sure exactly what that is or how to identify it. All I know is that it totally pisses me off.

The best way I can explain it would be to say I resent the way Nashville is held up as some kind of goddess that everybody's supposed to worship. Then when you bow down to her feet she kicks you in the damn teeth. When I think of the good people Nashville has destroyed, or tried to destroy, it makes me kinda sick. When I think of the people it's forgotten, I get mad.

The first name that comes to my mind is Grady Martin. Now tell me, who ever heard of a country music "Hall of Fame" that doesn't include Grady Martin? I don't know of anybody who deserves it more than he does. He's been involved in more hit records in that town than anybody who ever walked on Music Row. When they wanted a hit, they called Grady. When Grady needed help, Nashville, with her cold heart, turned her damn back on him. It's no secret that I always wanted to be the greatest guitar player in the world. Well, there's no way that's gonna happen because the number one spot has long been filled by Grady. I guess I hold Nashville directly responsible for ignoring great talent like Grady Martin while they rolled a bunch of shit off that musical assembly line, canned and labeled for the general public.

So, when I say I'm on the outs with Nashville, I mean with those who don't give people like Grady his due. It's because they hype up some singer who can't sing for shit and bring in musicians who can't pick their noses, yet fail to give proper credit to people like Grady and Johnny Gimble.

Who's Johnny Gimble, you ask? See what I mean?

Johnny Gimble has been somebody I've enjoyed since I remember hearing him on the radio years ago. I knew he was one hell of a fiddle player but until I met him one night in the Columbia Studios parking lot, I didn't know what an unusual person he was.

Roy Nichols introduced us, and I got a chance to tell him how much I loved "Brown-Skinned Gal." He just kinda grinned and looked at me. Then he got out his fiddle right there in the parking lot and started to play. We all stood there soaking in the music and patting our feet. Hell, that's what Nashville oughta be about. Country music is feelin' and *heart*, not a bunch of stuff some asshole says the public wants just because he's made "an extensive study of the market." It's enough to make you puke.

And, since I've put my ass in a sling already, let me tell you something else that makes me even madder. The Grand Ole Opry—that sacred cow devoted to filling the pockets of a bunch of anonymous bastards who don't know doodle-shit about country music or what it means to those of us who love it.

Now, if you want to hear something contradictory—let me go on record as saying how much I love the Grand Ole Opry. God, I remember hearing it as a kid. I can close my eyes, even now, and remember exactly how that Solemn Old Judge, George D. Hay, sounded. I remember Roy Acuff taking over, and then Red Foley for awhile. I even remember the first time Hank Williams sang "Lovesick Blues" on the Opry. Damn! Stopped the show for fifteen minutes. So, don't make any mistakes and say Merle Haggard don't like the Grand Ole Opry—that's a lie.

But, as the years have gone by, I've grown to feel very sorry for what was once—and could be again—the greatest country music show on Earth. It's become a lot bigger with all the trappings of Opryland. It has a lot more to offer, and I'm not really taking offense at that. Unlike some people, I feel that the move from the old Ryman Auditorium to the new building at Opryland was a good thing. That had to happen. My question is, and I've asked it many times, why in the hell didn't they update the *entire* thing? Hell, it's like a mansion with an outhouse.

The fans want, and deserve, a better showcase of country music. How many times have you heard people say, "Well, I went down to the Opry last night but there wasn't nobody there. . . . " The management could put some of what they make back into the Opry. They could offer a live network show, keeping the historic flavor. It was done on Public Broadcasting a couple of times. They could turn loose of the purse strings enough to offer top-notch entertainment, and give the people the true picture of country music.

I know I'm getting into politics now, but I'm entitled to my opinion in my own book. Hell, if I can't give it here, where can I give it?

I've been asked to be a member of the Grand Ole Opry several times, and I consider even being asked an honor. But until my feelings are a little different it would be wrong of me to accept. There's never been a time when I've appeared as a guest that I didn't feel humbled, surrounded by the ghosts of long-gone greats standing somewhere in the wings. The floor of the old Ryman stage was taken up and placed in the new building. So, when a performer stands in front of that mike, he's standing right where Hank Williams stood, where Lefty's been, where Elvis performed and some fool told him to go back to driving a truck. You know, when you're standing there, you're on the sacred ground where all the grand old masters of country music have played.

The most frustrating thing is where do you go to complain? Hell, it ain't Roy Acuff's fault. He's not to blame. Hal Durham is doing everything he can, but somebody else is still calling the shots. If you went to the Board of Directors they'd send you to somebody else and the buck would keep being passed. I guess the only place where the buck's not passed is in the performers' paychecks.

Maybe I just don't understand *how things are.* That's what the critics will say about my criticism of the church of the mother country, but I'm not preaching heresy when I say there ought to be some changes.

I don't see why the Opry can't be divided into three divisions. They could devote at least a third of the time to the old-timers, the backbone of the entire show. It's so important to see Grandpa Jones, Minnie Pearl, and Roy Acuff out there on that stage. Then I believe there ought to be at least a third of the time devoted to the new country, the fresh new talent that comes along in our business every day struggling to gain some kind of recognition without selling out body and soul.

The third part I believe should be devoted to the best

SING ME BACK HOME

entertainment money (and a fair amount) can buy. Offer the fans names they can recognize, people who appear on the show because it's a good place to be, not just to plug a new record or something.

And there has to be a superstar at the helm of this great ship. The Opry needs a strong image. Roy Acuff will be the first to tell you he's not exactly in his prime. We need a well-known leader right out front.

Do I have somebody in mind? Sure do. I saw him that first time inside a California prison singing the pain and misery away from a bunch of convicts. This man has been down the bad roads, won his battles, and is one of the best examples of country music's living legends.

Although I have no idea what his thoughts are on this subject, I believe "the man in black" is the best choice. He's the one who should be at the center ring of the greatest country show on Earth.

Hello . . . it's *Johnny Cash*. . . .

Fifteen

Endings and Beginnings

I live the kind of life
that most men only dream of . . .
I make my living writing songs . . .
and singing them . . .
But I'm forty-one years old,
and I ain't got no place to go . . .
when its over . . .
So I'll hide my age and make the stage
. . .and try to kick the footlights out again.

"*Footlights*"   by Merle Haggard

"ARE YOU SURE that's what you wanna do, Bonnie?" I asked. She said she was very sure. I wasn't surprised, but I felt strangely sad, uncertain about what was really happening.

It was ending—this thing between Bonnie and me—and we both knew it. I don't think either of us actually knew when the ending began, but there was little doubt where it was going to end.

It was 1974. The music life was being good to me and I had reached that point where every performer looks around and realizes there aren't too many more mountains to climb. It was not what I'd hoped it would be. I'd find myself working a big show as a headliner and watching the opening act come on. I'd know he was wishing he was top dog. More than once I wanted to grab him by the collar and say, "You fool, you're climbing that great side of the mountain—that's where all the excitement is. The upper side is so overrated." But I knew nobody would believe that unless they'd been there.

That's what was going through my mind when Bonnie mentioned getting off the road.

"I need some time at home, Merle," she said, "and I feel like the kids need me too." There was more but she wasn't saying it.

"You really don't need me all that much. . . . "

"Aw, come on, Bonnie," I said, sitting down next to her. "I need you. I'll always need you. The show needs you."

"And *I* need to get off the road for awhile," she insisted. "You know I love the road family and you, but everythin' seems to be kinda growin' away from me. I feel like I felt when I realized my boys were grown up. It's time we face the facts that you've reached the point in your career when you don't need . . . "

"That's not true," I stopped her. "I don't want you sayin' I've got too *big* for my people. Hell, Bonnie, what kind of man do you think I am?"

"You're an important man, Merle," she said, looking at me almost like she was seeing me for the first time. "I don't think you even realize that you actually belong to the public out there now. You're not just some little guy playin' music down at the Barrel House for fun. It's all come true.

Everythin' me and Fuzzy dreamed of for you years ago . . . it's all happened. Merle, don't you *remember*?"

"Oh God, Bonnie," I said, as I got up and walked to the window. I looked out at the mountains and the canyon where I'd fished with my father as a boy. I just couldn't believe things had changed so much. When did all this happen? I was standing in a million dollar house we'd built by the Kern River just outside of Bakersfield and I still had the same feelings and fears I'd always had. Hell, it didn't seem like that long ago that I'd stood in a diner and agonized over spending an extra *nickel* for a cup of hot chocolate.

"Bonnie," I said, turning back toward her. Her head was down and I hoped to God she wasn't crying. "Bonnie I want you to do whatever makes you happy now. . . ."

"This is not somethin' I've just decided to do," she said. "I've thought about it a lot. It's just somethin' I *have* to do at this time and I hope you understand."

I did understand. There was still so much we couldn't say, even after all we'd been through together. There was still no talk about separation or divorce. We were just taking one step at a time.

"Merle," she said then. "Do you remember when you asked me what I was thinkin' about durin' the ceremony and I told you I thought you might change your mind?"

"I remember."

"Well, that was true," she said. "I was bein' totally realistic about our relationship, even then. I know that for the first few years I was number one in your life, but after that, there must have been several ahead of me. Still, I was happy that you loved me in your own way, and I know you did. I had planned in the beginnin' to be prepared for our marriage to last three weeks, three years, or whatever time. I've always been prepared for it to end—but never have I been ready for our friendship to end."

SING ME BACK HOME

"No need to worry about that, Bonnie," I said. "No matter what happens you're my good friend."

"Your good friend needs a rest," she said.

"You've got it," I told her. "But if you think you'll get any kind of rest with this lively bunch . . . "

"Me and the kids will do just fine," she said. "But Merle, there's one more thing I want from you."

"Name it," I said.

"I don't want to know anythin' about the road. I don't want you comin' home discussin' the shows . . . nothin'. I just want to be totally removed from it all for awhile."

"All right," I said. "I'll leave the road out there when I come home."

So, Bonnie and I became "just friends" again. When I'd come in off the road she'd be there. We'd talk about the kids, the price of eggs, whatever married people talk about. But we never talked about the road or what was going on. At night we shared the same bed without touching.

As Bonnie told me from the beginning, she expected there'd be other women in my life, and on the surface that never seemed to affect our relationship.

One woman, however, affected *everything*.

It was easy to understand why I was attracted to her. God, every man in the country was hot for her—they still are. I thought I was *different*. I was fool enough to believe that she loved me back. Even now my pride won't let me believe that she didn't—just a little bit.

I didn't just fall in love with the image of Dolly Parton. Hell, I fell in love with that exceptional human being who lives underneath all that bunch of fluffy hair, fluttery eyelashes, and super boobs. I was like a schoolboy. I would have carved "Merle loves Dolly" on every damn tree in the country if she'd asked me to.

We'd been booked on several tours together, and because of our love for the business, and what seemed to be our own little mutual admiration society, we began to spend more and more time together on the road. If she wasn't on my bus, then I was on hers. The roads between one date and the next never rolled off so damn fast.

Even now, my favorite image of America's sweetheart is not all that glitter and show, but the kidlike creature who used to sit herself down on a pillow on the floor of my bus aisle, lay her head on my knees, and talk on and on about her dreams and that plan of hers to be a STAR.

"I've always wanted to be somebody, Merle," she said, and I told her she'd be somebody no matter what she did. She was important as a person—as a human being.

"I'm gonna be a star though," she said. "I mean, in every sense of the word. I made up my mind a long time ago, and that's the way it's gonna be."

She was so sure of herself, so positive, and God, she just glowed with confidence and excitement when she talked about her plans. There was no way to listen to her and doubt her ability to succeed. Dolly Parton is sure not what the public sees—there is just so much more to the lady than that. I felt almost honored to be in the presence and see the "real" Dolly. I got the feeling she was afraid to show this side of herself to too many people. It was clear that she'd been hurt and betrayed more than once.

"Nothin' is gonna stand in my way," she told me again and again. Sometimes there were tears in those great eyes of hers. It was both a statement and a kind of warning when she'd say it.

"Sometimes it's so hard to get people to understand," she'd say, "that there's nothin' wrong with feelin' the way I do." I'd tell her I loved her but it never seemed to give her any comfort. Instead, it seemed to disturb her more and more until she began to move away from me. The more she retreated the more I advanced until I was doing crazy, stupid things. I even began to feel I was really losing my grip on everything. I didn't give a damn. All I could think about was Dolly.

When I'd go home, I didn't discuss the road with Bonnie, but I think that woman could read my mind most of the time. She knew me so well. In time we began to discuss divorce. By the middle of 1975 Bonnie filed for legal separation.

"I'm not ready for a divorce at this time, Merle," she said. "When I close the door between us as man and wife, I've got to make sure I'm ready to seal it up for good."

"Whatever you think, Bonnie." Hell, I couldn't think straight about nothin'.

Dolly wouldn't even come close to discussing any kind of future with me. It was as though it was all an impossible dream—of mine.

"I'm married, Merle," she said over and over. "Don't you understand that I *love* Carl? I really *do*."

No, I couldn't understand. I loved Bonnie, too, but if Dolly would just talk to me about us, we could work everything out.

"I love my music, too," she'd say then. "I've got to do what I set out to do. Don't you hear me when I say that nothin' and *nobody* is gonna stand in my way? I don't wanna hurt nobody Merle, but if I don't sing my songs and follow my dreams, then I ain't nothin'. What you claim to love wouldn't even exist anymore if I couldn't be me."

I understood a little.

Still, I couldn't get her off my mind. I'd see her when I walked out on stage, when I lay down at night, and when I woke up in the morning. I'd try to blot her out of my mind with all the well-known blotters. Nothing worked.

Sometimes I'd even remember her the way she looked the first time I saw her. It was way back in the 1960's. I worked her home town of Sevierville, Tennessee, and she was just local talent. She was a cute little thing with a little-girl voice and a talent that had no limits. I thought she was best when she worked on stage alone, just her and her guitar. I still like Dolly like that. I think we all, including Dolly, lost a lot in the country field when she made changes.

Of course I never could see too clear when it came to Dolly, and I've no right to say how she handles her life or her career. At one point somebody said Dolly was telling around Nashville that she was afraid of me. I never knew if she thought I was a threat to her marriage, her career, or just to her. It might have been a combination of all three.

I can understand why she thought I might be a threat to her marriage. I didn't always use good sense. One night I remember stands out as a good example of my bad timing.

"Let me talk to Dolly," I snapped at the voice answering the telephone.

"It's three o'clock in the mornin'," came the sleepy answer. I figured I was talking to her housekeeper.

"Hell, I didn't call up to find out what time it is," I hollered. "Why is it when you call somebody in the middle of the night they ask you if you know what time it is? If I wanna know the time I'll look at a clock, dammit. Lemme talk to Dolly."

"She's asleep."

"Then wake her up."

"I can't do that," the voice said.

"Wake her up!" I was demanding. There was silence on the other end for awhile. Then she came back.

"I can't wake her up," the voice said again. "She's under the covers, head and all . . . way down at the foot of the bed. She won't answer. I can't wake her up."

Damn you Dolly. You know it's me, don't you?

"This is Merle Haggard." I tried to sound as threatening as I could. "If you don't wake her up and get her to the phone right now, I'm comin' over there and talk to her in person. I'm talkin' to her tonight . . . one way or another."

SING ME BACK HOME

I didn't see no point in tellin' her I was in Reno. After several minutes and some mumbling in the background she got on the phone. I knew before she spoke that it was Dolly on the other end. I could feel her right through the telephone wires.

"What is it, Merle?" She sounded a little scared.

"I wrote you a song, babe . . . ," I said. I started feeling a little foolish. I wondered if the song I'd been so pleased with was gonna hold up when I sung it for her. I couldn't hear nothin' on the other end, so I reached for the joint I'd been smoking and took another drag. I tried to imagine what she'd look like holding the phone while some crazy man on the other end talked about a song he'd wrote for her.

"Are you ready to hear the song, Dolly?"

"It's three o'clock in the mornin', Merle."

"If I want to know what time it is, I'll look at a clock," I said. "Now do you wanna hear my song or not?"

"What's the matter with you, Merle?" she asked then. I couldn't hear the fear any longer. She'd gathered up her strength.

"You're the matter with me, Dolly," I said. "You know that."

"Merle we've been all through this . . . there's no . . . "

I stopped her. I didn't want to hear what she was gonna say. I knew it by heart. There was nothing between us . . . never had been . . . never would be. . . .

"Dolly, listen to my song." Hell, I was almost begging. "I wrote it for you. I been sittin' here in this goddamned hotel room with my grass and my guitar and I wrote one of the dangest songs you ever heard. I want you to be the first one to hear it. It's the *least* you can do, Dolly, hell, it's your song. It's about my feelin's for you."

"All right." I could tell that she was just humoring me. She knew neither of us would get any rest till she let me sing my song.

254

Endings and Beginnings

I propped the phone on the side of the bed and scooted in as close as I could with my guitar.

> *"Always wantin' you . . . but never havin' you . . .*
> *makes it hard to face tomorrow . . .*
> *'cause I know I'll wake up wantin' you again . . .*
> *Always lovin' you . . . but never touchin' you . . .*
> *Sometimes it hurts me more than I can stand . . . "*

I would have given anything to have seen her face. Then I'd know what she thought, what she felt about the song—and me. All I could do was stare into the black plastic receiver connecting us together.

> *"I'd been better off . . . if I'd turned away*
> *. . . and never looked at you . . .*
> *the second time . . .*
> *'cause I really had my life together . . .*
> *'til your eyes met mine . . .*
> *then I saw a yearnin' and a feelin' 'cross*
> *the room . . . that you felt for me . . .*
> *Wish I'd had a way of knowin' . . .*
> *that the things we had in mind . . .*
> *could never be . . . "*

By the time I finished, my mind had cancelled out on me. I don't even remember what she said, if anything. Long after she hung up, I sat holding the receiver in my hand. Finally I was aware of another voice.

"Sir, this is the operator. You've been disconnected."

You got that right, lady.

I don't know how long I stayed crazy for Dolly, but it was quite awhile. It's damned embarrassing to talk about it, but if I leave it out I'll be accused of coverin' up, and I sure as hell wouldn't want to be accused of coverin' up Dolly Parton.

But you know what they say. Life goes on. Little by little I faced the fact that Dolly really meant it when she said there was no future for us. But hell, what did I care, I still had my music and one of the best danged songs I'd ever written.

What I needed then, I decided, was a singer to take Bonnie's place on the road. A girl singer, of course.

Several years before I'd heard a voice on the radio. And at the time I'd asked somebody who she was. I was told that her name was Leona Williams and she was from Missouri. I couldn't help but wonder what she looked like. If she looked half as good as she sounded, I knew she'd be a knockout.

So when I began to think about a new singer on the road, Leona Williams was one of the first to come to my mind. As luck would have it, Ronnie Reno knew her pretty well and offered to call her one night when we were in Nashville. She'd just gotten a divorce, he told me, and had three kids to raise.

"She's quite a fan of yours," Ronnie said, "and you won't find a better singer in this town than Leona Williams."

"Call her," I said, "and ask her to meet us at Ireland's." Ireland's was a restaurant right in the Music Row area.

While waiting for her to come through the door I tried to imagine how she'd look. I hadn't even seen a picture of her. When I tried to put a face with the voice, I drew a blank. I wasn't prepared for the lady who walked in at all.

She appeared taller than she really was because she stood so straight and held that chin up in the air. She looked proud, handsome, and strong. I liked those qualities, but what I liked best was the way she looked at me.

She looked me straight in the eye in such an honest way that it kinda threw me off. There was none of the cutesy stuff and flirting even though I felt like she was attracted to me. I knew this wasn't just another "girl singer" I could con into toeing the mark and warming the sheets. Leona Belle Williams was different—hell, she was fantastic. Besides that, she had more talent, I found out later, than any ten women I'd met.

Leona was almost too good to be true, I thought. I remember telling myself not to lose my head again so soon. I wasn't really over Dolly yet, but across the table from me in Ireland's sat some of the best medicine in the world.

There was no question about it, right from the first meeting. Leona was gonna be part of my life. I didn't know exactly how much she would come to mean to me, but I knew, sure as hell, she'd be somethin' special.

I studied her pretty close. There was a cautious edge to her voice, and it was easy to see that, like me, she was coming off an experience that had left her hurting. But she could laugh, and that impressed me. She had the kind of laugh that made everybody around her want to laugh too. I sure did need to laugh. I'd almost forgot how.

I wanted to say right off, "I *like* you, Leona Belle," but all I did was talk about music and look at her a lot. I couldn't help noticing how she kept pushing her dark hair back out of her face and how she seemed a little nervous. I hoped it was because of me. Wonder what she'd do, I thought, if I just blurted out that I wanted her even then. I figured she might just walk out the door and never come back. I sure didn't want that. I knew that much.

Finally, we said good night and I told her I'd call her about the show.

"You do that," she said as she headed toward the door. I sure as hell would do that.

In fact, it was the early hours of the following morning that I did that, or had Ronnie do it. I was in the studio, doing a session.

"Call Leona," I told him. "See if she'll come down here to the studio and put some harmony on that last song."

A little bit later Ronnie came running back in the studio and asked me to guess who had just pulled up in the parking lot. Since it was too soon for Leona, I figured only one other person could cause that much excitement. It was Dolly.

"How about that?" I said.

If heads don't turn when Dolly comes through a door then you might as well call the undertaker. If she's in a room, all attention just naturally turns in her direction.

"How ya doin' Dolly?" I said as she walked into the control room.

"Fine Merle, and you?"

"Doin' good," I answered, and realized I wasn't just making conversation. I *was* doin' good.

Then the door behind her opened and in walked Leona. I didn't try to hide my pleasure at seeing her, and in fact, probably went a little overboard in my greetings to her. My act was not lost on Dolly. Leona seemed unaware of any tension in the air at first.

So I stood there for awhile in the same room with two of the most beautiful women I've ever seen. I'd be lying if I said I didn't enjoy the situation. Neither of the women seemed comfortable and I liked that. If I'd been the gentleman I should have been I wouldn't have enjoyed the tension between them, but shit, there were two great looking ladies and I think I was on *both* their minds. It was quite an ego trip.

Although Leona told me later she and Dolly had always been pretty good friends, this night they didn't seem friendly at all. So, I did what any red-blooded male would have done. I played one against the other. I did everything I could to stir the two of them up—hoping I guess to make the other one jealous. Rotten thing to do. I loved it.

During a break from the session, I walked over to Dolly,

looped my arm through hers, and pulled her toward the door.

"Let's get some fresh air," I said. As I walked past Leona, I put my other arm around her shoulder and pulled her along, too.

"Come on, Leona," I said. "Let's all go outside."

I didn't have to look around to know that there wasn't a man in that studio who wouldn't have died to be in my place. Behind me I heard somebody say "son of a bitch" under his breath.

As we walked out into the alley, I could feel Dolly tense up. Leona, who was not sure what was happening, was a little more relaxed. In a few minutes Dolly, who hadn't had much to say, excused herself, remembering some place she had to be.

Then she was gone. I turned to Leona. My arm was still around her shoulder. I leaned over and kissed her on the cheek.

"Thank you," I said. She turned those blue-green eyes on me with that unbelievable look of sex and innocence mixed, and asked me what for.

"For settin' me free," I told her.

"I didn't do nothin' . . . ," she said, but she was grinning.

"I know," I said, taking her by the hand as we walked back into the studio, "but you will, babe, you will. . . . "

259

Sixteen

Leona Belle Williams

It's all in the movies,
   It can't happen to us I know,
It's all in the movies,
   Just a sad picture show . . .

"It's All in the Movies"   by Merle Haggard
                                              & Kelli Haggard

WELL, THERE IT WAS in the local newspaper in Lake
Tahoe. It said I was marrying a former backup singer in my
group. Hell, Leona was gonna love that, I thought. She'd
spent more than fifteen years in a business that still hadn't
given her her due and now some half-assed writer was
calling her a "former backup singer," like that's all she'd
ever done.

They were also making a big deal about Bonnie Owens,
"my former wife" serving as bridesmaid. What was so damn
unusual about that? It's true, I'd never heard of it. I hadn't

even seen it in the movies, but I didn't think it was all that newsworthy. Bonnie was, after all, a member of my family and it was only right that she share what was going to be one of the happiest days of my life.

I stuffed the newspaper into a wastebasket. No point in upsetting Leona this close to the wedding. God knows there was enough happening all around to drive us all up the wall, including side bets among the invited guests as to how long this marriage would last.

Our decision to get married hadn't been an easy one. It had been an on-again, off-again deal several times. From that first meeting back in Nashville, till the wedding day, October 7, 1978, we'd had more than our share of disagreements. That's putting it very nicely.

Leona Williams had been good for me, though, in spite of our clashes. I felt we had something going that could very well be the answer to a lot of things for both of us. She hadn't had an easy time in her life either, and since our feelings for each other were so strong we figured together we could set a lot of things right.

She had joined my road show, partly because she was the best talent I could find and partly because—well hell, I wanted to get in her pants. Besides, she was sure curing me of the feeling I had for Dolly Parton. That took a lot of woman.

As for Dolly, I don't know if she ever loved me or not. The songwriter would like to think she did. I found it hard to believe that face could look me straight in the eye and talk about life and love the way she did and not mean a word of it. I don't believe she's that good of an actress—but if she is—look out Hollywood!

After that night at the recording studio, I only saw her once when there was time for us to talk. She came on my bus between shows one night but we were both at a loss for words, which was sure unusual for Dolly. All the ease and comfort we'd shared in the past was gone. It was understood then that Leona had become important in my life. Dolly knew that, and I'd like to think she came on the bus to wish me well. She stood in the aisle and talked for only a few minutes. Then she said she had to leave. She got to the door before she turned around.

"I love you, Merle," she said in that direct way she had. I couldn't tell if it was just one of those friendship feelings or if it was more than that. I didn't know what to say, and when I looked at her closer I could see the tears rolling down her face. I knew then I was looking at one hell of a special human being. I felt proud to have been even a small part of her life, and I knew that determination of hers would take her any place she wanted to go. I watched her from the bus window, and she never looked back once. They say that's the way you can tell somebody has gone for good. I knew then that's what I wanted. It was best for her and it was best for me. I'd been fascinated by her, believed I loved her for awhile, but then what man who's ever seen her up close don't?

There was no question about my feelings for Leona. For what I thought was the first time in my life, I believed I was completely in love with a woman. It wasn't that first love kind of thing I had with my first Leona. It wasn't the comfort I felt with Bonnie. It wasn't that one-night fling I'd repeated over and over. It was real, and I hoped to God I could get it right this time.

I believed she felt the same way about me.

One thing I didn't believe though was that myth about "living happily ever after." Me and Leona were a long way away from agreeing on everything. I'd reached the point in my career where I felt in charge of my music. Nobody in my group argued with me much except Fuzzy, and we always worked things out. When Leona tried to make a suggestion, I resented it. She resented my resentment. So it went. She kept saying she felt like an outsider. I couldn't understand what she was talking about.

I couldn't understand why she got so upset by the press leaning toward good ol' Bonnie and the snide remarks about Leona coming in and breaking up my "happy home."

"Why don't you tell them how it really was?" she'd say. "Tell them I didn't break up your marriage to Bonnie. Everybody goes around sayin' how happy you were till I came along. They're callin' me all kinds of things, Merle, and I hate what they think of me. You don't understand how that makes me feel."

She was right. I didn't. It was no big deal.

I also resented her struggle to establish her own career. After all, I could offer her a permanent place on the stage with my show. She could even have a segment all her own. What *more* could she want?

"I'll always be just a backup singer in your band," she said. "Some of these people don't remember—or maybe they never even knew—that I have a career of my own. It hurts me real bad. I'm playin' to your fans, Merle. They love you and they love Bonnie. They *hate* me. I can feel it."

They didn't hate her. She was talented and she'd go out on stage and knock 'em dead. Still, if there was any negative feeling out there at all, she'd pick up on it.

So, she was hurt often, and she'd hurt me. I'd hurt her back and she'd return the favor. She'd hear the snickers and talk about "that ol' girl Merle's foolin' around with," and the whispers about "pore ol' Bonnie standin' up there singin' behind Merle with a broken heart . . . what a woman!"

"Do you know what one of the guys in the band said about us?" she asked me one day, and she was crying. I shook my head.

"He said if we wasn't fightin' we was . . . uh, you know. . . . " I couldn't help it, I laughed. That hurt her even more.

SING ME BACK HOME

Well, hell, it was funny, and it was almost true for awhile. Leona stood up to me when others wouldn't. She argued with me, sometimes telling me what I could do and where I could go. I'd give her the same general instructions. I hated her for the disruptions she caused in my life and loved her for being herself. There was no pretense about her but she was forever changing. I never knew from one minute to the next what her mood would be. She said the same about me. Our moods hardly ever hit the top together. But when they did, gangbusters! God, I'd never felt that way about nobody. I couldn't even *explain* it, much less understand it.

During all the time we had together there was hardly ever time alone. Only once did we share a time that was just about perfect. In fact, even now when I think about it, it hardly seems real. I wasn't used to things working out so right for me.

We went up to my houseboat on Lake Shasta, near Redding. That's one of the few places I feel I can get away from everything even now. It was winter time, and I can't describe how beautiful it was. There was nobody around and it seemed like we were the last two people left on Earth.

We spent thirteen days together. No phone. No interruptions. No kids. No shows. And no arguments. Just thirteen of the most beautiful and indescribable days and nights I've ever spent. Hell, I don't know, maybe a man shouldn't expect no more outta life than that.

Sometimes we just sat and talked. Other times we played like a couple of kids. She went out on the deck one morning and scooped up a big bowl of fresh snow.

"What are you doing?" I asked when she came back inside.

"I'm gonna make you some snow cream," she said. "Some good cold snow cream like I used to make when I was a kid back in Missouri. You California kids missed all the good stuff." I didn't agree with her about that, but I didn't argue.

She got some milk out of the refrigerator, put in some sugar and vanilla flavoring, and stirred it up.

I couldn't believe how good it was. She fed me spoon after spoonful of the cold snow cream. We laughed at how crazy we both were. I never see fresh snow that I don't remember that time.

When we went back to civilization, our problems were waiting for us. That crazy stubborn Missouri woman had a lot of strange ideas. Well, they must have been strange, they were different from mine. She *loved* Nashville. I hated it. She dreamed of being a member of the Grand Ole Opry. I told her she was a danged fool. I loved California. Leona hated it. She said it was too far from home. Hell, it *was* home.

We'd break up, both saying that was it. Then we'd get back together and in spite of the pain we'd caused each other, the feelings were stronger between us than ever.

We'd talk about getting married and everybody would say it would never happen—and wouldn't last if it did. This hurt her even more.

We finally decided if we got married maybe it would shut everybody up. Leona would no longer feel like an outsider, and we could start building a life together with her children, Kathy, Ronnie, and Brady Lee, along with my son Noel, who was living with me. We honestly believed we could make it work if we set our hard heads to it.

We didn't do it halfway either. We decided we'd have ourselves a big wedding, proving once and for all we were danged serious.

Now this whole wedding scene may seem totally out of character with the rest of my life, but I'm telling you it was the prettiest thing I've ever seen. As ridiculous as it sounds,

SING ME BACK HOME

I felt like I was in the middle of one of them storybook deals. I swear it was like a scene from *Dr. Zhivago*.

The wedding had been planned by Stu and Lorrie Carnell at their home in Gardenerville, just outside of Reno. The setting was also right out of the movies. It was the old Crosby ranch and Lorrie had the wedding party stand in the back yard by a trout stream, surrounded by flowers and greenery, while we waited for the horse-drawn carriage to bring the bride.

Hell, what would the gang at Bunkie's drive-in think of this? Some of 'em were there of course, and still making bets we'd never bring it off.

The weather was even perfect, and with the Sierra Nevada mountains in the background, I expected someone to yell "action" any minute.

All kinds of thoughts were going through my head as we stood there waiting for Leona. I hadn't seen her in over a week, and I felt exactly like I believed a bridegroom ought to feel. Hell, this was the first time I'd even thought of myself as a "bridegroom." I doubt if I'd ever used the word before.

I couldn't help remembering the day I'd first seen Stu and Lorrie back in San Quentin with the Cash show. How far we'd all come. I glanced around me at my band family and my natural family, and in spite of what anybody thought, I felt I was doing the right thing.

I looked over at Stu's mother, Mary Carnell, and she smiled at me. I felt even better. Mary and I had long had our own little mutual admiration deal going. She was getting way along in years and I knew we probably wouldn't have her around too much longer. Just before the ceremony she'd told me she wanted me to sing at her funeral services. There was nothing sad about the way she asked. She was just making her plans ahead of time. I kissed her and told her I would but I'd probably be an old man by that time. She laughed, but she knew better. Less than a year later I was standing in church singing "Swing Low Sweet Chariot" for Mary Carnell.

But on this day of mine she had stood there smiling—approving of my choice and decision. That meant a lot to me.

I looked down the road and saw the carriage coming. Even the horse, jet black and stepping high, was perfect. All at once though, he balked. I could hear mumbles in the crowd.

"Now's your chance to run . . . "

"Looks like Leona's changed her mind."

"The horse knows more than anybody . . . "

He straightened up though and galloped on up to the edge of the yard. When Leona stepped down from the carriage I just about lost my breath. I'd never seen anybody so beautiful. She came across the lawn toward me and I thought about the snow cream. I smiled at her and she smiled back.

The ceremony started.

"Mama, I'm sick." It was Brady Lee. Leona reached down to comfort him, and when she did, he sat down on the edge of her dress. She couldn't stand up straight after that so she had to hunker over for the rest of the ceremony.

After the final words from the minister, Rose Maddox began to sing and play the guitar. Her voice was still strong and clear as she sang "You Light Up My Life."

I looked at Leona and she was crying. Hell, I was crying, too.

From another direction then came the sound of a bass fiddle as Fred Maddox broke loose with "If You've Got the Hoss, I've Got the Saddle." And everybody started laughing.

We walked out to the front of the house where my friend Doug Butler had parked Leona's wedding present.

"Well, there it is, Leona," I said, pointing to the bright red

SING ME BACK HOME

Lincoln coupe. She hollered like a kid and hugged me. "You know how I love red cars," she said. "Oh thank you. I love it. I love you."

"Think it'll make a good honeymoon car?"

"Let's find out," she answered.

We drove back up to our hotel at Lake Tahoe, packed our clothes for the trip we'd planned across the country, and headed back down the mountain on the other side.

Coming down the mountain I pointed out Stu and Lorrie's ranch to her.

"Let's stop by and thank them again for the wedding," I said. "We won't stay long." Leona agreed.

"Do you feel married?" I asked her then. She nodded and moved over closer to me.

"I know you think it's silly," she said, "but I was never comfortable before. I wasn't brought up to just live with somebody and not be married. I didn't like what my friends were sayin' about me, how I'd changed."

"If they were your friends, Leona," I said, "they'd only want you to be happy."

"Well, maybe," she said, "but at least this way maybe people will stop treatin' me like I was some kind of trash."

"Nobody thought that, Leona."

"Don't you believe it," she said. "I could *feel* it."

"All in your mind, babe," I said, as I pulled into Stu's driveway.

There were still several people at the Carnell house. Grady Martin was out in the front yard looking over a silver Trans-Am I'd just sold him. One of Leona's friends, Susie Lepner, was still there. She lived in Denver, and everybody got to calling her "Susie-from-Denver" at the reception and it stuck.

I looked up on the front porch, and there was a kid named Auben. He was staying with Stu and Lorrie for some reason. He was only about five years old and the craziest little dude you ever saw. Him and Stu had this rapport going that was completely out of the ordinary for a man and a child. Of course Stu wasn't really an ordinary person and neither was Auben. Auben did have good taste though. He'd decided the first time he saw Leona that he was in love. The little dude cussed like a sailor every time he opened his mouth, and I must say Stu didn't do much to discourage him.

We had said our thank-yous and were heading for the car when Stu mentioned something about going fishing. I stopped and looked back at him.

"You know, that's not a bad idea," I said. "Maybe me and Leona will go along too." I looked at her and she just grinned. She knew me pretty well but she was still not sure I was serious.

"Well, if you're goin' fishin', you old gray-haired son of a bitch, I'm goin' too," came this little voice from the porch.

"No you're not, you little turd," Stu yelled back at him. "One reason I'm goin' is to get away from you."

"Well, I'm goin'," Auben said, "and I'm ridin' in the car with *her*." He pointed to Leona.

By the time our honeymoon caravan left the Carnell ranch, it consisted of Stu, Grady, Susie-from-Denver (who'd never been on a honeymoon before), the bride, the groom, and sweet little Auben.

"Goddamn," I said, as I looked down at the kid wedged in the front seat between me and Leona. "If I'da wanted a kid along on our honeymoon, I'da brought one of ours. Lord knows, we've got enough between us." There was no talking him into riding in Stu's pickup or Grady's Trans-Am. He'd found his place and he wasn't budging from it.

We stopped by a sporting goods store and bought about nine hundred dollars worth of fishing and camping equipment. Hell, it cost me more than the bridal suite at Harrah's, but of course it was worth it. No point in being cheap on a honeymoon.

SING ME BACK HOME

Even the trip out to the fishing place was nothing short of ridiculous. We stopped in a little town to get a drink and our presence there caused all kinds of commotion. They must have thought we were some kind of gangsters considering the crowd we collected while we played a little poker in one of the local taverns. I guess we were a pretty strange looking bunch.

By the time we got to the river I didn't care if I never saw another fish. I'd lost all interest in this expedition, and we were all tired and worn out.

"I'm hungry," Auben said. For once I agreed with the little squirt. Stu said he'd build a campfire if Auben would carry the wood. Grady took his fishing pole and went off downstream so the trip wouldn't be a total waste. Susie-from-Denver crawled in the back of the Lincoln and went to sleep.

"Let's put our sleepin' bags in the back of Stu's pickup," I said to Leona. "We may not get much sleep but at least we can watch the entertainment."

"Entertainment?" she asked.

"Stu and Auben fixin' a campfire breakfast," I said, pointing down toward the two of them who were already screaming all kinds of things at each other.

We put our sleeping bags side by side in the back of the truck and it was almost daylight by the time we'd got ourselves zipped into them.

"I wonder if they have honeymoon sleepin' bags," Leona said, looking over at me.

"Well, if they do," I said as I pulled one arm free from the bag and reached over toward her, "this ain't them."

"Hurry up, you little varmint," Stu called out to Auben. Auben told him what he could do with himself. Leona started laughing, and it was catching. We both lay there and laughed till our sides hurt.

It wasn't long till we could smell the bacon frying. I saw Stu squat down to turn it. He only had a plastic fork and the minute he touched the skillet, it melted. The smell was awful.

"Yuk, what have you done, you old bastard?" Auben yelled as he threw down another load of brush. Stu told him to shut up or he'd throw him in the river.

Just about that time one of the sticks in the campfire popped and shot a charcoal right over the top of Stu's head. He had on a green baseball cap with the bill pointing straight up and the coal came so close that it knocked it off. That scared Stu and made him mad at the same time. He started picking up all the stuff around him and throwing it in the river. First went the skillet with the plastic fork stuck to it, then the camping gear, the eggs and the rest of the bacon. All this time Auben jumped up and down screaming names and threatening to die of hunger. It was a threat Stu seemed to welcome.

"Can you believe this?" Leona said, as she raised up on her elbows and looked at the scene in front of us.

"What in the world is going on?" came the sleepy voice of Susie-from-Denver.

"Breakfast has been cancelled," I hollered back at her.

"This is crazy," she said. "What kind of a honeymoon is this anyway?"

"Why it's perfectly normal," I told her and Leona started laughing again. "This is the way *all* honeymoons are."

"Well, I've sure not missed nothin', have I?" she said, as she lay back down in the car.

From down the river we could see Grady coming back with his fishing pole and nothing to show for his efforts.

"Didn't get nothin', huh?" I called out as me and Leona crawled out of our sleeping bags. He shook his head.

"Well, they're all probably up here eatin' our breakfast bacon." I pointed toward the river where both Stu and Auben were sitting on the bank looking like they wanted to jump in.

"Leona Belle," I said then. "What would you say to

getting out of this crazy place and finding us somewhere where we can have breakfast in bed?"

"That sounds great," she said, holding out her hand. I took it and we made a run toward the car.

"Move out, Susie," I said, "we're leavin'."

As we got in the car I heard Auben holler for us to wait, but we didn't answer. We sure didn't stop.

As we took off across the desert away from the river, I looked over at Leona. Her hair was messed up, there were smudges on her face, and her makeup was all gone. She didn't look at all like the woman who'd stepped out of the carriage the day before—but she was just as pretty—maybe even more so.

"Well, the honeymoon's over," I said.

"Yeah, and everybody said it wouldn't last."

"I think they meant the marriage, babe."

"Well then," she grinned, "let's just show 'em."

We rode on down the road a little farther and I reached over for her hand.

"It ain't gonna be easy, girl," I said.

"It ain't been so far," she answered.

"But you love me, don't you?"

"I sure do," she said.

"Well, better hold on tight. It might be a rough road up ahead."

She squeezed my hand. She knew I wasn't talking about the desert road we were driving over right then.

She leaned her head against my shoulder and closed her eyes. I hoped this was as right as I felt like it was.

In the rear-view mirror, all I could see was a bunch of dust. Up ahead, hell, I didn't know. I was never one to look too far ahead. . . .

Epilogue

AROUND ME NOW I hear voices and people laughing. I reach out and touch the seat beside me. It's empty.

I am aware of all the activity around me but I feel very much isolated from it. Sometimes—no matter where I am and how far I've come—I still feel the chill of that danged fog rollin' in off the bay. Then I'm back there again in that nine-by-five room surrounded by all my doubts.

From the window of Harrah's private jet I can tell that we're still climbing. Below me I can still see the lights from "the biggest little city in the world," Reno, Nevada.

It's the early morning of July 3, 1980. I can see daylight beginning to show across the mountains in front of us. Ahead is Austin, Texas, where the Willie Nelson picnic is already in full swing. Another day—another show.

To my left I can see Pyramid Lake, and I can't help but think about all the different ways I've left Reno. Sometimes I've left with that feeling only a winner has, other times like a down-and-out loser. This morning, strangely enough, I feel neither one of those. I'm just leaving Reno behind.

I've been up all night unwinding from what has been another of those seesaw weeks in my life. It's been great professionally. The crowds and I, at Harrah's club, have given as much as we could to each other. Every night I've left the stage feeling like we've done better than the night before. The band felt it, too. It's not only left us satisfied, but proud. In a business where it's quite normal to have things go wrong, it's great to have everything go as right as it has this week.

Offstage, things ain't been so great.

We're flying at about sixteen thousand feet now, and if I tried real hard I could almost see the ranch where Leona and I were married about a year and a half ago. In one way it seems like just a few days—the fishing trip—the laughing, and the good times. Then again, it seems like a lifetime. So damn much has happened and a lot of it's been bad. We've tried—God knows we've tried—but too many things keep getting in our way. There was a time when we couldn't get enough of each other. Now sometimes a little bit is too much.

God, I miss that woman so damn bad when she's not with me. If she could only be here this morning, sitting beside me, we could talk. But she left yesterday on an early morning flight to Missouri. Her sister-in-law is dying of cancer and Leona is really tore up about it. If I could only be there, beside her, maybe I could be some comfort, but I've got a show to do in Austin. And so, hell, here we are again, in different parts of the country for different reasons.

Things between us are at an all-time low, and I don't know what to do. We just can't figure out how to work things out. I need her in my corner all the time, and she needs me in hers. Trouble is, our corners are usually at different parts of the country.

The plane has leveled off now and I can see some of the clouds breaking away. Looks like it's gonna be a pretty day after all. It rained all day in Reno yesterday, which didn't do a hell of a lot for my frame of mind. But late in the afternoon there was a big double rainbow over the city. I hoped it was some kind of a good sign, but it'll probably turn out to be just another line in a song sometime.

I wish to hell I didn't feel so alone. I'm surrounded by my band family—but with all due respect to their good company, I don't know when I've ever felt so lonely. To make matters even worse, Tuffy, my little dog, is not even with me. She went on to Cody, Wyoming, with Fuzzy on one of the busses. It was just too hot down in Texas to risk her getting sick. Louie took the other bus on to Austin, and Tex had to fly off in the direction of Nashville to take care of some kind of business.

I thought sure there'd be a note from Leona when I got up this morning, but there wasn't. Maybe she felt like there was nothin' we hadn't already said.

Hell, I can't sit here and look out the window of this damned airplane. I've got to get up and move around.

"Hey, you ugly bunch," I call out to the band. "I'm gonna walk up and down the aisle and look you all over." Stu Carnell, with his yellow T-shirt and red suspenders, shakes his head and waves in my direction.

"Now, if you all ain't a sorry lookin' bunch," I say to nobody in particular. Ronnie is trying to figure up how much everybody lost at Harrah's and says there oughta be a floor named after us by the next time we come back. Roy and Don are both reading something, and most of the others are sleeping.

"Four hundred chickens just died from the heat in Texas," Stu informs me. I feel a little better about Tuffy not being with us.

"You're lookin' pretty good for roarin' all night," I say to my piano player. God, I used to be able to do the same thing. Don't seem like that long ago I was that young and that strong. Hell, I'm not old now—just not *that* young. He opens one eye and grins, then goes back to sleep.

I even have my chiropractor, Doc Benson, on this trip. He's been going along on some of my tours to relieve the pain and stress in my back and neck. Wonder what adjustments he could make on a marriage that's kinda outta line.

I walk by Bonnie and she is looking out the window, lost, I guess, in her own thoughts. I get the feeling she's making some plans of her own, but I'm not sure. The time has long past that I know what Bonnie's thinking the way I used to.

Might as well sit back down.

Since it hurts to think about Leona, I turn my mind toward other people in my life. My children—who are no longer children. Noel, who is almost seventeen, still comes and goes out of my home and my life. He's still growing, and we're still trying to understand each other. Dana has two children now, and even though she's very talented musically, she's chosen the domestic life by becoming Mrs. Alan Stevens. Marty has signed a deal with a recording company, and I hope his music gives him the satisfaction mine has given me. At the same time I hope the rest of his life falls together a little better than mine has. Kelli and I are finally friends. I know we are because she called me not too long ago and told me that. Maybe I was cut out to be a father after all—but only after they're grown-up.

"I'm only eatin' fish and fowl," I tell the stewardess when she mentions food. "I've quit red meat all together and am takin' my vitamins—eatin' a lot of green vegetables, never felt better."

"Well, there's a lot of dead chickens in Texas," some insensitive asshole points out. I don't feel quite so hungry. "I think I'll have some fish," I say.

I can't stop looking out the window. I don't know what in the hell I'll see out there. The *answers*? I'm not even sure of the questions.

One thing I can't see from up here—the future. Putting my head back on the seat and closing my eyes, I can see a lot of the past though.

We won't be flying over Oklahoma this trip, but I know it's still down there. Some of my people, like Escar, are resting there in that Okie soil.

"This was a good and decent man," said the preacher, who held his funeral. "Escar Harp was the kind of man God would like to have around, the kind of man we should all strive to be like. . . . "

What a fitting thing to say. I wish Willie could have been there, but by then she was already in a nursing home. They didn't even tell her Escar had died. She's way past ninety now, and lately I've been feeling like I'd really like to see her again. What I'd really like to do is fry her some fish and make some good homemade biscuits to take to her. They say she don't remember nobody much, but I bet if I did that she'd remember that little ol' boy who used to spend his summers with her and Escar.

And don't nobody laugh about me makin' biscuits, from scratch, too. I *can*. My Missouri Leona taught me that.

Leona. There she is back on my mind again.

I wonder what Mama's doing today. God bless Mama. Didn't that woman really try? Never wrote a song that said the truth any more than "Mama Tried." I think if she lived to be a hundred and fifty, she would never give up believing that there was hope for me. There's a lot to be said for faith like that. She lives right across the street from Lillian, and she remarried a few years ago. Mama don't suffer the hard times like she once did, but I'm sure she worries just the same. It's her nature, I guess, and part of her charm.

Today must be my day for wishing. I wish I had some time to spend with Lillian and Bill. In the past few years I've come to love and understand Lillian a lot more than I used to. There was a time when we weren't close at all, but things have changed. Maybe we've both changed.

There is still a need for running away at times. When this urge strikes, I think about Deanrow and Bob Teague. Those were good old times, but they're long gone now, like Hank and Lefty and dear old Bob Wills.

I still wish I could have talked to Lomar that one last time. I remember the day Lowell took me up to the place where Lomar requested his remains be taken.

"Me and Lomar came up here fishing one time," Lowell said, "and he said then that this place was so pretty that he wanted to be brought here when he died." It was the second time I'd ever seen Lowell cry.

The other time is still hard to think about. But the years have made it easier to remember the man who lead me through the first nine years of my life. There are times now when it's hard to remember the exact sound of his voice, but his face is just as clear in my mind as it ever was. Sometimes it's like he never left me at all. I'm no longer feeling that anger I used to feel because he'd left me. I know he didn't want to go. I also know he gave more in those few years than most fathers are capable of giving their children. Daddy gave me love. Death only took *him* away. He left the love with all of us.

Some of the guys in the band are talking now and I open my eyes. It's back to reality and to the present. It's all anybody's got.

"You got both guitars on the plane, Ronnie?" I call out. He does.

"Where is 'Barroom Buddies' on the charts?" Stu wants to know.

"Hell, I dunno," I say. "Don't talk business today . . . I can't stand it. Besides it's 'Misery and Gin' that'll top the chart."

Leaning out in the aisle, I reach for the guitar. I try not to think about Leona and her jokes about her own guitar pickin'. Ronnie tunes up and we start pickin'. We settle on B-flat. Before we know it we're into an old Ernest Tubb favorite.

"Live and let live . . .
    don't break my heart . . . "

Ronnie joins in the harmony, and it sounds more than all right.

". . . don't leave me here to cry . . . "

"I can't wait to get to Austin," a voice from the front of the plane yells out. "Look out you Texas wimmen . . . !"

"Who was that?" I ask.

"Dunno," Ronnie answers, "but I'm sure it wasn't pore ol' Gordon."

Everybody laughs. Even I laugh.

"I never could live . . . if we should part . . . "

Hell, maybe we oughta take this show on the road. Sounds pretty good. Hear that, Rabbit. I guess a man can do something once he puts his mind to it. Especially if he wants it bad enough to go through the fire to get it. And, brother, I have been through the fire—sometimes fanning the damn flames myself.

". . . tell me you don't mean goodbye."

I never asked for much. Just wanted to pick a little guitar, sing a few songs. Ain't a lot to ask outta life, is it? A little love wouldn't hurt either. Strike that. A little love hurts like hell.

"Next verse, Ronnie . . . "

"Stayed awake last night . . . and walked the floor . . . "

Well, Leona, old girl, if you think I'm giving up without a

fight, you've got another think coming. Anything worth fighting about sure must be worth fighting for. In the meantime, the music's gonna give me some comfort.

I smile to myself. God, there it was again—the absolute magic of the music. How many times have I been washed clean by that sound—taken away by the feeling brought on by an old flat-top guitar and a country song?

Is *this* what I'm all about? I think maybe it is, and I'm not totally displeased with this rather obvious conclusion.

The years roll through my head, and song titles, like signposts, tell about living on the mountain and walking in the valley. From "beer-can hill," the honky-tonks of Bakersfield, the San Quentin yard, to the concert halls and our nation's capital, it's all there. It's been song after song, strung together from the sum total of all I am, all the places I've been, and all the people I've known and loved.

It's been some danged ride—and hey, we're just gettin' up a good head of steam.

"Let's sing right into Texas, Ronnie . . . ," I holler, and we hit the guitars again.

". . . what makes you treat me so . . . "

The music begins to fill all the cracks in my tired mind—touching and healing old wounds and new pain as it eases its way right into the corners of my soul—the way it always has.

The way it always will.

Acknowledgments

OUR AGREEMENT was simple. Before the tape ever rolled on this project, Merle and I sat down and talked about the overwhelming task we were about to tackle.

"I want you to know right off," he said, "that I'm not goin' to stay sober all through the writin' of this book."

"And I want you to know," I told him, "that I am."

We've kept our promises.

When time came to write the acknowledgments, Merle thought I ought to have a go at it—that is, if I can stop thinking in his mind and voice after all this time, and get back to my own conversation.

Danged right I can.

It's not very original or imaginative to say we didn't do this alone—but, we *didn't* do this alone.

Without the help and encouragement of Leona Williams, I might never have been part of this chance of a lifetime for a writer. And, without being aided and abetted by Tex Whitson, we might never have completed the job. It was not an easy task or totally without complications, but the completed work has made it worth it all.

There are so many who helped or were affected by the book that we feel it is necessary to thank them in print.

First of all, to The Strangers, we'd like to offer an apology. Whether they realized it or not, I was very much aware that every time I showed up on the road carrying "all of Merle's past" under my arm, there seemed to be a dark cloud looming over everything. Because of the pain of some of his recollections, your chief's mood was affected from time to time. Therefore everyone began to look upon me as some sort of a harbinger of doom. In spite of that, the cooperation, the kindness, and the acceptance of me by the band was never less than one hundred percent. Most of you began to breathe easier when you were told there wouldn't be a lot of road stories included. However, our idea of compiling a manuscript totally about the music and the band on the road was serious—so don't rest easy yet.

Other members of the "family" were equally important. Thanks to Bonnie Owens, whose recollections were sometimes more concise concerning dates and ages, and whose comments and contributions were much appreciated.

Thanks to Fuzzy Owen for his time and putting up with a writer who never ran out of questions. To Lewis Talley, who is a book unto himself, we offer our sincere gratitude for simply *being*.

To those who offered encouragement during the early days of work, Jackie and Kathy Lee, Judy Whitson, Bob Totten, Margie Miller, Stuart and Jane Taylor, Virginia and Gordon Terry, and Cindy Owens, thanks a whole bunch. Also, we are much indebted to Tom and Madalyne Pauley, in whose home this idea was first discussed several years ago.

To Dean Halloway and Bob Teague, who added much in the way of assistance, and especially for the roles they played in the real life of this book's main character.

To Merle's immediate family, especially Kelli, who wants to be a writer (and should be) but listened as a daughter to the stories of her father's early days—and cried right along with the rest of us.

To Dana, who told of her own feelings about being the child of an entertainer and who, regardless of what her father thinks, has not totally given up the idea of music in her own life.

To Marty and Noel, who have had to stand in the shadow

of their father's past and in the spotlight of his present, this book is offered as a loving legacy.

And to Flossie Haggard Scott—the Mama who really tried again and again. Whatever else we hope to show by this book, it is most of all that she succeeded. We worried about her when we first discussed this project. She will not approve of the language or some of the stories but she admires honesty—and that's what this is. We hope we've shown the strength and beauty of Flossie because above all else she is a woman of amazing character and tenacity. A woman of proud heritage who has never, even in times of much adversity, given up that absolute faith in God's overall plan for mankind—and for her son.

To Lowell, we are grateful for his cooperation and tolerance of being included as one of the prominent people in Merle's life. To Lillian, whose insight into those early years was extremely valuable in our research. Perhaps Lillian, more than anyone, has tried to set the records straight about the many misconceptions of the Haggard family. It is her comments in the photo section of this book that Merle has wanted to read again and again.

So many others had a part in building this book. People like Jerry Bailey and Martha Haggard at MCA Records, Stu Carnell and Candice Pearce, Harrah's in Reno, Billy Deaton, Nashville and New York editors Bob Weil (who did the work of three people and survived one of my stubborn streaks during the line editing) and Jim Fitzgerald.

To my own family, my husband, Kenneth, for telling me I'd never get it done—a great incentive to keep at it. To my daughter, Tina, who had to do much of the housework while I was tied to the typewriter, tape recorder, and telephone. To my son, Troy, who did nothing but make Merle laugh.

To the ones who transcribed tapes ("I can't believe he said *that*") and typed the manuscript ("*Nothing* surprises

SING ME BACK HOME

me now") words can't express our appreciation—which should please you since you expect to be paid. In any case, thanks Virginia Caple, Lorraine Lesney, Sandra Russell, Terri Caple, and Mary Langford.

And, most certainly, thanks to Sandra Palumbo, the lady who holds it all together in Merle's California office. Without her, none of us could ever find anybody else. Unlike the rest of us, Sandra's work will really begin after this book hits the stands. When fans are upset, Sandra comforts. In a recent magazine article it was stated that Merle had smoked pot. One impressionable young fan wrote that she was devastated to learn that her idol had feet of clay. Merle was on tour when the letter came and because of the urgency of the matter, it became Sandra's task to explain the situation to the young girl. Her answer, a portion of which follows, best expresses our feeling about certain reactions we know will come about as a result of Merle's candor:

> Merle is only a man, the same as anyone you know. We tend to idolize him because, through his music and warm manner of singing, he gives each of us something special in our lives. But he is only human, with a private life and problems and joys and sadness, just like you or me. Merle Haggard is great, because in spite of anything he may do and in spite of anything you or I may think, he has written and sung some of the finest songs ever recorded or heard. And that's the part of Merle Haggard that really belongs to you and to me and everyone else who has ever admired him or loved him. His work will stand up to be judged as the finest of our time. So, Audrey, if Merle has been a hero to you and important in your life, you don't have to give that up if he's done something you don't approve of or agree with. Just take those things that are good and positive—and there are so many—and hold

those dear to your heart. They are yours forever. His talent belongs to all of us but his life belongs only to him—and to God.

And so this book stands, not for a judgment, but as a statement concerning a very personal portion of a man's life. It is to this man, Merle Haggard, that I say thank you for the opportunity to share the joy, the pain, the laughter, and the tears of writing this personal account of one of the finest entertainers in the history of country music—and one of the most compelling characters—real or fictional—ever to come hitchhikin' down the pike. . . .

—Peggy Russell

Song Acknowledgments

Permission granted to quote from the following (ALL RIGHTS RESERVED):

"Sing Me Back Home" by Merle Haggard, copyright © 1967 Blue Book Music, Bakersfield, Ca.; "Mama Tried" by Merle Haggard, copyright © 1968 Blue Book Music, Bakersfield, Ca.; "I've Done It All" by Merle Haggard, copyright © 1970 Blue Book Music, Bakersfield, Ca.; "There's a Little Bit of Everything in Texas" by Ernest Tubb, copyright © 1946, copyright renewed, all rights controlled by Unichappel Music, Inc. (Rightsong, Publisher), New York, N.Y., International copyright secured, used by permission; "Always Late With Your Kisses" by Lefty Frizzell and Blackie Crawford, copyright © 1951, copyright renewed, by Hill and Range Songs, Inc., all rights controlled by Unichappel Music, Inc. (Rightsong, Publisher), New York, N.Y., Peer International Corp.; "Your Cheatin' Heart" by Hank Williams, copyright © 1952, copyright renewed 1980, co-published by Fred Rose Music, Inc., Nashville, Tenn., and Hiriam Music, New York, N.Y.; "Our Paths May Never Cross" by Merle Haggard, copyright © 1980 Shade Tree Music, Redding, Ca.; "Hey Good Lookin'" by Hank Williams, copyright © 1951, copyright renewed 1979, co-published by Fred Rose Music, Inc., Nashville, Tenn., and Hiriam Music, New York, N.Y.; "Runnin' Kind" by Merle Haggard, copyright © 1973 Shade Tree Music, Redding, Ca.; "California Blues" by Jimmie Rodgers, copyright © 1929, copyright renewed, Peer International Corp., New York, N.Y.; "You Don't Have Very Far to Go" by Merle Haggard and Red Simpson, copyright © 1964 Owen Publications,

Bakersfield, Ca.; "Keep Me From Cryin' Today" by Merle Haggard, copyright © 1968 Blue Book Music, Bakersfield, Ca.; "Unchained Melody" by H. Zaret and A. North, copyright © 1955 Frank Music Corp., New York, N.Y.; "Sing a Sad Song" by Wynn Stewart, copyright © 1974 Owen Publications, Bakersfield, Ca.; "I'm Movin' On" by Hank Snow, copyright © 1950, copyright renewed by Hill and Range Songs, Inc., all rights controlled by Unichappel Music, Inc. (Rightsong, Publisher), New York, N.Y.; "I Can't Hold Myself in Line" by Merle Haggard, copyright © 1968 Blue Book Music, Bakersfield, Ca.; "Branded Man" by Merle Haggard, copyright © 1967 Blue Book Music, Bakersfield, Ca.; "I Threw Away the Rose" by Merle Haggard, copyright © 1966 Blue Book Music, Bakersfield, Ca.; "Footlights" by Merle Haggard, copyright © 1980 Shade Tree Music, Redding, Ca.; "Always Wanting You" by Merle Haggard, copyright © 1975 Shade Tree Music, Redding Ca.; "It's All in the Movies" by Merle Haggard and Kelli Haggard, copyright © 1975 Shade Tree Music, Redding, Ca.; "Live and Let Live" by Wiley Walker and Gene Sullivan, copyright © 1941, copyright renewed, Peer International Corp., New York, N.Y.

BELFAST · PUBLIC LIBRARIES

BK DIST
Pd 55962
Price
£12.25